DEVELOPMENTS IN
HYDRAULIC ENGINEERING—2

CONTENTS OF VOLUME 1

Edited by P. NOVAK

DEVELOPMENTS IN HYDRAULIC ENGINEERING—2

Edited by

P. NOVAK

*Emeritus Professor of Civil and Hydraulic Engineering
University of Newcastle upon Tyne, UK*

ELSEVIER APPLIED SCIENCE PUBLISHERS
LONDON and NEW YORK

ELSEVIER APPLIED SCIENCE PUBLISHERS LTD
Ripple Road, Barking, Essex, England

Sole Distributor in the USA and Canada
ELSEVIER SCIENCE PUBLISHING CO., INC.,
52 Vanderbilt Avenue, New York, NY 10017, USA

British Library Cataloguing in Publication Data

Developments in hydraulic engineering.—2
 1. Hydraulic engineering—Periodicals
 627′.05   TC1

  ISBN 0-85334-228-8

WITH 3 TABLES AND 119 ILLUSTRATIONS

© ELSEVIER APPLIED SCIENCE PUBLISHERS LTD 1984

The selection and presentation of material and the opinions expressed
in this publication are the sole responsibility of the authors concerned.

Printed in Northern Ireland at The Universities Press (Belfast), Ltd.

PREFACE

Technical and scientific journals present papers where, owing to space restrictions, the author has to deal almost exclusively with his own work without being able to give a wider review of the subject and of the technical and scientific implications of his studies. These journals serve an extremely valuable purpose but there is a need for an outlet for statements of considerably greater length than those usually available in the journals, but shorter again than books and monographs on individual topics. The underlying concept behind this series *Developments in Hydraulic Engineering* is to provide such an outlet, giving in individual chapters an authoritative, comprehensive and up-to-date review of the subject by authors who themselves are active in the subject and have significantly contributed to it.

This second volume of the series is a logical continuation of the first volume with the same central theme of 'hydraulic structures'. After dealing in the first volume with computational methods related to hydraulic structures design, sediment transport and some special features of irrigation structures, the second volume concentrates on some important problems encountered in the design of hydraulic structures. The first chapter is orientated towards the general discussion of principles involved in vibration of hydraulic structures and is followed by a chapter discussing in detail vibration of gates. The third chapter is a fundamental treatment of the aeration problem which is followed by two chapters giving a wide-ranging account of approaches, pitfalls and recent developments in the design of spillways and energy dissipators at high dams.

The editor is aware that complete uniformity in style and presentation by the authors of individual chapters was not achieved—indeed it was not attempted. Nevertheless it is hoped that this volume—on its own and in conjunction with Volume 1—presents material which in its individual chapters and as a whole, is an up-to-date state-of-the-art publication and contribution towards progress in hydraulic engineering design.

P. NOVAK

CONTENTS

LIST OF CONTRIBUTORS

J. J. CASSIDY
  Chief Hydrologic Engineer, Bechtel Civil & Minerals, Inc., 50 Beale Street, PO Box 3965, San Francisco, California 94119, USA

R. A. ELDER
  Engineering Manager, Hydraulics/Hydrology Group, Bechtel Civil & Minerals, Inc., 50 Beale Street, PO Box 3965, San Francisco, California 94119, USA

K. HAINDL
  Associate Professor and Head of the Department of Hydromechanics and Applied Hydraulics, Water Research Institute, Prague, Czechoslovakia

S. T. HSU
  Chief Hydraulic Engineer, Bechtel Civil & Minerals, Inc., 50 Beale Street, PO Box 3965, San Francisco, California 94119, USA

P. A. KOLKMAN
  Head of the Locks, Weirs and Sluices Branch, Delft Hydraulics Laboratory, Rotterdamseweg 185, PO Box 177, 2600 MH Delft, The Netherlands; Senior Research Officer, Department of Civil Engineering, Delft University of Technology, Delft, The Netherlands

F. A. LOCHER
  Engineering Group Supervisor, Hydraulics/Hydrology Group, Bechtel Civil & Minerals, Inc., 50 Beale Street, PO Box 3965, San Francisco, California 94119, USA

Chapter 1

VIBRATIONS OF HYDRAULIC STRUCTURES

P. A. KOLKMAN

Locks, Weirs and Sluices Branch, Delft Hydraulics Laboratory; Department of Civil Engineering, Delft University of Technology, Delft, The Netherlands

1 INTRODUCTION

Vibrations of hydraulic structures is a subject between hydrodynamics and applied mechanics; notions from the two disciplines will be used without special introduction.

The intention of this introduction is particularly to show the most important phenomena of the interaction between the fluid and structure behaviour. This will be done in broad outline only; data and graphs included are meant as illustrations, they do not comprise complete design information. Blevins,[6] and for structures with cylindrical sections Griffin,[19] for instance, give more design-oriented information with a special orientation to offshore engineering, and additional information and insights are already becoming available.

Before flow-induced vibrations are discussed, the following differentiation (in the order of increasing level of danger) is introduced:

1. The passive response to excitation by turbulence, also called forced vibration. This turbulence can be present in the oncoming flow (external turbulence excitation), or it can be induced in the flow by the structure itself (internal turbulence excitation). The character of excitation can be either a broad-band spectrum or a narrow-band one (nearly periodic).

2. Body-controlled excitation, where initially unstable flow phenomena can be amplified by body vibration, or where vibration of the body synchronises the random turbulence excitation

1

acting on different parts. The resulting amplification of the excitation is a limited one.

3. Self-excitation or negative damping, where the dynamic flow excitation is purely induced by the body vibration itself (feedback). At smaller amplitudes, the excitation force will increase linearly with the vibration movement; this results in an exponential growth of the amplitude and a limit to the vibration amplitude is only reached when non-linear effects interfere.

Further definitions will be derived from the basic dynamic equation of a single mass–spring system (single resonator), which will be introduced in Section 2. In Section 3 the natural-mode analysis for continuously elastic structures (partly) submerged in water will be explained. In Sections 4 to 8 the influence of fluid flow on the different terms of the basic oscillator equation will be introduced. Section 9 focuses especially on the dynamic behaviour of cylinders in flow; an important part of the literature on flow-induced vibrations deals with cylinders owing to their wide applicability and their striking dynamic behaviour. In Section 10 flow instabilities are discussed, which in their turn can cause a dynamic loading of structures.

The reasons why knowledge of the dynamic behaviour of hydraulic structures is of importance are:

1. Vibrations can endanger the construction and the environment which is protected by it, and noise can be unacceptable. A wider knowledge of the causes can prevent design errors, or at least indicate the aspects which need special attention in the design.
2. Extrapolation of design experiences to large-scale structures can be hampered by lack of knowledge of dynamic behaviour.
3. Some structures are difficult to modify when vibrations are encountered.
4. When vibrations occur only in extreme conditions, it is not certain that they will be recognised or detected in time.

The knowledge in the field of hydroelasticity is rapidly developing; theoretical efforts are made from the fluid dynamics viewpoint, as well as from the applied mechanics. New experimental techniques in prototypes and scale models are becoming available (instrumentation and data acquisition) and new test rigs with high-speed and/or large-scale measuring sections are applied.

Besides vibration phenomena, there can be other causes of dynamic loads. Load impacts occur when water hits a structural surface (wave attack, hydraulic jump, fully developed cavitation); this can also occur when there are voids in the fluid (cavitation, aeration of culvert or pipe flow). These aspects are not treated in this chapter. Periodic or random wave loads have to be considered as dynamic loading, although the frequency of excitation is generally low compared to the resonance frequencies of structures.

Remedies for flow-induced vibrations may consist in reshaping the structure (e.g. to stabilise the flow pattern by fixation of the flow separation and/or the flow reattachment point, to shift the excitation frequency, or to disturb the regularity of vortex shedding), in increasing the rigidity (which reduces initial deflections and the possibility of self-excitation and which also results in a shift of the resonance frequency), and in the application of mechanical damping. There always remains a certain amount of dynamic excitation due to local turbulence induced in the flow by the body itself.

2 THE SINGLE RESONATOR IN A FLOW FIELD

The classical equation of an oscillator or resonator is

$$m\ddot{y} + c\dot{y} + ky = F(t) \tag{1}$$

where y = displacement, $\dot{y} = \partial y/\partial t$, etc., m = mass, c = damping, k = rigidity, F = external force and t = time.

The natural frequency is defined as

$$f_n = \omega_n/2\pi = \sqrt{(k/m)}/2\pi \tag{2}$$

Dimensionless damping is represented by δ or by γ

$$\gamma = \frac{1}{2\pi}\,\delta = \frac{1}{2\pi}\ln\,(a_n/a_{n+1}) = \frac{c}{2m\omega_n} = \frac{c}{2\sqrt{(km)}} = \frac{c\omega_n}{2k} \tag{3}$$

where γ is the relative damping, this being the ratio of the damping factor and the critical damping. F can be seen as the hydrodynamic force, to be introduced as F_w.

The following properties of eqn. (1) and its solutions will be used in this chapter:

1. Any force (working on the mass) proportional to $\dot{y}$ and hence in phase with the velocity of vibration, but in opposite direction, is

in fact a damping force. When it is in the direction of the vibration velocity, the term negative damping is introduced (equivalent to self-excitation).

2. At resonance, and when γ is not too high, the vibration frequency is close to the natural frequency and hence $my + ky \approx 0$. The remaining terms of eqn. (1) show that the equilibrium amplitude depends on the ratio of the harmonic force component in the resonance frequency to the damping force (being $c\dot{y}$).

3. At a periodic oscillation, the internal (or spring) force $k\hat{y}$ (the $\hat{}$ sign denotes the amplitude of the oscillating value) can be expressed as a factor A times the external force amplitude $\hat{F}_w$. The factor A depends on the ratio f/f_n, where f is the excitation frequency. A_{max} equals $1/2\gamma$ when γ is not too high.

Concerning the design of structures it can be concluded:

4. Excitation frequencies should be remote from the resonance frequencies unless the damping is high enough.

5. Negative damping should be prevented, because it makes the system dynamically unstable.

When water flow interferes, it is convenient to write eqn. (1) as follows

$$(m + m_w)\ddot{y} + (c + c_w)\dot{y} + (k + k_w)y = F_w(t, y, \dot{y}, \text{etc.}) \qquad (4)$$

where the right-hand side terms $F_w(y, \dot{y}, \text{etc.})$ are coupled forces and $F_w(t)$ is non-coupled force.

This means that the fluid forces which are linearly coupled with the body movement are introduced as left-hand side terms (m_w = added mass, c_w = added damping, k_w = added rigidity), but in principle they can all have positive or negative values; moreover, it can happen that m_w, etc., still depend on the frequency of the body oscillation. In the right-hand side term one can have excitation forces which are independent of or non-coupled with the vibratory movement, but there also remain the non-linearly coupled terms.

For the design it is helpful when the dominant excitation frequency, f, is known. In this paragraph only some general remarks are presented. The hydrodynamic force can be written as $F = \bar{F} + F'$ (where $\bar{F}$ is the time-averaged or static force component and F' is the dynamic part). When the flow pattern shows oscillations, a dominant frequency f can be distinguished in F' for which

$$S = fL/V \qquad (5)$$

applies, where S = the dimensionless Strouhal number, V = velocity of the oncoming flow, and L = a representative length of the body. L should be clearly defined, and also the quantity to which f is related (local pressure, in-line or transverse force).

For those bodies where the flow separation point is not fixed by a sharp edge or where flow separation is combined with flow reattachment, one finds that S is dependent on the Reynolds number, on the surface roughness and on the initial flow turbulence.

In the same way as S has been introduced for the excitation frequency, we introduce S_n for the natural frequency

$$S_n = f_n L / V \qquad (6)$$

S_n is called the reduced natural frequency. Some authors use the symbol $V_r = S_n^{-1}$ and call this the reduced water velocity (as in Fig. 23). When the excitation is induced only by external turbulence or by turbulence created by the body itself, F' has in general the character of broad-band excitation and is then described in terms of a spectral density function wherein the following definition is used for the representative time-averaged force amplitude

$$\overline{F'^2} = \lim_{t \to \infty} \frac{1}{t} \int_0^t F'^2(t)\, \mathrm{d}t \qquad (7)$$

The force amplitude is related to the flow velocity and the fluid density

$$\sqrt{(F'^2)} = (C_D' \quad \text{or} \quad C_L')(\tfrac{1}{2}\rho V^2 L^2) \qquad (8)$$

where C_L' = dynamic lift coefficient, C_D' = dynamic drag coefficient which in fact represents the rms value and the bar in $\overline{F'^2}$ indicates the time-averaged value.

For the spectral density function $W(f)$

$$\int_0^\infty W(f)\, \mathrm{d}f = \overline{F'^2} \qquad (9)$$

It is common practice to introduce the frequency in a dimensionless way by replacing f by the Strouhal number S (and hence $\mathrm{d}f = (V/L)\,\mathrm{d}S$) and to replace $W(f)$ by the uniformed spectral distribution function $\phi(S)$, for which

$$\int_0^\infty \phi(S)\, \mathrm{d}S = 1 \qquad (10)$$

It can be shown that

$$W(f) = [C'(\tfrac{1}{2}\rho V^2 L^2)]^2 L V^{-1} \phi(S) \tag{11}$$

It turns out that $\phi(S)$ and C' are still dependent on the Reynolds number, but not on the velocity and the absolute size of L itself; there still remains the influence of the shape of the body and other flow contours.

When the flow pattern is stable (when sharp edges determine the flow separation and when the separated flow is not reattached again), the influence of body vibration on the excitation is small.

2.1 Response Calculations

It is possible to calculate numerically the spectral distribution of the passive response of the oscillator to the excitation spectrum by multiplying $W(f)$ by the square of the amplification curve A (A as function of the frequency). This calculation is illustrated in Figs. 1 and 2.

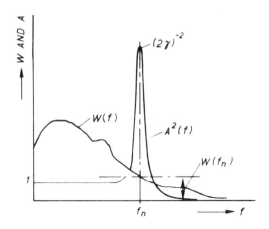

Fig. 1.   Excitation and amplification function.

It is common practice to design hydraulic structures such that the resonance frequency lies above the dominant excitation frequency.†
The response $k^2 y'^2$ can now be approximately calculated by the

---

† Because the velocity V can vary from 0 to V_{max}, eqn. (5) shows that f varies from 0 to $f_{max} = SV_{max}/L$; so it is not feasible to have f_n below f_{max}.

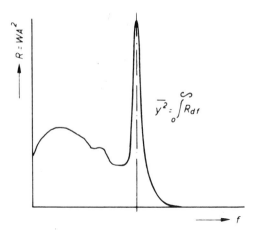

FIG. 2. Response of an oscillator.

summation of $\int_0^\infty W \, df$ (this is the quasi-static part, because for a great range of f the amplification factor A equals unity) and the dynamic part $\int_0^\infty A^2(f) W(f_n) \, dF$. $W(f_n)$ is schematised as a new function with a constant excitation level over the whole frequency band. In this summation there is a small double counting.

The last integral can be expressed analytically when γ is small (for instance up to 20%, see ref. 25) by

$$F_{\text{int}}'^2 = k^2 \overline{y'^2} = \frac{\pi f_n}{4\gamma} W(f_n) \tag{12}$$

When expressed in a dimensionless way the following can be derived

$$F_{\text{int}}'^2 = \frac{\pi}{4\gamma} S_n \phi(S_n)(C'\tfrac{1}{2}\rho V^2 L^2)^2 \tag{13}$$

Due to lack of design data it is common design practice not to calculate the response value for each part of the structure, but only to make f_n (five or more times) greater than f. This implies the neglect of the resonance effect of eqn. (13). Because, in general, the dynamic excitation coefficient C_L' or C_D' (eqn. (8)) is much smaller than the stationary drag coefficient, the dynamic force can be accounted for by an increased (fatigue) safety factor.

In the design of a structure the following points must be considered:

1. Negative hydrodynamic damping should be prevented; this is a matter of shaping.
2. Also, shapes sensitive to self-control are preferably not to be applied.
3. Resonance frequencies should be remote from dominant excitation frequencies; m_w and k_w interfere in the determination of f_n.
4. Dynamic phenomena caused by attack of steep waves, hydraulic jump and cavitation should be prevented.
5. Play in bearings and articulating points has to be avoided.
6. The remaining dynamic load has to be acceptable; response calculations will show the necessary strength and the remaining amplitudes.
7. It has to be verified whether the remaining vibrations still lead to a certain amplification of the dynamic load (self-control phenomena, see Section 9).

Remarks on the design procedure:

It is not always possible to prevent (1); in such a case a study is necessary to discover to what extent $(-c_w)$, and sometimes k_w and m_w, are amplitude-dependent. This study can lead to a still-acceptable limit amplitude.

Remarks on the use of scale models:

Often one will not be able to find all the data necessary for the procedure mentioned in the points above. Then, laboratory experiments may be necessary; they can often be of limited scope, due to the fact that partial information is already available. Such a limitation may also be necessary for other reasons, such as limitations of laboratory facilities in relation to scale effects, and because each type of scale model has only limited possibilities. In Chapter 2, Section 9, a short survey is given of different model types for gate research; this paragraph is also more generally applicable. An important point is whether the whole construction should be reproduced, or only parts. This is important in view of the model scale. Another point is whether the model will be a rigid one (with force or pressure gauges), a dynamic one with one or more degrees of freedom (naturally excited by the flow or artificially excited), or one with a simulation of the continuous elasticity. Much depends on whether information is needed only to be on the safe side, or for a quantitative prediction of the vibration magnitude.

3 COMPUTATION TECHNIQUES FOR CONTINUOUSLY ELASTIC STRUCTURES

Analysis of the dynamic behaviour of continuously elastic structures requires firstly a calculation of the natural modes and frequencies of vibration for the situation without damping. The added mass (see Section 4) is included in this calculation. When the system has n degrees of freedom $(y_1, y_2, \ldots, y_n)$, the displacement vector $\mathbf{Y}$ has to be combined with the mass matrix $\mathbf{M}$ (including added mass) and with the rigidity matrix $\mathbf{K}$ such that

$$\mathbf{M\ddot{Y}} + \mathbf{KY} = 0 \tag{14}$$

For each of the n natural modes, the amplitude Y_n is expressed as a reference amplitude $\hat{y}_n$ times the spatial distribution vector (or vibration mode) $\boldsymbol{\xi}_n$

$$Y_n = \boldsymbol{\xi}_n \hat{y}_n \tag{15}$$

Calculation techniques for $\boldsymbol{\xi}_n$ and also for the natural frequency, f_n, are the lumped-mass or the finite-element methods.

Now a linear damping can be introduced, but the natural modes remain only mutually non-coupled (orthogonal) when the spatial distribution of the damping is the same as the mass distribution or the rigidity distribution. Physically, this condition is fulfilled for that part of the structural damping where the dimensionless damping, γ, is a property related to the hysteresis characteristics of the material. For composite structures, and especially for hydraulic structures which are partly in water and partly in air, this is not the case. However, it can be argued that for low damping the coupling effect between vibrations in the different modes caused by the damping is small and, consequently, the ξ solutions and the resonance frequencies are only a little affected. When one assumes that the ξ solution is not affected by the fluid damping at all, it is possible to calculate (for each mode separately) the energy dissipation by the damping, and one can determine an equivalent γ_w value at which the same amount of energy is dissipated.

Before one can apply the theory and laboratory results of single resonators in flow to continuously elastic structures, each of the natural modes of eqn. (15) has to be analysed separately and replaced by an equivalent single oscillator, oscillating in a stationary position with amplitude $\hat{y}_n$ (and having its appropriate mass m_n, damping c_n and rigidity k_n).

After the natural modes have been calculated, one gets the properties of the equivalent resonator of the nth mode as follows:

A. The maximum potential energy of the equivalent spring $(\frac{1}{2}k_n\hat{y}_n^2)$ is assumed to be equal to the potential (deformation) energy of the nth mode of the whole structure; this determines k_n. There are no special problems in also taking into account elements of the fluid rigidity, k_w.

B.' The maximum kinetic energy, $\frac{1}{2}m_n\omega_n^2\hat{y}_n^2$, of the equivalent mass should be equal to the kinetic energy of the whole structure. Easier and more direct to apply is $m_n = k_n/\omega_n^2$.

C. The energy dissipation per period of the damping, $\pi c_n\omega_n\hat{y}_n^2$, should be equal to the dissipation of the whole system. The latter can be divided into a part which directly equals the structural damping, γ_s, and a part due to the water and which is transformed into γ_w; the total dissipation per period now becomes $2\pi(\gamma_s + \gamma_w)m_n\omega_n^2\hat{y}_n^2$.

D. The energy brought in by a periodic excitation in the resonance frequency per period is $\pi\hat{F}_n\hat{y}_n$, and this should be equal to the energy brought into the whole structure.

E. For random excitation, the dynamic response $\sqrt{(\overline{y'^2})}$, as found in eqn. (12), can be transformed into a quasi-response, $\hat{y}$, to a purely periodic excitation with a force amplitude $\hat{F}^2 = \pi\gamma f_n W(f_n),$† and hence the same technique as used in point D for periodic excitation can be applied to establish the equivalent excitation.

F. At different points of the structure, the dynamic loads due to flow are not fully correlated and a correlation coefficient r is introduced. The absolute value of r is smaller than unity and r is, in general, a function continuously decreasing with the distance between two locations and increasing when the vibration amplitude is strong enough to trigger turbulence or vortex shedding. In addition, r is also a function of the frequency (or better of S_n); this is often neglected.

For flexural vibrations of a one-dimensional structure with ordinate z, for instance a cantilever cylinder which is partly in flowing water and partly in air, the foregoing leads to the following equations (a) to (f),

---

† This relation is found by comparing $k(\overline{y'^2})^{1/2}$ of eqn. (12) with the maximum internal force obtained by resonance excitation, $k\hat{y} = F/2$. It neglects that for a harmonic oscillation $y = \hat{y}\sin\omega t$ counts $(\overline{y'^2})^{1/2} = \frac{1}{2}\sqrt{(2)}\hat{y}$.

which are related to, respectively, the points A to F. The derivation can be found, for instance, in Blevins.[6]

$$k = \int_0^L EI(\partial^2\xi(z)/\partial z^2)^2 \, dz \qquad (a)$$

(Here EI can also be introduced as a function of z.)

$$m = \int_0^L \{m(z) + m_w(z)\}\xi^2(z) \, dz \qquad (b)$$

This, however, is a simplified form (see Section 4) which is only admissible when the added mass acts at each point only as an addition to the proper mass of the structure and does not show coupling effects. For bending vibrations of slender structures this assumption is valid when the wavelength of the vibration mode is long compared to the width of the structure. More in general, one can apply

$$m = k/\omega_n^2 \qquad (b1)$$

When the force due to water damping is proportional to the local vibration velocity one gets (L_1 being the part in water)

$$c_w = \int_0^{L_1} c_w(z)\xi^2(z) \, dz \qquad (c)$$

and so

$$\gamma_w = c_w/2m\omega_n \qquad (c1)$$

To this value the structural damping γ_s is added. The equivalent periodic force amplitude becomes

$$\hat{F} = \int_0^{L_1} \hat{F}(z)\xi_z \, dz \qquad (d)$$

With random excitation, and introducing the correlation coefficient r, one can introduce the equivalent excitation coefficient C' (defined as for eqn. (8))

$$\overline{C'^2} = \frac{\int_0^L \int_0^L C'(z_1)C'(z_2)r(z_1, z_2)\xi(z_1)\xi(z_2) \, dz_1 \, dz_2}{\left(\int_0^L \xi(z) \, dz\right)^2} \qquad (e \text{ and } f)$$

In this equation $C'(z_1)$ and $C'(z_2)$ are the local excitation coefficients.

Here it is assumed that r (at one certain frequency) depends only on z_1 and z_2. It might also be possible that the mode of vibration $\xi(z)$ interferes with r, but such experiments have not yet been done.

This approach is based on linearised equations. When the vibration amplitude affects m_w, c_w, k_w or the excitation force, an iteration procedure is needed.

In principle, the reduction formulae (a) to (f) make the various considerations about a single-degree-of-freedom resonator applicable to continuous structures.

4   ADDED MASS, m_w

Studies of added mass are done for analysis of flow-induced vibrations, but there are also several other applications:

1. Dams in earthquake regions.
2. Periodic wave forces on rigid structures.
3. Oscillations of floating structures in waves.
4. Wave impact forces.
5. Impact forces on ships (at moorings and collisions).
6. Slamming (an object falling on the water surface).

4.1   Stagnant Water Conditions
In its simplest form, m_w is introduced as the cylindrical volume of water which is forced to oscillate due to piston movement (Fig. 3). The

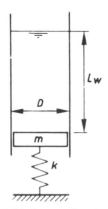

FIG. 3.   Added mass of a piston.

water is confined and hence all particles are obliged to move with the same velocity, $\dot{y}$, as the piston, and in the combined potential and kinetic energy of a freely vibrating, undamped single oscillator ($E_{pot} + E_{kin}$ = constant) each particle contributes proportionally to its mass.

This is different when a submerged body oscillates with small amplitude in stagnant fluid (Fig. 4). It is permissible to calculate the flow field with the potential flow theory (see Lamb[27]). This means that all fluid particles will oscillate in phase with the body vibration. But the farther the fluid is away from the body, the smaller its velocity is compared to $\dot{y}$ of the body, while its contribution to E_{kin} decreases proportionally to $(V_{fluid}/\dot{y})^2$. The total kinetic energy of the fluid has a limit value which can now be expressed as an added mass, m_w, such that $E_{kin} = \frac{1}{2}m_w\dot{y}^2$. The added mass, m_w, has the dimension of a virtual volume of fluid with density $\rho(= \rho_{fluid})$. Like Fig. 3, local pressure on the body can be expressed as a local fluid column with a length L_w, but this length generally will depend on the location of the body surface. L_w is proportional to the representative body dimension, L, and depends on the direction in which the body vibrates.

When the body is asymmetric (Fig. 5), the resultant pressures are asymmetric too, which results in a resultant hydraulic force which is not in line with the body movement. Also, when there are several

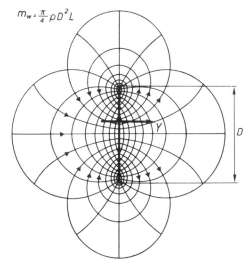

FIG. 4. Added mass flow of an oscillating strip (after Lamb[27]).

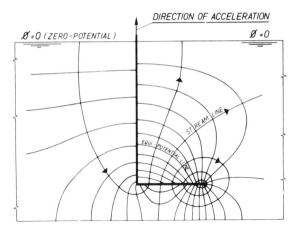

FIG. 5.   Added mass of a hooked gate (after Kolkman[25]).

objects in the fluid, the acceleration of one of them will exert 'added mass forces' on the other ones. This has an important consequence for the behaviour of a system with more degrees of freedom.

The basic equation in matrix notation of a system with n degrees of freedom was presented in Section 3

$$\mathbf{M}\ddot{\mathbf{Y}} + \mathbf{K}\mathbf{Y} = 0 \tag{16}$$

In the mass matrix, components are normally found only on the main diagonal, because each mass only gives inertial forces at its centre point and in the direction in which this point accelerates. When, however, the added mass matrix $\mathbf{M}_w$ is considered, this is not true any more. The fluid causes inertial interaction forces between different mass points and, as has been shown before, also between different directions of movement of one single mass point; this has a certain parallel in a coupled pendulum system.[25] This means that eqn. (16) changes character and that a new equation where $\mathbf{M}$ has been replaced by $(\mathbf{M} + \mathbf{M}_w)$ has to be solved. Reference 25 also shows an example of how the first symmetrical vibration modes of a visor weir were completely changed by the water.

For bending vibrations of a slender structure, it is the relation between the wavelength, λ, of the vibration mode and the diameter which determines whether the coupling effect between m_w at different sections interferes. As long as λ is more than a few diameters, no great influence of the coupling effect is to be expected; nearly all literature dealing with slender structures assumes only fluid mass is added to the local mass of the structure.

4.2 The Influence of Flow Velocity

When the body is oscillating in a flowing fluid, the added mass can be affected by the flow velocity. The stationary flow conditions can be seen as a solution of the Navier–Stokes equations (continuity and dynamic equations)

$$\frac{\partial p}{\partial x} = -\rho \frac{\partial v_x}{\partial t} - \rho v_x \frac{\partial v_x}{\partial x} - \rho v_y \frac{\partial v_x}{\partial y}, \text{etc.} \tag{17}$$

When it is supposed that the oscillating body causes a periodic small-amplitude disturbance where all disturbance velocities, v', are in phase with the body vibration velocity (a first approximation which is only really valid for stagnant fluid conditions), the resultant dynamic pressure fluctuations follow from

$$\frac{\partial(p + p')}{\partial x} = -\rho \frac{\partial(v + v')}{\partial t} - \rho(v_x + v'_x) \frac{\partial(v_x + v'_x)}{\partial x}, \text{etc.} \tag{18}$$

When only the periodic oscillation terms with p' and v' are considered and the term proportional to v'^2 is neglected because of the small amplitudes, one gets

$$\frac{\partial p'}{\partial x} = -\rho \frac{\partial v'_x}{\partial t} - \rho v'_x \frac{\partial v'_x}{\partial x} - \rho v_x \frac{\partial v'_x}{\partial x}, \text{etc.} \tag{19}$$

Introducing $v' = \hat{v} \sin \omega t$ and at an order of magnitude $\partial v_x / \partial x \simeq V/L$ (V = reference velocity, L = reference length), the first of the three right-hand side terms dominates when $\omega > V/L$ or when

$$\frac{\omega L}{V} (= 2\pi S) \gg 1 \tag{20}$$

When eqn. (20) holds, one finds again the m_w of the stagnant flow solution (because the influence of v_x is negligible), and the condition holds that all disturbance velocities, v'_x, are in phase with the vibration velocity of the body.

Precise data on when m_w gets affected by too low an S value have to be determined experimentally.[†]

Even when the $\rho \, \partial v_x / \partial t$ term dominates, the last two terms of eqn. (19) are still of importance, because they result in pressures proportional to v_x' and to the vibration velocity, $\dot{y}$, of the body. These pressures result by definition in damping forces, because they are proportional to $\dot{y}$.

4.3 Computation Methods for m_w

The computation methods available for establishing the value of m_w all assume stagnant fluid conditions with potential flow induced by a body in harmonic vibration. The small-amplitude vibration is replaced by a non-vibrating body with a source distribution on its contours such that the source discharge equals the quantity of water displaced by the vibration. This transformation is one of the reasons why its validity is limited to small-amplitude vibrations. When there is a free fluid surface, the simplified assumption (valid for high-frequency vibration) is that the disturbed surface plane is replaced by the non-disturbed surface plane, for which the condition of constant atmospheric pressure remains valid; this signifies a neglect of wave radiation. The more advanced methods introduce surface conditions corresponding to those applied in the linear wave theory.

The computation methods for a harmonic vibration are:

1. Conformal mapping (two-dimensional and simplified free-surface conditions); see Wendel.[55]
2. Electric analogy (in general: two-dimensional and simplified free-surface conditions, like Fig. 5); Zienkiewicz et al.[61] extended this method for three-dimensional shapes.
3. Boundary elements or boundary integral methods (three-dimensional, linear wave theory), also called wave diffraction computation; see Derunz et al.[10]
4. Finite-element method (three-dimensional, linear wave theory), where the computation grid concerns the surrounding fluid.

The latter two methods calculate the force components in phase with the vibration acceleration (added mass) and the ones in phase with the

---

[†] See for one of the few examples the Sarpkaya experiments on cylinders in Section 9; these results are strongly influenced by the S value in the range where the dynamic vortex shedding is dominant.

vibration velocity (added damping due to the effect of wave radiation). Both methods have about equal validity. Because another application of these methods lies in the computation of wave forces on rigid structures of large size, much literature has become available with the development of offshore engineering. A review of both methods in relation to the latter application is found in Mei.[28] Applications of the methods in relation to added mass are found in ref. 35. Institutes which apply finite-element methods for mechanical problems also prefer this method for m_w determination.

An example of natural mode analysis, using the added mass matrix (determined by the finite-element method) in combination with the structural properties of a ship's hull, is presented by Meyers.[29]

4.4 Computation Results

For slender rigid structures of round or elliptical cylindrical shape which vibrate perpendicular to their axis, two-dimensional flow analysis (see Lamb[27] and Fig. 4) results in an added mass of $\rho \pi D^2/4$ per unit length (D = circle diameter or, for an ellipse, the width perpendicular to the direction of vibration). For an ellipse this is only valid for vibration in the direction of one of the main axes. For other shapes, see Wendel.[55]

When the object has a finite length, m_w decreases. This is often neglected in vibration analysis (overestimation of m_w means generally that one remains on the safe side). A free surface of the fluid results in a decrease of m_w, an adjacent fixed boundary in an increase of m_w. When the effect of wave radiation is introduced, the free surface tends, for the very low frequencies, to act as a fixed boundary, which results in an important increase of m_w. For 'half-space' conditions, as shown in Figs. 6 and 10, however, m_w tends to decrease at lower frequencies.

For a vertical wall, of height h with water at one side, vibrating horizontally, Westergaart found (with neglect of wave radiation and compressibility) in his 'classical' paper[56]

$$m_w = 0 \cdot 54 \rho h^2 \text{ per unit length} \tag{21}$$

He also presented the pressure distribution and the effect of water compressibility.

Schoemaker[48] presented similar results for a gate standing on a step and with water only at the deep side—see Fig. 6.

For an example of the effect of the radiation of surface waves at lower frequencies on m_w and on the occurrence of damping forces at

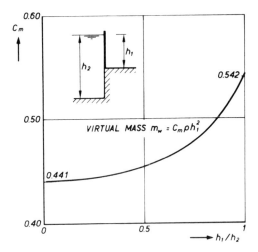

FIG. 6. Added mass coefficient as function of h_1/h_2 (after Schoemaker[48]).

half-space conditions, see Fig. 10 (for $h/\delta = 1$, these are the results for a horizontally vibrating vertical wall).

For the effect of wave radiation on a three-dimensional case see Fig. 7. The same tendencies are found for a ship vibrating in the transverse (sway) direction.[16] In this case one finds that for low frequencies the water surface tends to act as a rigid boundary, while for high frequencies the water surface is a boundary with the condition of atmospheric pressure. In between there is a frequency range in which the relation (body width)/(wavelength of radiated wave) is of importance.

Added masses related to responses to impact forces can be derived by a Fourier or Laplace transformation; the pulse force in the time domain is transformed into a function in the frequency domain, and now the added masses (which are known for harmonic oscillations) can be introduced. When the added mass is constant for all frequencies (e.g. when only high frequencies are involved, which leads to a neglect of wave radiation), its constant value is also directly valid for impacts. Schoemaker's results apply, for instance, for a calculation of the momentum of wave impact when the front height is h_1.

When a ship is decelerated by impact against a fender structure, Fontijn[16] shows that m_w can only be determined by using the Laplace

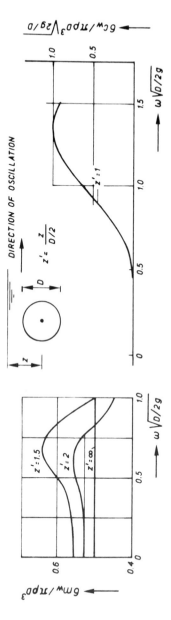

FIG. 7. Added mass and damping of a submerged sphere (after Hooft[22]).

transformation of the impact, subsequently using the frequency-dependent added mass and damping, and finally using the inverse transformation. When $m_w = f(\omega)$, this is a numerical procedure.

For the computation of periodic wave forces on slender structures, m_w interferes in the Morison equation[30]

$$F_w = C_m * (\text{section area}) * \rho \frac{dV}{dt} + C_D * (\text{width}) * \tfrac{1}{2}\rho V |V| \qquad (22)$$

where V = local horizontal flow velocity component in the undisturbed wave, F_w = force per unit length, C_m = added mass coefficient, C_D = drag coefficient; the added mass is $m_w = C_m \rho$ (sect. area).

For more information on precise wave forces, field of application and restrictions of Morison's equation, see refs. 9 and 46. Dynamic lift forces and resulting vibrations are not included in the Morison equation.

The m_w value in the Morison equation is not the same as that found for the vibrating cylinder. Suppose a cylinder with $\rho = \rho_{\text{water}}$ oscillates with the same velocity, V, as the water; then no external force has to be applied. To stop this vibration, m_w plus the mass of the cylinder have to be stopped. The same stopping force would have to be applied for any cylinder, independent of its weight, so

$$m_{w(\text{Morison})} = m_{w(\text{vibration})} + \rho * (\text{sect. area}) \qquad (23)$$

5 ADDED RIGIDITY, k_w

There are only a few elements which can potentially lead to a hydrodynamic rigidity:

1. Variation of the submergence of a semi-submerged object (heave or roll).
2. Restoring force on a wind vane which deviates from the wind direction; a negative rigidity is obtained when the wind direction is opposite to the vane direction. Looking at the diagram of an elastic wing (Fig. 11), one can also see an element of negative (polar) flow rigidity: when the incidence angle, Φ, increases, the lift force, L, will increase and this causes a rotational moment.
3. A plug valve at the downstream end of a pipe undergoes, when the discharge remains constant, a decrease in head difference when the leak gap increases (see Chapter 2, Section 2). This

results in a positive added rigidity. When the valve is at the upstream end of the pipe the added rigidity is negative.

When the negative added rigidity $(-k_w)$ is greater than the (positive) structural rigidity, the structure is statically unstable; in the literature this is referred to as 'divergence'.

Remarks

Sometimes one finds experimental results showing that the added mass is varying with the vibration frequencies, but, because in the resulting in-line force k_w also interferes, it is difficult to draw conclusions about m_w or k_w. In such a case, it is better to speak of the total in-line forces without further distinction. For example: at a vibrating plug valve in combination with a long pipe, where water compressibility contributes, the relation between the local pressure and the plug vibration depends on the vibration frequency, and changes sign when there is a standing compression wave.

6 ADDED DAMPING, c_w

Hydrodynamic damping occurs when energy is radiated (in the form of free-surface or compression waves), transformed into turbulence (drag force, lift force), or directly dissipated by viscous shear forces. For the dynamic computation of hydraulic structures, only the damping by drag forces and radiation of gravity waves contributes. Only in hydraulic models can viscous shear forces and the influence of surface tension on wave radiation interfere. For flow-induced vibrations the drag force is generally the dominant one. Two examples will illustrate the damping induced by drag force (see Figs 8 and 9).

Figure 8 shows the derivation for the in-line vibration of a circular

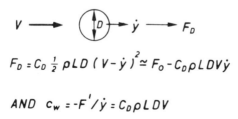

$$F_D = C_D \tfrac{1}{2}\, \rho L D\, (V - \dot{y})^2 \simeq F_0 - C_D \rho L D V \dot{y}$$

$$AND \quad c_w = -F'/\dot{y} = C_D \rho L D V$$

FIG. 8. Derivation of c_w for in-line vibration of a cylinder.

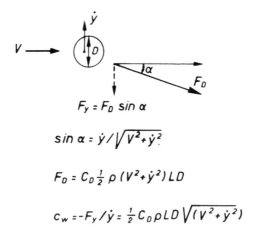

$$F_y = F_D \sin \alpha$$

$$\sin \alpha = \dot{y} / \sqrt{V^2 + \dot{y}^2}$$

$$F_D = C_D \tfrac{1}{2} \rho (V^2 + \dot{y}^2) LD$$

$$c_w = -F_y / \dot{y} = \tfrac{1}{2} C_D \rho LD \sqrt{(V^2 + \dot{y}^2)}$$

FIG. 9.   Derivation of c_w for cross-flow vibration of a cylinder.

cylinder, assuming that C_D remains constant. This is a reasonable assumption when the frequency is low (low Strouhal number).

It is common practice to express flow damping as a dimensionless damping coefficient, C_{da}

$$C_{da} = c_w/\rho VL^2 \qquad \text{or} \qquad c_w/\rho VLD \tag{24}$$

and hence there follows from Fig. 8 an expression for in-line vibration

$$C_{dai} = C_D \tag{25}$$

C_{da} depends on the geometry of the object and other flow contours and is often determined experimentally. Moreover, C_{da} is a function of S; this depends on whether the $\partial v'/\partial t$ or the $v' \, \partial v/\partial x$ is dominant in eqn. (19). C_{da} is also affected by the Reynolds number.

In the case of cross-flow vibration, there follows from Fig. 9 that

$$c_w = C_D \tfrac{1}{2}\rho DL \sqrt{(V^2 + \dot{y}^2)} \tag{26}$$

and as long as $\dot{y}$ is small compared to V, the equation linearises and one finds for cross-flow vibration

$$C_{dac} = \tfrac{1}{2}C_D \tag{27}$$

In Section 4 it was discussed that in eqn. (19) the terms $\rho V'_x$, $\partial v_x/\partial x$, etc., result in a hydrodynamic damping and, in fact, this is also the damping due to the change in the drag and lift forces. Furthermore,

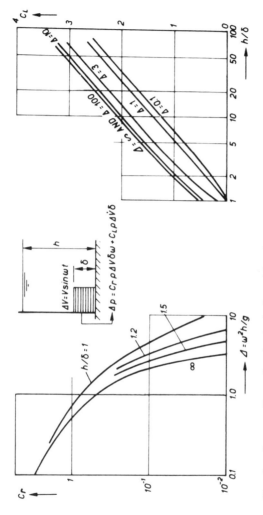

FIG. 10. Results of a two-dimensional calculation of in-phase and out-of-phase pressures at a vibrating gate.[25]

there also follows that at high S values a constant damping coefficient is found, but its value is different from the one at low S values.

Résumé

   At low S values, cross-flow damping results from a flow pattern related to a quasi-change in magnitude and direction of the oncoming flow; and at high S values, the flow pattern is a combination of the stationary flow pattern and the 'added mass flow pattern in stagnant fluid'.

As has already been mentioned in Section 4, Fig. 10 illustrates the influence of wave radiation (at lower Δ values) on c_w and on the decrease of added mass, m_w. These results were obtained by a two-dimensional calculation of a vibrating gate underneath a non-vibrating wall. The results for $h/\delta = 1$ represent a horizontally vibrating wall.

   The average pressure over the gate area is expressed in an in-phase term for which the added mass, m_w, per unit length follows from

$$m_w = C_L \rho \delta^2 \tag{28}$$

and in an out-of-phase term for which the damping, c_w, becomes

$$c_w = C_r \rho \omega \delta^2 \tag{29}$$

It can be seen that for higher frequencies (or Δ values) C_r decreases rapidly and m_w tends to become independent of Δ.

   As discussed in Section 4, the tendencies for m_w and c_w, as functions of the vibration frequency, are different when the structure is a three-dimensional one. In Fig. 7 wave radiation damping is shown for a sphere.

7 NEGATIVE ADDED DAMPING ($-c_w$) OR SELF-EXCITATION

The two ways in which self-excitation normally manifests itself are flutter and galloping. Flutter occurs mainly when relatively slender sections with a low torsional rigidity are involved (aeroplane wings, bridge decks and, for instance, venetian blinds). This vibration is a combination of flexural and torsional vibrations. Galloping (and, closely related to it, stall-flutter) is a low-frequency high-amplitude vibration and has only one degree of freedom involved, being in general a cross-flow flexural vibration. Other types of self-exciting vibration can be found in gates; these are extensively presented in Chapter 2.

In analysing whether there is positive or negative damping by flow, the coefficients of lift and drag can be taken from stationary flow tests (as has been done for positive damping in the examples of Figs. 8 and 9), but this holds only for low-frequency vibrations. A complete analysis should always include the influence of the reduced vibration frequency (a Strouhal number related to the vibration frequency of the structure). The analysis can generally be restricted to a check of the dynamic stability at the onset of vibration; the limitation to a small-amplitude vibration has the advantage that the disturbance terms of the Navier–Stokes equation can be linearised (see Section 4, eqn. (19)) so that the principles of superposition can also be applied.

7.1 Flutter Analysis

Although not negligible *a priori*, flutter vibrations are rarely mentioned in relation to hydraulic structures. Only the principles of flutter analysis will be shown here; extensive treatment can be found in handbooks on aero-elasticity, for example in ref. 17.

In general, one finds the analysis executed for the combination of torsion and cross-flow vibrations; and the lift force, L, and the moment, M, induced by the lift force are considered while the drag force is neglected. A convenient approach is to start with a stationary vibration (for explanation of symbols see Fig. 11):

$$\text{translation } y = \hat{y}e^{i\omega t} \text{ and rotation } \Phi' = \hat{\phi}e^{i(\omega t + \theta)} \qquad (30)$$

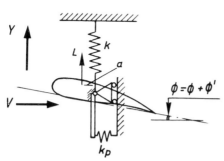

Fig. 11. Scheme for flutter calculations. k = rigidity (vertical), k_p = polar rigidity, m = mass, I_p = polar moment of inertia, L = lift force, V = fluid velocity, ϕ = wing angle, $M = aL$ = moment of force.

Each of these movements produces forces linear with $\hat{y}$ and Φ (in-phase and out-of-phase forces), which are also a function of the reduced frequency, S.† The influence of S is again related to the ratio of the different terms in eqn. (19). Oscillation tests will in general serve to obtain all the coupled forces but, in his classical paper, Theodorsen[50] showed a theoretical derivation for aeroplane wings, based on potential flow theory. The complete set of equations for the two degrees of freedom is

$$m\ddot{y} + c\dot{y} + ky = L_y y + L_{\dot{y}}\dot{y} + L_{\ddot{y}}\ddot{y} + L_\Phi \Phi + L_{\dot{\Phi}}\dot{\Phi} + L_{\ddot{\Phi}}\ddot{\Phi} \quad (31a)$$

$$m_p\ddot{\Phi} + c_p\dot{\Phi} + k_p\Phi = M_\Phi\Phi + M_{\dot{\Phi}}\dot{\Phi} + M_{\ddot{\Phi}}\ddot{\Phi} + M_y y + M_{\dot{y}}\dot{y} + M_{\ddot{y}}\ddot{y}$$
$$(31b)$$

When all the coefficients and masses are known, one can investigate systematically what are the necessary c, c_p, k and k_p values as functions of, respectively $(\hat{\Phi}/\hat{y})$, θ and ω. The values of c and c_p indicate the minimum damping necessary to prevent vibration.

The mechanism of self-excitation can only occur due to coupling (the last three terms in both eqns. 31a and b); an example for $\omega = 0$ was the divergence introduced in Section 5.

For bridge decks it is also possible to suppress flutter vibrations by altering the cross-section, perforating the bridge deck and/or increasing the torsional rigidity.

7.2 Galloping

The approach for calculations of vibrations in a cross-flow direction is the same as for the hydrodynamic damping in the case of Fig. 9. In Fig. 12 is shown how the vibration velocity, $\dot{y}$, transforms V_0 into a relative velocity V: its magnitude and angle of attack are changed by the values

$$\Delta V = \dot{y} \sin \alpha \quad (32)$$

and

$$\Delta\alpha = -\dot{y} \cos \alpha / V \quad (33)$$

For a stationary condition with flow under an angle of attack α

$$F_y = L \cos \alpha + D \sin \alpha = \tfrac{1}{2}\rho V^2 LD(C_L \cos \alpha + C_D \sin \alpha) = C_{F_y}\tfrac{1}{2}\rho V^2 LD$$
$$(34)$$

† Here S is not precisely the Strouhal number, which is only related to the periodic component of the non-coupled term of the flow excitation.

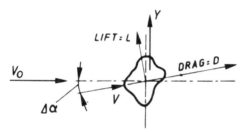

F IG. 12. Scheme for galloping calculations.

Now one can calculate the extra force, ΔF_y, induced by the vibration velocity, $\dot{y}$, using a linearised expression

$$\Delta F_y = (\partial F_y/\partial\alpha)\Delta\alpha + (\partial F_y/\partial V)\Delta V \qquad (35)$$

When the vibration is in a cross-flow direction, $\Delta\alpha$ can be replaced by $\dot{y}/V$. When eqn. (34) is introduced in eqn. (35) and $\Delta\alpha$ and ΔV are introduced using eqns. (32) and (33), a new equation is found where $\sin\alpha = 0$ and $\cos\alpha = 1$ approximately holds. This results in

$$\Delta F_y = \tfrac{1}{2}\rho LDV_0\dot{y}(-\partial C_L/\partial\alpha - C_D) \qquad (36)$$

Because the fluid only transfers energy to the structure when ΔF_y is in phase with $\dot{y}$, the system is dynamically unstable when

$$\partial C_L/\partial\alpha + C_D < 0 \qquad (37)$$

This is the well-known expression of Den Hartog,[21] where $(\partial C_L/\partial\alpha + C_D)$ can also be expressed as $\partial(C_{F_y})/\partial(\dot{y}/V)$. The analysis is possible for other vibration directions as well. Blevins presents values of $\partial(C_{F_y})/\partial(\dot{y}/V)$ for different cross-sections;[6] and an example of a cross-section sensitive to self-excitation is the square prism of Fig. 13.

The character of the negative damping is exactly the same as found for the positive damping in Figs. 8 and 9 and it is possible to define a negative damping coefficient $(-C_{dac})$ similar to eqn. (27)

$$(-C_{dac}) = (-c_w)/\rho VLD = \Delta F_y/\rho VLD\dot{y} = (-\partial C_L/\partial\alpha - C_D) \qquad (38)$$

Whether the system is really unstable depends also on the mechanical damping; when $(c + c_\omega) < 0$ the vibration will increase incrementally. If it is not possible to find a cross-section which is dynamically stable, it is of interest to continue the analysis with a calculation of an equilibrium amplitude. This means the introduction into the equations of higher order terms of $(\dot{y}/V)$, and a more extended range of the function $F_y = f(\dot{y}/V)$ has to be used. Novak[34] presented such an analysis for a square prism, using the measurement data of Fig. 13. By introducing a limit cycle

$$y = \hat{y} \sin \omega t \tag{39}$$

one can calculate the energy transfer per period

$$E = \int_0^T \dot{y} F_y \, dt \tag{40}$$

and the mechanical damping, c, which dissipates the same amount of energy. When this is done for several $\hat{y}$ values, the relation between mechanical damping and the amplitude is found. If the damping is too small, the amplitude tends to increase. The relation between c, $\hat{y}$ and ω for a square prism is presented in Fig. 14.

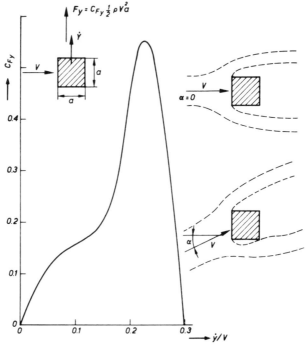

FIG. 13.   Cross-flow force coefficient for a square prism (after Novak[34]).

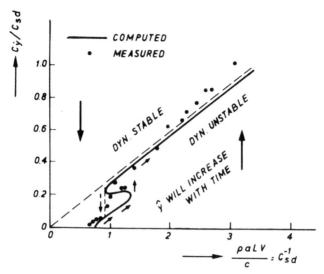

FIG. 14. Response curve as a function of the damping coefficient (after Novak[34]).

The reason why self-excitation occurs is that the body has a certain extra dimension in the flow direction (afterbody) and that at the non-vibration condition there exists a flow pattern without reattachment of flow (see Fig. 13). When there is an angle of incidence of the flow, there is a tendency to one-sided reattachment and a low-pressure zone is formed, resulting in a ΔF_y in the direction of $\dot{y}$.

Like the negative fluid damping of eqn. (38), in Fig. 14 the structural damping, c, of the system is also introduced as a dimensionless damping factor

$$C_{sd} = c/\rho a L V \tag{41}$$

To take into account the non-linearity effects and the maximum velocity, $\omega \hat{y}$ must be considered in relation to the water velocity, V

$$C_{\dot{y}} = \omega \hat{y} / V \tag{42}$$

The presentation of Fig. 14 is such that, when for instance the mechanical parameters are known (and c is especially important), the equilibrium vibration velocity, $\omega \hat{y}$, can be read as a function of the fluid velocity. When the momentary vibration amplitude is smaller than its equilibrium value, it will grow (dynamic instability); when it is greater than its equilibrium value, it will decrease. There is a range of velocities where two equilibrium values of $\omega\hat{y}$ exist; these are related to the fact that in Fig. 13, at increased $\dot{y}/V$ values, an extra-steep slope, $\partial(-C_{F_y})/\partial(\dot{y}/V)$, is found. The arrows show how $\omega\hat{y}$ increases when the velocity increases, and the dotted arrow how $\omega\hat{y}$ decreases when the velocity decreases. A hysteresis is found; the measurements do not show this hysteresis, but only a wide scattering in that region. The tests were performed in air; in water similar results will be obtained, but the frequency of vibration will then be reduced by the water. For practical applications one should know up to which S value the stationary flow value of C_{F_y} is still applicable.

A similar analysis, not for galloping but for cross-flow vibrations of circular cylinders in water, has been presented by Sarpkaya.[45] He did not use the stationary flow coefficient for C_L, nor a constant added mass coefficient, C_m, but first he did laboratory experiments with an oscillating cylinder to find the forces in-phase and out-of-phase with the vibration (say, added mass and added damping terms) as a function of the reduced frequency, S (see Figs. 24–27).

7.3 Vibrations Similar to Gate Vibrations

In Chapter 2 there is an extensive presentation of a mechanism of self-excitation related to a periodic variation of the gate opening, wherein the pressure head across the gate appears to vary in proportion to the vibration velocity, $\dot{y}$. A similar mechanism can occur when a pipe in cross-flow condition is placed at a small distance above the bottom. If the pipe vibrates vertically, the discharge, Q, under the pipe will vary. When Q varies in phase with the vibrational displacement, y, $\partial Q/\partial t$ will vary with $\dot{y}$ and, due to the inertia of the fluid, up- and downstream pressures may arise proportional to $(-\partial Q/\partial t)$. Hence the suction force acting at the underside of the pipe may also vary in phase with $(-\dot{y})$, and this might be a condition for negative hydrodynamic damping.

8   EXCITATION FORCES

8.1   Non-Coupled Forces

Of the dynamic lift (cross-flow) and drag (in-flow) forces on slender bodies, the first are dominant. This is due to the character of the wake: it tends to stabilise with a flow pattern with vortices having alternating rotation directions and shifting away from the object (the Von Kàrmàn vortex street). Because the total quantity of fluid rotation is not abruptly changing, a compensating opposite rotation forms around the body. This rotation is responsible for the periodic lift force (a kind of Magnus effect which causes a low-pressure zone on the side where the initial flow velocity and the rotational velocity are in the same direction). The strongest lift forces are found with circular cylinders where the 'compensating' rotation is not hampered.

The stable pattern of vortices results in a fixed relation between vortex spacing and wake width, and this again results in a correlation between the stationary drag coefficient and the Strouhal number of the lift forces. This is illustrated in Fig. 15 which shows C_D and S variations as a function of the Reynolds number for a circular cylinder. More recent test results for higher Re values are found in refs. 23 and 1; these lead to somewhat deviating values of S and C_D, but their correlation remains.

S and C_D are dependent on the Reynolds number, but only for shapes with rounded edges where the point of flow separation is unstable and influenced by minor effects (boundary layer development, surface roughness and initial flow turbulence). Figure 16 gives some examples of approximate S values for steel profiles; the original paper presents many more shapes. Delany et al.[8] present S values for various

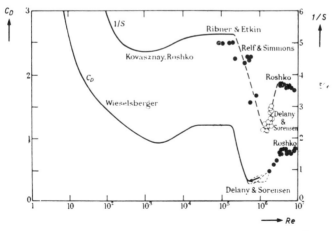

FIG. 15. C_D and S as function of Re (after Bishop et al.[5]).

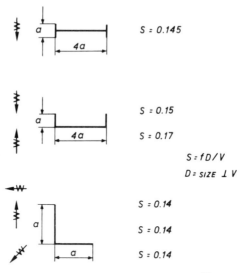

FIG. 16. S values of steel profiles.[54]

shapes with rounded edges where again an important influence of the Re value is found.

For the dynamic lift or drag coefficients not many data are available, with the exception of circular cylinders. In general, the excitation will have a spectral distribution and the S values mentioned should be seen as the values at which the 'energy' is maximal (or better, where $S_n \phi(S_n)$ has its maximum, see eqn. (13)). But for cylinders, when $Re < 10^5$, the bandwidth of the excitation spectrum is small and the excitation is nearly periodic.

When the body is symmetric with respect to the flow direction, there are dynamic in-line forces (often of small amplitude only) with a doubled frequency. This can be seen as follows: consider a momentary flow pattern at an arbitrary moment, and then half a period later; the flow pattern is then mirrored and hence the same in-line force occurs. It was only quite recently that Wootton discovered the relevance of this phenomenon for circular cylinders.[59,60]

Other sources of excitation are the trailing-edge vortices of plates and wing-shaped bodies[12] and shear layer instabilities.[40] The shear layer is formed by flow separation, when the flow is divided into a dead-water region and a full-flow region. High shear tensions occur and vortices are generated. When the shear layer has a limited length (due to flow reattachment), vortices can be locked in; pressure pulsations will become stronger and dominant S values occur.

8.2 Self-Control Phenomena

One speaks of body-controlled or self-controlling vibrations, when the excitation force is amplified by the vibration itself. In this section a few examples of self-control will be presented. The amplification of the excitation force is limited, because self-control phenomena concentrate only initially available energy at the resonance frequency. In practice it is sometimes difficult to make a sharp distinction from self-excitation.

Especially in those conditions where small disturbances can affect the flow excitation (bodies with rounded edges), even a small-amplitude vibration of the body can have the effect of (a) synchronisation in length direction of the vortex shedding (see Fig. 17) and (b) concentration of the excitation energy into the resonance frequency. This concentration is illustrated in Fig. 18; the test with lower damping (γ value) not only results in higher amplitudes, but also in a greater range of Strouhal numbers ($S^{-1} = V/fD$), where the excitation remains concentrated near the resonance frequency.

Another presentation of how the excitation force is influenced by the vibration is shown in Fig. 19. (The great differences between the curves in Fig. 19 may be partially explained by the different Reynolds numbers of the tests.)

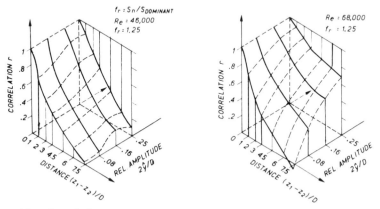

FIG. 17. Correlation coefficient over the length of a cylinder vibrating in cross-flow (after Toebes[51]).

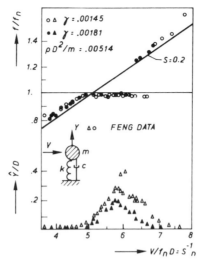

FIG. 18. Vibration amplitude and frequency of a circular cylinder as a function of $S_n = f_n D/V$ (after Blevins[6]).

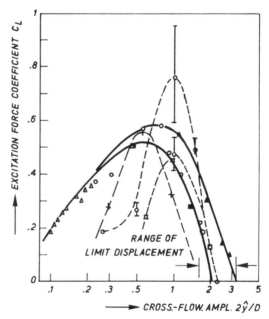

FIG. 19. Dynamic lift force coefficient as function of amplitude (after Griffin[19]).

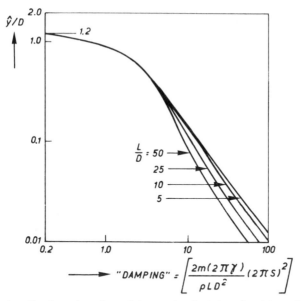

$$\text{"DAMPING"} = \left[\frac{2m(2\pi\gamma)}{\rho L D^2}(2\pi S)^2\right]$$

Fig. 20. Amplitude as function of the mechanical damping (sinusoidal deflection) (after Blevins[6]).

From such data one can, for a given mechanical system, calculate the equilibrium amplitude (at resonance), assuming that the amplitude of the mechanical damping $(c\omega\hat{y})$ equals the excitation amplitude $(C'_{L\frac{1}{2}}\rho V^2 DL)$. When one introduces $\gamma = c/2m\omega_n$ (eqn. (3)),† this results in a function like the one presented in Fig. 20.

Figure 20 introduces the correction due to the correlation coefficient of Fig. 17 (this explains why for greater lengths the amplitude decreases), while use is made of the calculation methods for continuously elastic structures introduced in Section 2. With a cantilever beam, a short length results in smaller amplitudes;[57] this is due to its free end (different S value, less correlation, flow damping).

Considering the introduction of the added mass, it has already been mentioned that Sarpkaya[45] has found that for circular cylinders, m_w, or more generally the ratio (in phase forces)/$\ddot{y}$, varies strongly with the S value, especially near the critical S value of 0·2 (where m_w even tends to be absent).

† For structures in water one should apply $(m + m_w)$ instead of m, and then use the natural angular frequency in the submerged condition.

Normally, one will take care that no resonance occurs, but for very long beams (risers, etc.) higher modes always interfere and therefore greater amplitudes cannot be prevented. Hence data as mentioned in Figs. 19 and 20 are fully relevant.

Another type of self-controlling vibration arises from the locking-in phenomenon of vortices at in-line vibrations of circular cylinders. At S_n values above 0·5, the occurrence of vibration changes the character of vortex shedding from the shedding of single vortices of alternating sense of rotation to the shedding of twin vortices having opposite sense of rotation (see Wootton[60] and next paragraph).

For this locking-in phenomenon two conditions have to be fulfilled:

1. The dominant excitation frequency, f, should be close to the natural frequency, f_n.
2. The amplitude of the response, when f equals f_n, should be greater than a limit value, i.e. $\hat{y}_{max} > \alpha_{cr}D$ (D = diameter of the cylinder).

King and Prosser[24] proposed another presentation. They introduced two components to prevent in-line vibrations of circular cylinders

$$S_n = f_n D / V \text{ should not come below a certain value (about 0·55)} \tag{43}$$

or, when this is not possible

$$2(m + m_w)\delta/\rho D^2 L \text{ should not be below } 1·2 \tag{44}$$

(δ is defined as log decrement $= 2\pi\gamma$).

The second parameter can be understood from the following. When the amplitude of the periodic excitation force equals $C'_{D2}^{\frac{1}{2}}\rho V^2 DL$, then, at resonance conditions, this force is neutralised by the amplitude of the mechanical damping force, $\omega\hat{y}c$. Because the relative vibration amplitude should remain below a critical value, or $\hat{y} \ll \alpha_{cr}D$, one gets as stability parameter

$$\frac{\omega Dc}{C'_{D2}^{\frac{1}{2}}\rho V^2 DL} > \frac{1}{\alpha_{cr}} \tag{45}$$

When we introduce $f_n = \omega_n/2\pi$, $\delta = 2\pi\gamma$ and $\gamma = c/2 (m + m_w)\omega_n$ (see eqn. (3)), eqn. (45) is transformed into

$$\left(\frac{f_n D}{V}\right)^2 \frac{m + m_w}{\rho D^2 L} \delta_s > \frac{C'_D}{8\pi\alpha_{crit}} \tag{46}$$

Because C_D and $S_n = f_n D/V$ must be taken for the most critical condition of resonance, they can be introduced as constants. The right-hand term of eqn. (46) is also a constant and when it is divided by the constant value of S_n^2 the expression of eqn. (44) is obtained.

King and Prosser calculated the damping, δ, from the logarithmic decrement of the freely damped cylinder in stagnant water. From eqn. (46) it can also be seen that for conditions where C_D' is small no danger exists; this is in fact the criterion of eqn. (43).

Another stability criterion (Connors's) is used for the design of cross-flow-positioned pipes and pipe bundles in atomic reactors and heat exchangers (see Paidoussis[37] and Connors[7]). This criterion is

$$(V/f_n D)/(m\delta/\rho D^2 L)^{1/2} < K \tag{47}$$

It is based on the following concept. When a cylinder is placed in the wake of another body, the force exerted by the flow has a magnitude and direction dependent on the relative location of the cylinder. When, now, the vibration is not in one direction but follows a closed loop (circular, elliptical, figure-of-eight-shaped, etc.), there is a possibility of a net energy flux E per period, being $\alpha(\rho V^2 DL) * \hat{y}$ (like force multiplied by travel distance). Meanwhile, the energy dissipation by any mechanical damper with a damping value c equals $E_d = \pi c \omega \hat{y}^2$. But the factor α is also dependent on $\hat{y}$, and for small amplitudes it will be linear with $\hat{y}/D$, say $\alpha = \beta \hat{y}/D$. When the ratio of the two energies (E/E_d) is smaller than unity, the system is stable; this is when

$$\frac{(\beta\hat{y}/D)(\rho V^2 DL\hat{y})}{\pi c \omega \hat{y}^2} < 1 \tag{48}$$

When $c = 2m\omega_n\gamma$ (eqn. (3)) is introduced for the damping, or expressed in δ_s (subscript s means structural), $c = m\omega_n\delta_s/\pi$, and when one transforms $\omega = 2\pi f_n$, one gets

$$\left(\frac{V}{f_n D}\right)^2 \frac{\rho LD^2}{m\delta} < 4\pi^2/\beta \tag{49}$$

This result agrees with the square of eqn. (47), because in eqn. (49) the right-hand term is a constant. However, a few remarks must be made:

1. The factor β is certainly a function of the reduced natural frequency, S_n, although instability occurs, especially when the cylinder is in resonance with the vortex shedding. The vortex shedding frequency, however, depends (within a certain range) on

the vibration frequency and one cannot say beforehand at which precise frequency the energy flux has its maximum.

2. When the cylinder is vibrating just in period with a periodically changing flow pattern, the vibration may be in one direction, because on the way back and forth of the vibration path the same forces are not met, and hence it is possible still to have a net energy flux.

3. Equation (3), namely $c = 2m\omega_n\gamma$, is valid only when ω_n and m are both taken either in dry or in submerged condition. Because in point 1 S_n has to be seen for submerged condition, the best thing to do is to combine (S_n^{-2}), eqn. (49) (but now for submerged condition) and $\beta = f(S_n)$ of point 1 into a new function of S_n; in this case one should introduce for the damping

$$c = 2(m + m_w)\omega_{n_{subm}}\gamma \qquad (50)$$

4. When eqn. (50) is introduced in eqn. (48), one obtains a modified eqn. (49) which then is similar to eqn. (46).

Paidoussis[37] indicated that the power of (S_n^{-1}), which in eqn. (47) is 0·5, has been found to vary between 0·3 and 0·5. He also indicated that results of experiments gave a great scatter of K values in eqn. (47); a safe value for K seems to be 3·3.

9   ADDITIONAL REMARKS ON FLOW-EXCITED CYLINDERS

This section is included because a great deal of the research effort on flow-induced vibrations concerns circular cylinders and many aspects have hardly, or not at all, been touched on in the foregoing sections. This research effort is on the one hand due to the wide range of applications of circular cylinders (easy to manufacture, high strength and logical in shape when multi-directional flow is involved) and on the other hand because the circular cylinders, especially, experience considerable dynamic excitation.

The unstable flow separation related to the round shape means that small influences can cause an important change in the flow pattern, and this results in a sensitivity to

1. Boundary layer development at the cylinder wall upstream of the flow separation point (influenced by Reynolds number, surface roughness and initial turbulence of the water).

2. Vibration of the cylinder in in-flow and cross-flow directions.
3. Interactions of various kinds when more cylinders are involved.
4. Interactions between the left-hand side terms m_w, c_w and k_w and between the left- and right-hand side terms of eqn. (4).
5. Scale effects in hydraulic modelling, related to point 1 and also to other factors, such as confined flow in test rigs.

In a short context, however, it is only possible to make a few remarks on each of the points 1–5 above as follows.

Remarks on point 1

Concerning the influence of the Reynolds number, the following flow regimes are met (see Fig. 21).

The quantitative values of the stationary drag coefficient and the S values have already been indicated in Fig. 15. The effect of initial turbulence, and on some points also the roughness, is that the

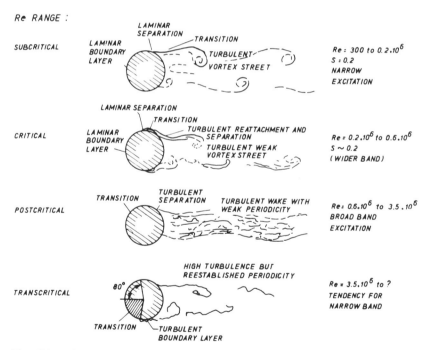

FIG. 21.   Flow regimes for flow across circular sections at higher Re values (after Wootton *et al.*[59] and Morkovin[31]).

boundary layer gets more turbulent, which results in a quasi-shift to higher Reynolds numbers. Encrustation by sea-shells, etc., also causes an increased diameter. Tests with different roughnesses are presented by Sarpkaya[44,47] and Achenbach et al.[1] (high Re values).

A remarkable point is that in the subcritical flow regime the vortex shedding and hence the excitation are periodical, but that this periodicity gets disturbed from the critical regime on. At higher Re values, the character of excitation gets random and spread over a wide frequency range. Thereafter, at $Re > 3.5 \times 10^6$, a certain regularity is re-established.

Figure 22 shows three spectra for cross-flow excitation at different Re values.

Where slight disturbances cause important changes in the flow and excitation character, small remedies might be able to stabilise the flow.

One of the remedies to reduce vibration lies in the fixation of the flow separation points. The sensitivity to Re will then also disappear. Longitudinal fins have disadvantages (quasi-increase of diameter, two-dimensional flow pattern and hence great correlation of excitation in the length direction), but the idea of helical fins appears to be effective. In Wootton et al.[58] and Blevins[6] this and similar remedies are discussed.

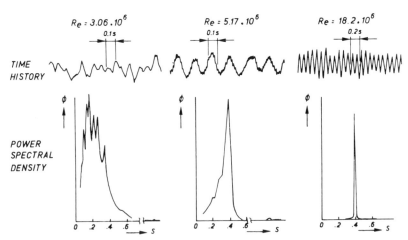

FIG. 22.   Spectra for cross-flow excitation at different Re values (after Jones et al.[23]).

Another remedy is the attachment to cables and small-diameter cylinders of rigid or flexible 'flags' which are rotatable in the flow direction. These disturb the alternating sense of rotation of the vortices and establish a symmetric regime with two half-vortex streets. This results in smaller vortex spacings and hence a higher excitation frequency, low dynamic lift coefficient (because of symmetry $C'_L = 0$ is to be expected, but the vane is also moving) and no increase of stationary drag (see Apelt et al.[2]).

Remarks on point 2

Symmetrical vortex shedding will only result in in-line forces, but now it appears that the in-line vibrations tend to generate symmetrical vortex shedding! This is still an additional phenomenon to the one mentioned in Section 8, stating that with alternate vortex shedding a double-frequency in-line excitation occurs. Both phenomena lead to a relatively high (but different) S value. Hence a lower velocity is needed to develop an excitation at the resonance frequency of the structure. Figure 23 shows test results for a tested single pile in prototype. The value $V_r = 2 \cdot 5$ (or $S = V_r^{-1} = 0 \cdot 4$) shows double the frequency of the alternating vortex shedding. A similar picture, but now extended to V_r values of 9, and hence including cross-flow vibrations, is presented by Walshe.[53] This one was assembled during wind tunnel tests of a scale model of a high chimney.

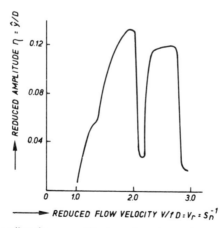

FIG. 23. In-flow vibration; amplitudes of a clamped prototype cylinder in tidal flow (after Wootton et al.[60]).

Unlike the results of Fig. 23, his picture shows only one peak in the V_r range 1·5 to 3.

The critical S values for cross-flow and in-flow vibrations together cover, when the cylinder is able to vibrate at large amplitudes, a wide range (from 0·1 to 1) in which cylinder vibrations can occur.

There seems to be a tendency that vibrations cause a sort of locking-in of the vortex pattern, by which the great Reynolds sensitivity of the excitation is decreased. Hardwick and Wootton[20] reported model tests (which have low Re values) whose results for in-line vibrations were quite similar to prototype measurements of Wootton et al.

The influence of the vibration amplitude on the excitation in cross-flow direction has (for the subcritical range of Reynolds numbers) already been introduced in Section 8 (see Figs. 18 and 19).

In the critical and supercritical range of Reynolds numbers the amplitude of vibration also increases the excitation magnitude. Fung[18] still found an absence of influence in the critical Re range (wherein the excitation has a random character), but he investigated only small vibration amplitudes. Prototype tests by Fischer et al.[15] in the same Re range show such large amplitudes that they are probably related to a re-established periodic excitation. For tests with a vibrating cylinder in the supercritical Re range, see Jones et al.[23]

Remarks on point 3

The interaction between cylinders is important, but depends completely on the lay-out (see refs. 6, 7 and 38). With chimneys, for instance, it has been found that more stacks cause higher excitation, especially when a row of stacks lies nearly in the wind direction; Ruscheweyh[43] and Dudgeon[11] presented extensive wind tunnel experiments. Ozker and Smith[36] reported on tests in prototype.

Remarks on point 4

In order to study the interactions between excitation, hydrodynamic damping and added mass, Sarpkaya performed tests where the periodic components of the cross-flow forces were measured at different forced oscillation amplitudes and at various water velocities.[45] These tests have already been mentioned a few times in preceding sections. Sarpkaya presented his results as forces in phase with the vibration (where normally m_w and k_w effects are included) and out-of-phase forces (including c_w and excitation forces). Figures

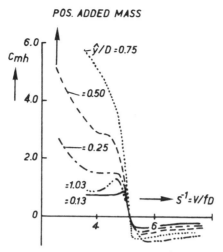

FIG. 24. In-phase forces; $C_{mh} = \hat{F}/\frac{1}{2}\rho V^2 DL$.

24 and 25 show these forces in a dimensionless way (divided by $\frac{1}{2}\rho DV^2L$).

In order to see whether an added mass can still be recognised, Fig. 26 shows the in-phase force divided by $(\pi/4)\rho D^2 \ddot{y}L$. It can be seen that (apart from the very great amplitude $\hat{y}/D = 1\cdot03$) the added

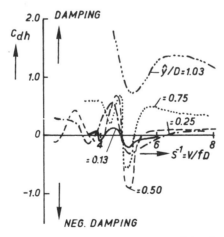

FIG. 25. Out-of-phase forces; $C_{dh} = \hat{F}/\frac{1}{2}\rho V^2 DL$.

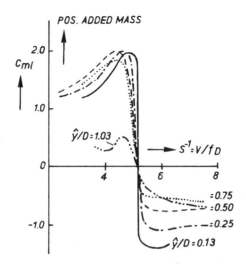

FIG. 26.   In phase forces; $C_{ml} = \hat{F}/(\pi/4)D^2 L\ddot{y}$.

mass is more or less independent of the vibration amplitude as long as the vibration frequency is above the main vortex shedding frequency† (or $V_r < 5$), but even then the V_r value itself has an important influence. The theoretical value of Lamb,[27] $m_w = (\pi/4)\rho D^2 L$, holds only in a global way and at small V_r values only. Sarpkaya also expressed the out-of-phase force in another way, namely as a C_D value, by dividing $\hat{F}$ by $\frac{1}{2}\rho\dot{y}\,|\dot{y}|\,DL$, similar to what has been used, for instance, in the Morison equation (eqn. (22)); this is presented in Fig. 27. His results would have been less scattered if he had divided the force, F, by $\rho DLV\dot{y}$, thus considering the out-of-phase forces as a (positive or negative) hydrodynamic damping, as has been done in Section 6. It can indeed be seen in the results that all factors, m_w, c_w, k_w and $F(t)$, interfere in a mixed way, and therefore application of these factors for cylinders is difficult.

Sarpkaya made a theoretical study where, for the most critical V_r value, the growth of the amplitude from the non-vibrating situation to equilibrium vibration was studied, using his experimental results. This was done for several values of the mechanical damping. It

† The main excitation frequency is at the flow regime investigated, about $S = 0.2$; resonance occurs when $S_n = 0.2$ or $V_r = V/f_n D = 5$.

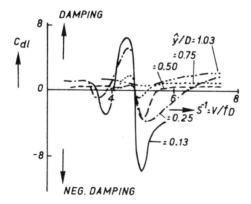

FIG. 27.   Out-of-phase forces; $C_{dl} = \hat{F}/\frac{1}{2}\rho\dot{y}\,|\dot{y}|\,DL$.

appears that in the transient condition a temporary overshoot of the amplitude can occur.

Similar tests with in-flow cylinder oscillations are presented by Verley *et al.*[52]

Remarks on point 5

Scale modelling of structures with circular sections has its merits for design, but there are also relatively important scale effects due to the strong influence of the Reynolds number on the flow regime. A laboratory investigation with dynamic force measurements at a stationary and at an oscillating cylinder performed at the highest Reynolds numbers is presented by Jones *et al.*[23] Other limitations of scale models can be due to the confined flow conditions (see Richter *et al.*[39]) and the small section length of the model. This means that only a part of the structure can be reproduced, problems occur with tip effects, and reproduction of the correlation of the excitation over the entire cylinder length is impossible. Data obtained at prototype structures are therefore most valuable; Wootton *et al.*[60] have already been mentioned. In ref. 42 more experiences and further references are found relating to dynamic pressures and vibrations in prototype structures. It is often found that the flow pattern in the prototype is less pure than in the schematised laboratory conditions (flow distribution varies over the length in magnitude and direction; initial turbulence; non-stationary flow conditions) and hence it is always difficult to obtain pertinent data from prototype measurements.

46   P. A. KOLKMAN

10 OTHER ELEMENTS OF FLOW INSTABILITIES

Flow instabilities are important because they can cause considerable dynamic loads on structures. Just like a mechanical system, a fluid system can also be a resonator with its own natural frequencies (standing waves, communicating vessels, etc.), and it can be excited in the same way as mentioned for structural vibrations. Moreover, the dynamic flow excitation force exerted on a structure is at the same time a dynamic excitation force exerted by the structure on the fluid.

Hence, unstable flow conditions in one of the components can, together with resonance properties of the whole fluid system, lead to fluid oscillations.

10.1 Phenomena of Self-Excitation

In the same way as vibration of a mechanical structure gives a destabilising feedback to the flow-induced forces, a fluid oscillation can also have this effect, resulting in self-exciting fluid oscillation. Again this will lead to an exponentially growing amplitude, till a level is reached where non-linear components interfere.

A recent example experienced in the Delft Hydraulics Laboratory was the functioning of a free-surface-flow discharge sluice model (Fig. 28). When, for instance, only six openings discharged while the

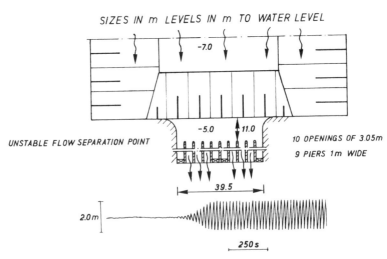

FIG. 28.   Self-exciting wave oscillations in the upstream basin of a sluice.

other openings (and especially the outer ones) were closed by gates, a transverse wave oscillation occurred, resulting in a wave amplitude in the prototype of $H = 2\hat{y} = 2$ m near the closed gates. The transverse flow component related to the water level oscillations interacted most probably at the point where the main flow seperated from the side walls.

The instability of a flow reattachment point can also cause a self-exciting fluid oscillation. This is related, among others, to the fact that a flow contraction coefficient decreases at an acceleration of flow, while a deceleration causes an increase. The reason is related to what has been shown in Section 4 for the added mass calculations; when the term $\rho \, \partial v'/\partial t$ in eqn. (19) gets more important, the flow pattern tends to approach the one obtained by potential flow theory.

The original condition of Fig. 29 resulted in a pulsating flow and, related to it, a vibration of the downstream butterfly valve. This phenomenon was cured by the application of gradual bends of constant cross-section.

In the case of the bifurcating pipe in a power plant circuit of Fig. 30, fluid oscillations were cured by reshaping the circuit in such way that no flow separation occurred.

It is possible to generalise, as an indicator for unstable flow, that instability occurs when there is a component in a pipe which tends to decrease the discharge when the head difference is increasing. In Chapter 2, Section 2 this is illustrated for a bath-tub plug or a gate in a short pipe. Streeter and Wylie[49] presented the use of this indicator for the prediction of flow instabilities in the standing compression wave

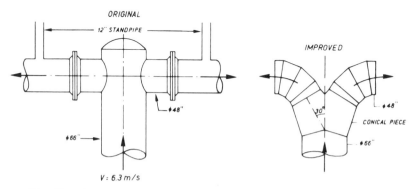

FIG. 29.   Original T-junction and improved design (after Bakes *et al.*[3]).

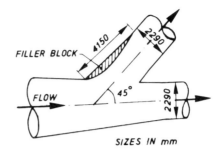

FIG. 30.   Y-junction and improvement (after Falvey[13]).

period in penstocks, etc. The component can be a valve, but can also
be a pump or a turbine, of which the Q-H characteristic shows a point
where the derivative $\partial Q/\partial H$ becomes positive. This is close to the
regime where $\partial Q/\partial H = 0$ and where the working conditions are known
to be unstable. Fanelli[14] reported such an instability for a pump in a
conduit. Also, draught tube surges in hydro-turbines can be induced
by the same mechanism (see Falvey[13]).

The same indicator may also be applicable for free-surface flow. A
raised gate just touching the water level causes a flow contraction
which becomes smaller when the upstream water level rises. In this
case a standing wave in the upstream basin can occur (see Binnie[4] and
Kolkman[26]). In the case of a weir with several openings, transverse
oscillations of the upstream water level can also occur, provoked by
the same mechanism.

10.2   Forced Excitation and Self-Control Phenomena

Resonance of a fluid system occurs when the fluid is periodically
excited at or near a resonance frequency of the fluid basin. Because,
for instance, a non-vibrating cylinder is periodically excited by the
flow, this cylinder periodically excites the fluid. An example is the
wave oscillation in a river induced by bridge piers. The oscillation
occurs in one of the standing wave periods of the canal section. This
phenomenon, among others, has been studied by Rohde et al.[41]

An important phenomenon of periodic excitation of a fluid is the
instability of a shear layer behind a flow separation. The shear layer is
the zone between the through-going flow and the eddy with a high
velocity gradient. Especially when the shear layer has a limited length
(because of reattachment of the flow), pressure pulsations increase and

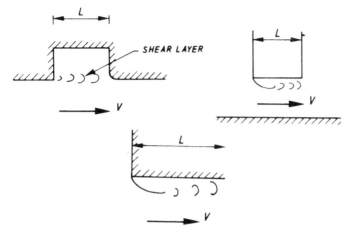

FIG. 31. Definition scheme for L and V.

periodic flow oscillations occur. The length, L, of this zone (between flow separation and reattachment—Fig. 31 shows the definitions for different situations) and the velocity, V, result in a periodic oscillation of the flow pattern, of which the frequency, f, can again be expressed in a Strouhal number, $S = fL/V$. A review of experimental results for a great number of configurations is presented by Rockwell and Naudascher.[40]

REFERENCES

1. ACHENBACH, E. and HEINECKE, E. On vortex shedding from smooth and rough cylinders in the range of Reynolds numbers 6×10^3 to 5×10^6, J. Fluid Mech., **109** (1981), 239–51.
2. APELT, C. J., WEST, C. S. and SZEWCZYK, A. A. The effect of water splitter plates on the flow past a circular cylinder in the range $10^4 < R < 5 \times 10^4$, J. Fluid Mech., **61** (1973), 187–98; **71** (1975), 145–60.
3. BAKES, F. and GOODWIN, P. MC. Flow induced vibrations in circulating water system, Proc. ASCE, **HY8** (Aug. 1980), paper 1394.
4. BINNIE, A. M. Unstable flow under a sluice gate, Proc. Roy. Soc., London, **367** (1730) (1979).
5. BISHOP, R. E. D. and HASSAN, A. Y. The lift and drag forces on a circular cylinder oscillating in flowing fluid, Proc. Roy. Soc., London, **277** (1368) (1964).
6. BLEVINS, R. D. Flow-Induced Vibration, Van Nostrand Reinhold Co., New York, 1977.

7. CONNORS, H. J. Fluidelastic vibration of tube arrays excited by cross flow, *Proc. ASME Symp. Winter Annual Meeting*, December 1970, 42–56.

8. DELANY, N. K. and SORENSEN, N. E. *Low speed drag of cylinders of various shapes*, NACA Tech. Note 3038, November 1953.

9. Delft Hydr. Lab. *Golf- en Stroomkrachten op Slanke Cylinders*, Report R1155, 1977.

10. DERUNZ, J. A. and GEERS, T. L. Added mass computation by the boundary integral method, *Int. J. Numerical Methods Eng.*, **12** (1978), 531–49.

11. DUDGEON, C. R. *Wind-induced oscillations of power station stacks*, Report 46, Water Res. Lab, Univ. New South Wales, 1962.

12. EAGLESON, P. and DAILY, J. W. The effect of boundary layer thickness and vibrational amplitude on the Strouhal number for plates, *IAHR Congress*, London 1963, paper 3–10.

13. FALVEY, T. Bureau of Reclamation experience with flow-induced vibrations. In: *Practical Experiences with Flow-Induced Vibrations IAHR/IUTAM Symp.*, *Karlsruhe*, 1978, E. Naudascher and D. Rockwell, Eds., Springer Verlag, Berlin, 1980.

14. FANELLI, M. A. Theoretical treatment of a spontaneous instability of a system of pump, valve and conduit, *8th IAHR Symp.*, *Sect. Hydr. Mach. Equipm. and Cavitation*, Leningrad, 1976, paper IV-4.

15. FISCHER, F. J., JONES, W. T. and KING, R. Current induced oscillations of cognac piles during installation—prediction and measurement. In: *Practical Experiences with Flow-Induced Vibrations IAHR/IUTAM Symp.*, *Karlsruhe*, 1978, E. Naudascher and D. Rockwell, Eds., Springer Verlag, Berlin, 1980.

16. FONTIJN, H. L. *The berthing ship problem: forces on berthing structures from moving ships*, Rep. 78–2, Lab. of Fluid Mech., Delft Univ. of Technology, Dept. Civ. Eng., 1978.

17. FORSCHING, H. W. *Grundlagen der Aeroelastik*, Springer Verlag, Berlin 1974.

18. FUNG, Y. C. Fluctuating lift and drag on a cylinder in flow at supercritical Reynolds numbers, *IAS 28th Annual Meeting*, N.Y., Jan., 1960, Inst. of Aerospace Sciences, Paper 60–6.

19. GRIFFIN, O. M. *OTEC cold water pipe design for problems caused by vortex-excited oscillations*, Ref. 4157, Naval Research Lab., Washington D.C., 1980.

20. HARDWICK, J. D. and WOOTTON, L. R. The use of model and full-scale investigations on marine structures, *Int. Symp. on Vibr. Problems in Industry*, Keswick (U.K.), 1973, paper 127.

21. DEN HARTOG, J. P. *Mechanical Vibrations*, McGraw-Hill Book Co., New York, 1956.

22. HOOFT, J. P. Hydrodynamic aspects of semi-submersible platforms, Thesis, Delft Univ. of Technology, Dept. Naval Arch., 1972.

23. JONES, G. W., CINCOTTA, J. J. and WALKER, W. *Aerodynamic forces on a stationary and oscillating circular cylinder at high Reynolds numbers*, NASA Report TR-300, Febr., 1969.

24. KING, R. and PROSSER, M. J. Criteria for flow-induced oscillations of a cantilevered cylinder in water. In: *Flow-Induced Structural Vibrations*,

IAHR/IUTAM Symp., Karlsruhe, 1972, E. Naudascher, Ed., Springer-Verlag, Berlin, 1974.

25. KOLKMAN, P. A. Flow-induced gate vibrations, Thesis, Delft Univ. of Technol., 1976; Publ. 164, Delft Hydr. Lab.

26. KOLKMAN, P. A. Development of vibration-free gate design. In: *Practical Experiences with Flow-Induced Vibrations, IAHR/IUTAM Symp., Karlsruhe*, 1978, Springer Verlag, Berlin.

27. LAMB, H. *Hydrodynamics*, 6th ed., Cambridge Univ. Press, Cambridge, 1932.

28. MEI, C. C. Numerical methods in water-wave diffraction and radiation, *Ann. Rev. Fluid Mech.* (1978.10), 393–416.

29. MEYERS, P. *Numerical hull vibration analysis of a far-east container ship*, Report 195 S, Netherlands Ship Research Centre, TNO, 1974.

30. MORISON, J. R., O'BRIEN, M. P., JOHNSON, J. W. and SCHAAF, S. A. The force exerted by surface waves on piles, *Petroleum Transactions AIME*, **189** (1950), 149.

31. MORKOVIN, M. V. Flow around circular cylinder—a kaleidoscope of challenging fluid phenomena, *Symp. on Fully Separated Flow, Proc. of Eng. Div. Conference ASME, Philadelphia, May, 1964*, A. G. Hansen, Ed., New York, 1964.

32. NAUDASCHER, E. (Ed.) *Flow-Induced Structural Vibrations, IAHR/IUTAM Symp., Karlsruhe*, 1972, Springer Verlag, Berlin, 1974.

33. NAUDASCHER, E. and ROCKWELL, D. (Eds.) *Practical Experiences with Flow-Induced Vibrations, IAHR/IUTAM Symp., Karlsruhe*, 1978, Springer Verlag, Berlin, 1980.

34. NOVAK, M. Aeroelastic galloping of prismatic bodies, *Proc. ASCE, J. Mech. Div.*, **EM1** (Febr. 1969), paper 6394.

35. *Int. J. Numerical Methods Eng.* **13** (1) (1978). Special issue on Fluid–Structure Interaction.

36. OZKER, M. S. and SMITH, J. O. Factors influencing the dynamic behaviour of tall stacks under the action of wind, *Trans. ASME*, **78** (6) (Aug. 1956), 1381–91.

37. PAIDOUSSIS, M. Flow-induced vibrations in nuclear reactors and heat exchangers In: *Practical Experiences with Flow-Induced Vibrations, IAHR/IUTAM Symp., Karlsruhe*, 1978, E. Naudascher and D. Rockwell, Eds., Springer Verlag, Berlin, 1980.

38. PAIDOUSSIS, M. P. Fluidelastic vibration of cylinder arrays in axial and cross flow: state of the art, *J. Sound Vibration*, **76** (3) (1981), 329–60.

39. RICHTER, A. and NAUDASCHER, E. Fluctuating forces on a rigid circular cylinder in confined flow, *J. Fluid Mech.*, **78** (part 3) (1976).

40. ROCKWELL, D. and NAUDASCHER, E. Review: Self-sustaining oscillations of flow past cavities, *ASME J. Fluid Eng.*, **100** (part 2) (1978).

41. ROHDE, F. G., ROUVE, G. and PASCHE, E. Self-excited oscillatory surface waves around cylinders. In: *Practical Experiences with Flow-Induced Vibrations, IAHR/IUTAM Symp., Karlsruhe*, 1978, E. Naudascher and D. Rockwell, Eds., Springer Verlag, Berlin, 1980.

42. RUSCHEWEYH, H. *Statische und dynamische Windkräfte an Kreiszylindrischen Bauwerken*, Forschungsberichte des Landes Nordrhein-Westfalen

Nr. 2685, Fachgruppe Maschinenbau, Verfahrenstechnik, Westdeutscher Verlag, 1977.

43. RUSCHEWEYH, H. Winderregte Schwingungen zweier engstehender Kamine, *3rd Colloq. on Industrial Aerodynamics*, June, 1978, Aachen, part II, 175–84.

44. SARPKAYA, T. *In-line and transverse forces on smooth and sand-roughened cylinders in oscillatory flow at high Reynolds numbers*, Naval Postgrad. School, Monterey, Calif., Rep. NPS-69 SL, 76062, June, 1976.

45. SARPKAYA, T. Fluid forces on oscillating cylinders, *Proc. ASCE, J. Waterway, Port, Coastal and Ocean Div.*, **WW4** (Aug. 1978), paper 13941.

46. SARPKAYA, T. A critical assessment of Morison's equation, *Int. Symp. on Hydrodyn. in Ocean Engn., Trondheim, Aug., 1981*, Norw. Inst. of Technology, 447.

47. SARPKAYA, T. Flow-induced vibration of roughened cylinders, *BHRA, Int. Conf. on Flow Induced Vibrations in Fluid Engn.*, Reading, paper D1, Sept., 1982.

48. SCHOEMAKER, H. J. Virtuele massa bij golfklappen en daarop volgende trillingen in een constructie, In: *Manuscripten van H. J. Schoemaker in de periode 1946–1971*, Delft Hydr. Lab., paper G6, 1971.

49. STREETER, V. L. and WYLIE, E. B. *Hydraulic Transients*, McGraw-Hill Book Co., New York, 1967.

50. THEODORSEN, Th. *General theory of aerodynamical instability and the mechanism of flutter*, NACA Rep. 496, 1935.

51. TOEBES, G. H. The unsteady flow and wake near an oscillating cylinder, *Trans. ASME, J. Basic Eng.* (Sept. 1969), 493–505.

52. VERLEY, R. L. P. and MOE, G. *The forces on a cylinder oscillating in a current*, Proj. 608018, Harbour & River Lab., Univ. of Trondheim, 1979.

53. WALSHE, D. E. J. *The aerodynamic investigation for the proposed 850-ft. chimney stack for the Drax power station*, Nat. Phys. Lab., Aero. Rep. 1227, Apr. 1967 (reference taken from ref. 59).

54. University of Washington Engineering Expt. Stat. *The role of vortex in the aerodynamic excitation of suspension bridges*, University of Washington Press (eds), Bull. 116, Part III, Appendix III, 1952.

55. WENDEL. K. Hydrodynamische Massen und hydrodynamische Massentragheitsmomente, *Jahrbuch der Schiffsbautechnischer Gesellschaft*, **44** (1950), 207–55.

56. WESTERGAART, H. M. Water pressures on dams during earthquakes, *Trans. ASCE* (1933), paper 1835.

57. WOOTTON, L. R. Wind-induced oscillations of circular stacks. *Proc. Conf. on Tower Shaped Structures*, The Hague, 1969, 164–84.

58. WOOTTON, L. R. and SCRUTON, C. *Aerodynamic stability, Proc. Seminar on the Modern Design of Wind-Sensitive Structures*, CIRIA, June, 1970, 65–81.

59. WOOTTON, L. R., WARNER, M. H., SAINSBURY, R. N. and COOPER, D. H. *Oscillation of piles in marine structures*, CIRIA, London, Techn. Note 40, Aug., 1972.

60. WOOTTON, L. R., WARNER, M. H. and COOPER, D. H. Some aspects of

the oscillations of full scale piles. In: *Flow-Induced Structural Vibrations, IAHR/IUTAM Symp., Karlsruhe,* 1972, E. Naudascher, Ed., Springer Verlag, Berlin, 1974.

61. ZIENKIEWICZ, O. C. and NATH, B. Analogue procedure for determination of virtual mass, *Proc. ASCE, J. Hydr. Div.,* **HY5** (Sept. 1964), 69.

Chapter 2

GATE VIBRATIONS

P. A. KOLKMAN

Locks, Weirs and Sluices Branch, Delft Hydraulics Laboratory; Department of Civil Engineering, Delft University of Technology, Delft, The Netherlands

1 CHARACTERISTIC ELEMENTS RELATED TO GATE VIBRATIONS

Gates in hydraulic structures can be fully opened or closed, but in practice they often serve for the regulation of discharge, pressure or water level. Over sometimes long periods, partly opened gates induce energy dissipation resulting in high turbulence, and this turbulence excites gate vibration. Moreover, there are several mechanisms which may cause heavy, self-excited (or negatively damped) vibrations leading to great amplitudes and this is, even for a short duration, never acceptable. These mechanisms can be related to underflow or to overflow, while the combination of both can lead to other important dynamic phenomena related to a so-called Von Kármán vortex street. The long periods involved, in which vibrations can potentially arise, make it absolutely necessary to design the gates in such a way that only low-level vibrations can occur.

Although a gate can be considered to be an object in flow, its most striking characteristic is that it throttles the flow; and when it is vibrating with a certain frequency the discharge capacity will vary with the same frequency. It is this element that leads to a type of vibration mechanism which is not encountered with an object in free flow.

Apart from the analysis of vibrations, it is seen that the flow pattern is often quite complex due to the complexity of flow boundaries and discontinuities of the flow profile caused by gate shafts, slots, etc.; this flow pattern is almost always three-dimensional. Moreover, the whole variety of gate positions has to be considered in relation to the variations of the upstream and downstream water levels. Viewed mechanically, it can be seen that vibrations with several degrees of freedom may be involved, where the elasticity of rubber seals may also interfere.

Gates generally belong to a system comprising other resonating components, such as shafts acting as communicating vessels and standing free-surface oscillations in shafts or in upstream and downstream basins. Considering all these elements, which are typical for gate vibrations, it makes sense to introduce this subject separately.

At first, gates will be introduced with their gate members, culverts and shafts as parts of one single system to illustrate the potential interaction of these components.

In Fig. 1, shaft I presents, together with the upstream canal, a communicating vessel system whose inertia is related to the fluid density times the culvert length (ρL_1) and whose 'rigidity' is related to the gravity force. When the head difference, z_1, is varying in time $(z_1 = \bar{z}_1 + z_1')$, the gravity force $\rho g z_1'$ can accelerate the culvert fluid. But the total system consists of upstream canal + shaft I + shaft II + downstream canal and has the degrees of freedom z_1' and z_2' (which are the dynamic components of the non-stationary values z_1 and z_2). When the upstream and downstream levels are constant, the system will have two resonance frequencies.

However, the gate member also forms part of the system. Suppose the movements in X and Y directions are coupled with separate rigidities (two springs, see Fig. 1); now the flow resistance (which is a

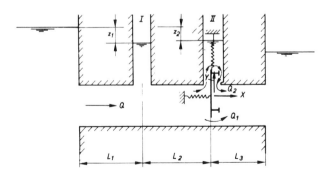

FIG. 1.   Presentation of gate–culvert–shaft system.

measure of the hydraulic forces acting on the gate) is determined by the width of the opening under the gate and of the narrow slit at the top of the gate (flow over its top via shaft II), and both widths vary through oscillation of the gate. Moreover, the gate vibration (especially in the X direction) is pistoning the fluid in the culvert. When all these elements are considered, it is possible to describe the whole system in a series of coupled equations. All these equations can be linearised when only small-amplitude disturbances are considered and it is possible to calculate the different natural frequencies of the system, while the damping of each mode can also be determined (to check whether or not the system is dynamically stable at initially small amplitudes).

Such linearisation is possible when the oscillation velocity components are small compared with the initial fluid velocities. (Example: the non-linear pressure relation $p = \alpha V^2$ becomes linear by stating $\Delta p = 2\alpha V \Delta v$.) In Section 2 the point of dynamic stability or instability is further introduced for a system having two degrees of freedom, one being the gate movement the other the flow variation in the culvert. When the system is dynamically stable (i.e. when it has positive damping), the flow turbulence is the only remaining source of excitation. Quantification of the response of a complex system of this type to turbulence excitation, however, is not yet attempted. The turbulence excitation acts on several points simultaneously, and how this occurs is not sufficiently well known.

Other elements leading to dynamic loads on a gate can be water hammer, cavitation, wave impact, an unstable hydraulic jump, and water column separation related to (partial) aeration or cavitation. Also, the raising or lowering of the gate by an elastic hoist system can, through the occurrence of non-linear friction, lead to slip–stick vibrations which, in their turn, can induce dynamic water pressures. This shows that the gate design and the dynamic gate behaviour are fully related to the design of the total structure to which they belong.

Depending on the speed of closing or opening the gate, a virtual extra head difference has to be introduced, because of the deceleration or acceleration of water in the culvert.

Recently, compilatory literature has become available on flow-induced gate vibrations as follows:

1. A fairly complete collection of gate vibrations experienced in practice and their remedies.[19]
2. Theories on the mechanisms of self-exciting gate vibrations (see Sections 2 and 3).

Much insight is gained by the use of hydraulic and, especially, hydroelastic models (systems with single or multiple degrees of freedom and continuously elastic similarity models), where a great refinement has been reached. The structure of this chapter is that gate vibrations are mainly discussed in their simplest form, this being the behaviour of a gate with a single degree of freedom. To this end, its passive reaction to turbulence excitation, the character of this excitation, the added mass, the added damping, the added rigidity and, finally, the negative damping (dynamic instability) will be introduced in Section 2. The important phenomenon of negative damping will be analysed in more detail, including some theoretical background, in Section 3. This is done because a detailed understanding of the phenomenon can prevent design errors and is the basis of an approach wherein the gate member is considered as a part of the entire system.

Section 4 will present examples of gate vibrations experienced in practice, which occurred due to dynamic instability. Subsequently, in Section 5, some examples of self-control phenomena (wherein the vibration itself can amplify the hydrodynamic excitation, but to a limited extent only) will be shown. The importance of gate seal design in relation to dynamic gate behaviour is discussed in Section 6; and in Section 7 vibrations due to overflow of gates are treated (and also the influence of the compressibility of the air cushion which can be enclosed between gate and overflow nappe).

In Section 8 the design aspects of vibration prevention are discussed, for which the use of hydroelastic scale models is often necessary. Their field of application and their limitations are discussed in the final section, Section 10. In Section 9 cavitation aspects are discussed.

2 COMPONENTS OF THE DYNAMIC EQUATION OF A SYSTEM HAVING A SINGLE DEGREE OF FREEDOM

Parallel to the text in Chapter 1, special features of gate behaviour will be presented in terms of the components of the classical equation of the oscillator, with added components for the fluid

$$(m + m_w)\ddot{y} + (c + c_w)\dot{y} + (k + k_w)y = F_w(t, y, \dot{y}, \ddot{y}) \tag{1}$$

where the right-hand side terms $F_w(y, \dot{y}, \text{etc.})$ are coupled forces and $F_w(t)$ is non-coupled force; $y = $ displacement, $\dot{y} = \partial y/\partial t$, etc., $m = $ mass, $c = $ damping, $k = $ rigidity, $F_w = $ hydrodynamic force, $t = $ time, $m_w = $ added mass, $c_w = $ added damping and $k_w = $ added rigidity.

2.1 The Passive Response

From Chapter 1, Section 2, the following expressions are adopted:
—for the excitation frequency of the flow

$$S = fL/V \qquad (2)$$

where S = Strouhal number, f = excitation frequency due to the flow, L = a reference length of the structure and V = a reference value of the flow velocity.
—for the intensity of excitation

$$F'^2 = C'^2(\tfrac{1}{2}\rho V^2 L^2)^2 \qquad (3)$$

where F' = dynamic part of the excitation force, F, and C' = excitation coefficient.
—for the frequency distribution function $\phi(S)$ of the excitation

$$\int_0^\infty \phi(S)\, dS = 1 \qquad (4)$$

—for the dimensionless expression of the natural frequency (or the reduced resonance frequency S_n)

$$S_n = f_n L/V \qquad (5)$$

where f_n = natural frequency.
—for the (internal) force in the spring

$$F_i = ky \qquad (6)$$

When the gate reacts only passively to the random excitation by turbulence (or when, in eqn. (1), F_w is only a function of t), there is a quasi-static part of the response where the excitation frequency is (far) below the resonance frequency and where F_i' is not amplified towards F'. There is a dynamic part where the amplification depends on the dimensionless damping, γ, $\gamma = (c + c_w)/2\sqrt{[(m + m_w)(k + k_w)]}$, on the intensity of the excitation and on the value of the frequency distribution function at the natural frequency, being $\phi(S_n)$.

Quantitatively this leads, similar to what has been introduced in Section 2 of Chapter 1, to

$$\overline{F_i'^2} = \frac{\pi}{4\gamma} S_n \phi(S_n)(C'\tfrac{1}{2}\rho V^2 L^2)^2 \qquad (7)$$

The validity of eqn. (7) has been proven by gate tests in hydroelastic scale models with variable gate mass, hoist rigidity and mechanical damping. From these tests it was concluded that for such a case a purely passive response occurs, without a tendency to self-control or self-excitation. The gates are excited by turbulence induced by the energy dissipation at the gate itself.[28,30] One should not generalise this conclusion to extend beyond the excitation by turbulence, because other elements can lead to self-control.

In the literature, in general, one does not find quantitative applications of eqn. (7) because it is implicitly assumed that when the resonance frequency is far from the main excitation frequency, the dynamic excitation forces are small. The total C' value in eqn. (3) can be up to about 10% of the maximum stationary hydrodynamic forces (say, gate area × local head difference) for a submerged condition of flow.

Abelev presented a number of studies to establish the dominant Strouhal numbers and C' values of different gates.[1,2] At the transition to free-surface flow, where an unstable hydraulic jump can occur, the load can greatly increase.

Some more data have been published by Naudascher et al.[33,38] What is still missing is a kind of catalogue of Strouhal numbers for a wide variety of configurations.

The S values for two configurations are presented in Figs. 2 and 3.

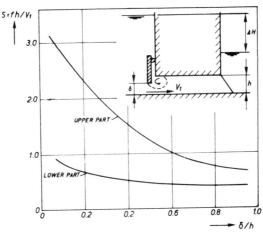

FIG. 2. Strouhal number for horizontal excitation of a culvert gate (after Abelev[1]).

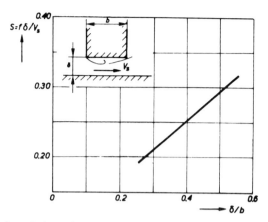

FIG. 3.   Strouhal number for vertical excitation (after Naudascher[38]).

For the culvert gate it is to be expected that the top leakage gap will influence the S value of its upper part.

2.2   Added Mass, m_w

The added mass of a horizontally vibrating gate, especially when the gate is placed in a closed conduit, depends on the gate position. When, as shown in Fig. 4, the gate is nearly closed, the situation is similar to that of a piston in a cylinder and the mass of the fluid in the culvert determines the m_w quantity.

Such a value of m_w is much greater than the m_w of an object oscillating in unconfined fluid. When a gate is partly opened, the fluid in the culvert will hardly follow the gate oscillation, but a flow through the gate opening will occur. This means that m_w is much reduced.

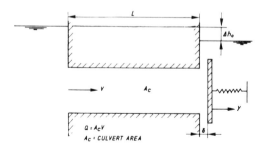

FIG. 4.   Plug-valve gate.

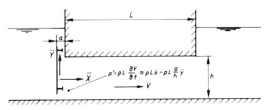

FIG. 5.   Pressures related to m_w.

The coupling term in m_w (introduced in Chapter 1, Section 3) is important in gates; this means that an acceleration in the X-direction also results in forces in the Y-direction (proportional to $\ddot{x}$) and vice versa. Figure 5 shows, for instance, that a horizontal gate oscillation causes pressures at the gate which also exercise a lift force; and, inversely, a vertical gate movement will also cause a horizontal force.

For a piston in a cylinder, the length of the water column (L in Fig. 4) determines m_w. In Fig. 6 one can also express the m_w of the oscillating gate under a rigid wall in terms of an imaginary cylinder of length L. This length is expressed by $C_L\delta$. The graph has been determined analytically, using potential flow theory neglecting wave radiation.[30] In Chapter 1, Section 5, the influence of wave radiation was mentioned for a similar case, but this influence is small because of the relatively high resonance frequencies of gates. The inertia of the water column in a culvert results in an extra pressure downstream of a gate when the water is accelerated. The reason for acceleration can be an increased discharge, but can also be a horizontal gate vibration where the water in the culvert acts as added mass (as in Fig. 4). This parallel between dq/dt and $\ddot{y}$ of the gate vibration is also shown in Fig. 6b and 6a, respectively.

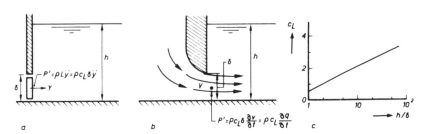

FIG. 6.   Flow inertia at a vibrating gate and fluctuating discharge. (a) Vibration; (b) velocity fluctuation; (c) c_L coefficient.

Concerning vertical vibrations, Thang[56] presented experimental results of m_w values for gates in free-surface flow and in culvert flow.

2.3 Added Rigidity, k_w

A cause of hydrodynamic rigidity which is typical for gates is the instantaneous or high-frequency rigidity, k_{wi}. Suppose, looking at Fig. 4, the gate opening, δ, decreases abruptly to an opening $(\delta - \delta')$: the discharge will at first remain the same, and then gradually adapt to the new situation; how slowly depends on the culvert length, L. But looking at the first moment only, the same discharge has to pass through a smaller opening; so the pressure difference which initially was

$$\Delta p \sim V^2 \sim Q^2/\delta^2 \qquad (8)$$

increases with an extra pressure head difference $\Delta p'$, due to the gap width reduction $(-\delta')$, and becomes

$$\Delta p' = \frac{\Delta p}{\partial \delta}(-\delta') \sim (-2Q^2/\delta_0^3)(-\delta') = \Delta p \frac{2\delta'}{\delta_0} \qquad (9)$$

where $\sim$ is used as a sign for proportionality.

This leads to the (instantaneous) hydrodynamic rigidity

$$k_{wi} = \frac{\Delta p' A_c}{\delta'} = \frac{2\rho g \Delta h_0}{\delta_0} A_c \qquad (10)$$

Because the extra pressure head results in a force which is in phase with the displacement, δ', this results in a rigidity. When the plug-valve is situated downstream of the culvert, as in Fig. 4, k_w is positive; when upstream, it becomes negative.

The same value is found for the hydrodynamic rigidity at a high-frequency oscillation of the gate; the discharge is then unable to follow the varying discharge capacity of the gate, and tends to remain constant.

2.4 Added Damping (c_w), or Added Negative Damping ($-c_w$), Due to Fluctuating Leak Gap

When a bath-tub is emptying, one can feel that when the plug is lowered to close the drain there is a great suction force at the last moment. This is related to the flow inertia, and hence to the pipe length, L. Once the plug has been seated, it is much easier to lift it

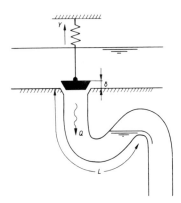

Fɪɢ. 7.   The vibrating bath-tub plug.

again. Now it is clear why L is also the factor involved in self-excitation.

Self-excitation occurs when the hydrodynamic force acts in the direction of and in phase with the vibration velocity, $\dot{y}$, of the plug, and $\int_0^T F'\dot{y}\,dt$ is the energy transferred into the mechanical system in a certain time period (F' = the dynamic component of the hydrodynamic force in the Y-direction).

The force is in phase with $\dot{y}$ when the plug in Fig. 7 oscillates at low frequency; the discharge will then roughly follow the variation in the discharge capacity. An increase of δ results in an increase of the discharge, Q, and dQ/dt is proportional to the velocity of vibration, $\dot{y}$. Due to the inertia of the fluid in the pipe, a pressure difference $\Delta p'$ is needed to accelerate the fluid. When the downstream pressure is constant, the upstream pressure in the pipe increases by $\Delta p'$ and is in phase with dQ/dt, which in its turn was already in phase with $\dot{y}$. The pressure $\Delta p'$ exercises a lift force on the plug, in phase with $\dot{y}$. This was introduced as the condition for a negative c_w or self-excitation.

If, however, the same plug is situated downstream of the pipe, c_w becomes positive and any vibration will damp out.

2.5   Application of an Instability Indicator

As has been seen, the same mechanism which, for low frequency vibration, leads to self-excitation, for high-frequency vibration (when Q tends to remain constant) leads to negative rigidity. This means that because self-excitation is unwanted a negative k_w value at high-frequency vibrations is also unacceptable. This leads to the following formulation of an instability indicator:

> When, assuming that the discharge remains constant, the gate moves in such a way that the gate opening or any leak gap becomes smaller and this causes a hydrodynamic force tending to reinforce the gate movement, there is a risk of self-excitation.

The application of this indicator shows that in nearly all cases one can say that the stronger the suction forces are, in stationary conditions, the more unstable the gate tends to be. This means, for instance, that horizontal girders should be placed well above the gate edge (to prevent flow reattachment), unless the girder is an open frame. More shapes susceptible to vibration are mentioned in ref. 30.

2.6 Wave Formation Due to Vibrating Gates

When gates in river barrages or open sluices vibrate, wave radiation occurs, being especially visible in the smooth water surface of the upstream basin. When the gate vibrates horizontally, the gate can act as a wave generator; for deep-water waves the wave amplitude becomes twice the vibration amplitude. The much bigger waves which are often produced are generally due to discharge variations. Examples of such wave patterns are presented by Petrikat[48] and Kolkman.[30]

In the first paper[48] it has been shown that even high spatters can occur. These indicate that very high pressures occur near the leak gap where the discharge variation is produced.

2.7 Coupling Forces Due to c_w and $-c_w$

In a similar way to the added mass, the pressures near the gate which are related to the positive or negative hydrodynamic damping can also act simultaneously in horizontal and vertical direction on the gate (for instance, in a configuration like Fig. 5); a vertical vibration can induce a horizontal force and vice versa.

2.8 Second Mechanism of Negative Hydrodynamic Damping; the Fluctuating Discharge Coefficient

With self-exciting vibrations of the 'bath-tub plug' type, the discharge is partly throttled due to the fact that the vibration is related to a variation of the leaking gap area. This mechanism is absent in the horizontal vibration of Fig. 8, but in such conditions high-frequency

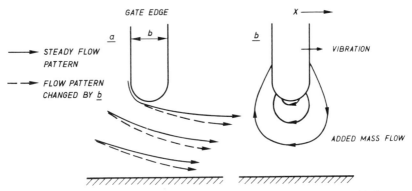

FIG. 8.   The elements of simultaneously occurring gap flow and added-mass flow.

vibrations were sometimes experienced which were probably horizontal lip vibrations causing undulations in the retaining plate of the weir gate.

Kolkman[27] suggested a possible mechanism of self-excitation. When the gate vibrates horizontally and the discharge remains constant (due to the flow inertia at a high-frequency vibration), the flow contraction presented in Fig. 8a (with a coefficient μ) will vary due to the influence of the flow pattern shown in Fig. 8b (which is the added-mass flow in stagnant fluid). When the contraction (or the discharge) coefficient varies proportionally to $(-\dot{y})$ and the discharge through the gap remains constant, one can see that an extra head across the gate occurs (due to the μ variation) which is proportional to $\dot{y}$.

$$\Delta p \sim V^2 \sim \frac{q^2}{(\mu\delta)^2}$$

and when δ remains constant

$$\Delta p' = \frac{\delta\Delta p}{\delta\mu}\Delta\mu = -2\frac{q^2\Delta\mu}{\mu^3\delta^2} = -2\Delta p\frac{\Delta\mu}{\mu}$$

When $\Delta\mu$ is assumed to be proportional to $(-\dot{y})$, this assumption leads to a pressure variation across the gate in phase with the vibration velocity, $\dot{y}$; this is the condition for self-excitation.

It has been mentioned that the experiences are related to gate lip profiles with an unstable flow separation point (semi-circular or quarter-elliptical profile) or with an unstable flow reattachment point (rectangular lip profile with a gate opening 60 to 100% of the thickness of the gate lip—see Fig. 26). The Strouhal numbers (fb/V) found are of the order 0.1 to 0.4 $(b = $ lip thickness—see Fig. 8; $V = $ velocity, $\sqrt{(2\Delta p/\rho)})$. The critical gate openings are in the range 0.6 to 3 times the edge thickness (and for the semi-circular edge even up to 5.5 times).

This type of vibration is not covered by the instability indicator just introduced. At sharp-edged gates, these Strouhal numbers result in high frequencies (up to 80 Hz were experienced), and thus higher harmonic vibrations (local plate vibrations) are involved.

2.9 Non-Linear Coupled Right-Hand Side Terms of Eqn. (1)

In the case of self-excitation, the linear approach leads to an infinite exponential growth of vibration amplitude. In reality, the amplitude will be limited and this is always due to non-linearities. In small-gap situations, the amplitude is sometimes limited because the gate hits the bottom!

It has been shown theoretically by Abelev et al.[3] that finite amplitudes can be obtained when non-linear terms are introduced. This refinement in the theory is not yet quantitatively applicable, because the behaviour of the discharge coefficient, which in fluctuating gap situations is supposed to be a constant, is not known. In practice, one will always try to prevent configurations where self-exciting vibrations occur.

In Section 5 considerations are presented about self-controlling vibrations where a certain amplification of the excitation amplitude takes place due to the vibration itself. This amplification, however, is limited; this is in contrast to self-excitation, where the excitation increases proportionally to the vibration amplitude.

3 THEORY OF SELF-EXCITATION; THE FLUCTUATING-GAP THEORY

The fluctuating-gap theory, which was qualitatively presented in Section 2, is now worked out quantitatively; firstly for the case of a plug-valve vibrating in the flow direction (in-flow vibration), and then for transverse vibrations (cross-flow vibration). More detailed information is found in ref. 30.

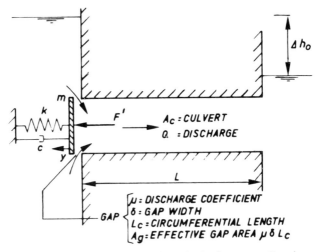

Fig. 9.   Diagram and notations for in-flow gate vibration.

Figure 9 shows the notation used in the following calculation of the in-flow gate vibrations.

What is looked for first is the external force needed to produce a periodic gate vibration described as

$$y = \hat{y}e^{i\omega t} \tag{11}$$

The hydrodynamic force component acting on the gate is introduced as a force linearly related to the vibration movement

$$F_w = yA(\omega) + iyB(\omega) \tag{12}$$

and the total external force needed to balance internal forces and the hydrodynamic force becomes

$$F = \{k - (m + m_w)\omega^2 - A(\omega)\}y + i\{c\omega - B(\omega)\}y \tag{13}$$

With eqn. (13) one can see if the system is dynamically stable (or positively damped), namely when

$$c\omega - B(\omega) > 0 \tag{14}$$

and in the absence of a mechanical damper when

$$B(\omega) < 0 \tag{15}$$

The natural frequency of the system follows from

$$k - (m + m_w)\omega^2 - A(\omega) = 0 \tag{16}$$

and it is now possible to see whether the system is dynamically stable at this frequency by applying eqns. (14) or (15). It is also possible, when the ω range for stability has been found from eqn. (14), to determine with the aid of eqn. (16) which rigidity, k, is needed to get into the desired natural frequency range. To calculate $A(\omega)$ and $B(\omega)$ the following assumptions are introduced:

1. The flow through the gate depends on the local head difference across the gate ($\Delta h_0 + \Delta h'$, in which $\Delta h'$ is the dynamic component).
2. The vibration amplitude, $\hat{y}$, is small compared to the gap width, δ.
3. The discharge coefficient remains constant.
4. Friction losses, etc., are negligible compared to the losses at the gate (so $\Delta h_0 = \Delta h_{\text{extern}}$).
5. The gap flow is immediately redistributed over the culvert cross-section and without extra inertia effects. (In refined calculations these effects can be taken into account.)
6. The added mass, m_w, depends only on the upstream conditions; the downstream part is included in the inertia of the culvert flow.

The hydrodynamic force ($A(\omega)$) is calculated as follows.
In the discharge relation for the gap (for symbols see Fig. 9)

$$Q = \mu \delta L_c \sqrt{(2g\Delta h)} \qquad (17)$$

δ and Δh oscillate around their average value with magnitudes y and $\Delta h'$, respectively; and due to assumption 2 above, linearisation is possible for the calculation of Q' (the dynamic component of Q)

$$Q' = \frac{\partial Q}{\partial \delta} y + \frac{\partial Q}{\partial \Delta h} \Delta h' = \mu y L_c \sqrt{(2g\Delta h_0)} + \tfrac{1}{2}\mu \delta_0 L_c \Delta h' \sqrt{(2g/\Delta h_0)} - A_c \dot{y}$$

$$(18)$$

(remember that $\dot{y} = \partial y/\partial t$). The last term is due to a piston effect of the vibrating gate.

The equation of the motion of the water column in the culvert leads to

$$\Delta h' = -(L/gA_c)\, \partial Q'/\partial t \qquad (19)$$

where L = culvert length. The dynamic part of the fluid forces is

$$F' = -\rho g A_c \Delta h' \qquad (20)$$

(this excludes the forces due to m_w upstream of the gate).
When eqn. (18) is differentiated, one can eliminate $\partial Q'/\partial T$ with eqn.

(19) and one can replace the $\Delta h'$ terms by the hydrodynamic force by using eqn. (20). This results in a linear relation between f' and y

$$F' + (\mu\delta_0 L_c L/A_c \sqrt{(2g\Delta h_0)})\dot{F}' = (\rho\mu LL_c \sqrt{(2g\Delta h_0)})\dot{y} - \rho LA_c\ddot{y} \quad (21)$$

The functions $A(\omega)$ and $B(\omega)$ can now be calculated when one introduces $F' = \hat{F}e^{i\omega t}$ and $y = \hat{y}e^{i\omega t}$, and one finds

$$A(\omega) = \frac{\omega^2 \rho LA_c(1 + \mu^2\delta_0 LL_c/A_c^2)}{1 + (\omega\mu\delta_0 L_c L/A_c \sqrt{(2g\Delta h_0)})^2} \quad (22)$$

$$B(\omega) = \omega \frac{\rho\mu LL_c \sqrt{(2g\Delta h_0)}(1 - \omega^2\delta_0 L/2g\Delta h_0)}{1 + (\omega\mu\delta_0 LL_c/A_c \sqrt{(2g\Delta h_0)})} \quad (23)$$

From eqn. (13) it can be seen that $B(\omega)/\omega$ can be regarded as the negative hydrodynamic water damping.

3.1 Limit of Stability of an Undamped Gate

The gate has its critical condition when no external force is needed in eqn. (13) to maintain a steady-state vibration. If $c = 0$, the imaginary term in eqn. (13) equals zero when $B(\omega) = 0$, or

$$\omega^2\delta_0 L/2g\Delta h_0 = 1 \quad (24)$$

Or, when one introduces the critical Strouhal number

$$S_c = \frac{1}{2\pi}\,\omega_c\delta_0/\sqrt{(2g\Delta h_0)} \quad (25)$$

one finds

$$S_c = \frac{1}{2\pi}\sqrt{\left(\frac{\delta_0}{L}\right)} \quad (26)$$

When S is greater than S_c the system is stable.

Another expression for the limit of dynamic stability is found when one introduces the condition of eqn. (24) into eqn. (22), knowing that in eqn. (13) the real term also has to be zero. Firstly, $A(\omega)$ is calculated

$$A(\omega) = 2\rho g\Delta h_0 A_c/\delta_0 \quad (27)$$

This is exactly the expression of the instantaneous negative hydrodynamic rigidity $(-k_{wi})$ which was found in Section 2 (negative because the gate is upstream of the culvert). So

$$A(\omega) = -k_{wi} \quad (28)$$

Remarks

One would have expected from eqn. (13) that $A(\omega)$ was the negative hydrodynamic rigidity and that $A(\omega)$ from eqn. (22) (after introducing $\omega \to \infty$) was the instantaneous rigidity. This is not the case, because in eqns. (22) and (23) the pistoning effect is included.

The real term of eqn. (13) being zero, one can introduce the conditions found for $A(\omega)$ in eqn. (28), and for ω in eqn. (24). This leads to

$$\frac{k}{-k_{wi}} = 1 + \frac{m + m_w}{\rho L A_c} \tag{29}$$

(because for this gate k_{wi} is negative, the relation $k/(-k_{wi})$ is positive).

Equation (29) leads to the expression

$$c_k = 1 + c_m \tag{30}$$

where c_k = rigidity coefficient, being the ratio of the rigidity and the

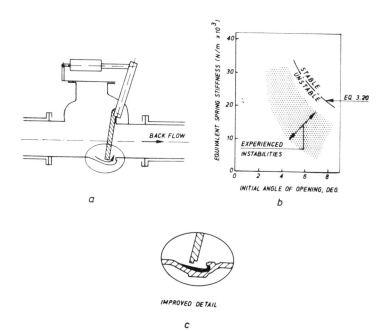

FIG. 10. (a) Damped check-valve, (b) test results and (c) reshaped housing (detail).

instantaneous negative hydrodynamic rigidity, and c_m = mass coefficient, being the ratio of gate mass (including upstream added mass) and the fluid mass in the culvert.

For stability, $k/(-k_{wi})$ needs to exceed a minimum value; but from eqns. (29), (28) and (27) it can be seen that however great the rigidity, a critical condition always occurs, but that the critical δ_0 range becomes smaller and smaller.

A direct application is demonstrated in a wheel-gate which is released from its seat before raising: the release distance should be greater than the critical δ_0.

Weaver[61] checked eqn. (30) for a mechanically damped check-valve (Fig. 10) and found that the minimum rigidity needed to prevent self-excitation was a little lower than predicted.

Kolkman[30] reported on results of two model investigations, one of a sliding gate with a release system which caused an initial circumferential leak gap, and the other of a reversed Tainter valve for a navigation lock. Both results were, roughly speaking, in agreement with theory.

Weaver found an interesting solution to prevent the self-excitation. By shaping the gate housing surface parallel to the gate edge path, the leak gap had a constant width during part of the closing movement (Fig. 10c).

3.2 Cross-Flow Gate Vibration

As an example, a vertically vibrating gate in free-surface flow will be taken. As is indicated in Fig. 11 and introduced in Section 2, a free-surface flow is also subject to inertia effects when the flow rate changes, and these effects can be introduced as an imaginary tube with a length L_u upstream and L_d downstream of the gate, using the graph in Fig. 6. (However, the potential flow calculation is only valid for higher S numbers, as discussed in Chapter 1, Section 3.)

The total tube length thus becomes $L = (L_u + L_d + b)$. When the gate gets into a stationary vibration, $y = \hat{y} e^{i\omega t}$, the discharge coefficient m remains constant and the fluctuating discharge can be calculated. At a low-frequency vibration (compare with Section 2), the discharge Q will 'follow' the momentary gap width $(\delta_0 + y)$. This means that for the variable part of the discharge $Q' \sim y$ and $\partial Q'/\partial t \sim \dot{y}$ holds; taking into account the tube length, L, and the approximation that the upstream and downstream levels remain constant, one gets an increase of the head difference, $\Delta h'$, across the gate proportional to $(-\partial Q/\partial t)$. When the gate edge is shaped such (Fig. 11) that suction occurs proportional

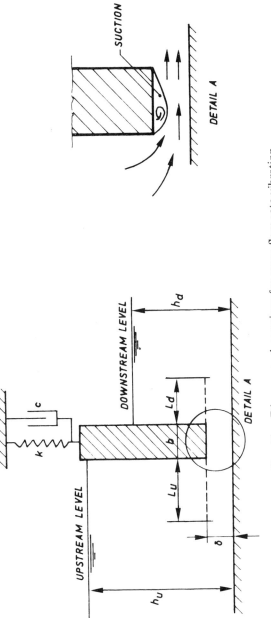

FIG. 11.   Diagram and notations for cross-flow gate vibration.

to $\Delta h'$, the suction force is in phase with the vibration velocity and the gate is unstable.

This suction force (per unit length) equals

$$F_s = c_s b \rho g \Delta h' = c_s b \rho L(-\partial v/\partial t) = (c_s b \rho L/\delta)(\partial q/\partial t) \tag{31}$$

where c_s = suction coefficient, b = gate edge thickness and L = virtual tube length. But now it is important to know where exactly the discharge is throttled—at either the upstream or the downstream edge point—because when $(\partial q/\partial t)$ becomes negative, there is a pressure increase due to the flow inertia upstream from the throttling point, and downstream from it there is a pressure decrease; and one of these two is also acting in a vertical sense. The gate tends to be unstable when the throttling point is at the upstream edge point, and the resulting suction force becomes the force of eqn. (31) plus the effect of the downstream inertia

$$\begin{aligned} F_s &= c_s \rho b(L/\delta)(\partial q/\partial t) + \rho b(\partial q/\partial t)(L_d + b)/\delta \\ &= \rho b\{c_s + (L_d + b)/(L_u + L_d + b)\}(L/\delta)(\partial q/\partial t) \\ &= c_s' b \rho (L/\delta)(\partial q/\partial t) \end{aligned} \tag{32}$$

The complete set of equations, similar to eqns. (11–14), is found in ref. 30; and a comparison of theoretical and experimental values of the

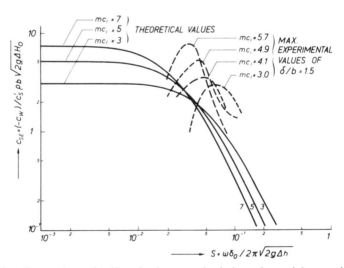

FIG. 12.   Comparison of self-excitation magnitude in scale model; experimental and theoretical (after ref. 31).

negative water damping is found in Fig. 12. In this figure, the negative water damping is expressed non-dimensionally by the self-excitation coefficient, c_{se}, as a function of the Strouhal number, S, and for different values of the factor mc_i, being the discharge coefficient times the ratio $(L_u + L_d + b)/\delta$.

The conclusion of these verification tests is that the order of magnitude of the maximum $(-c_w)$ value is confirmed. A further examination shows that when the L_u and L_d values are calculated not with h/δ, as in Fig. 12, but using $h/m\delta$, a still better agreement can be obtained. This is not an improbable proposition, because $m\delta_0$ is the thickness of the contracted jet, and the inertia effect in Fig. 4 is calculated without the influence of the contraction. At lower S values, when the calculation of L_u and L_d is no longer valid, the inertia effect probably decreases; this could possibly explain the disappearance of self-excitation.

Vrijer reported a theoretical approach and model tests[60] to develop edge designs, where use is made of the fact that downstream throttling of the discharge is preferable (all investigated situations were with stable flow separation)—see Fig. 13. Only shapes A and B in Fig. 13 are sensitive to self-excitation (A worst, B least), even at wider gate

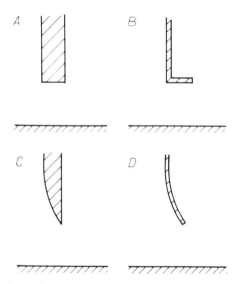

FIG. 13.   Comparison of the dynamic behaviour of different gate edge shapes (after Vrijer[60]).

openings where no flow reattachment and stationary suction occur. The shapes C and D result in a positive c_w (especially D).

Remark

The critical S values found in Fig. 12 are lower than those found in Fig. 3 or those found with in-flow vibrations due to a fluctuating discharge coefficient. Because gates sometimes have thin edges, with the advantage that only a small area can be excited by the flow, even at low S values excitation frequencies may still come within the range of resonance frequencies.

4 SELF-EXCITING VIBRATIONS FROM EXPERIENCE

4.1 Examples Illustrating the Fluctuating-Gap Theory

4.1.1 Example 1

After severe rotational vibrations, a Tainter gate was swept out by buckling of the lower strut which connected the gate plate to the pivot (Fig. 14). The cause of the vibrations was that the axis of the cylindrically curved plating was situated under the axis of rotation. When an initial disturbance tends to close the gate, the flow is throttled, and this increases the water pressure at the upstream side of the gate. Due to the low position of the weir plate axis, a closing moment results which amplifies the initial disturbance, and the instability indicator of Section 2 is now applicable. A detailed theoretical analysis of the dynamic instability of this gate was presented by Imaichi *et al.*[20]

At first sight, it is surprising that not the hoist system but the lower strut collapsed. But the increased upstream pressure, related to a heavy vibration, acts over the whole skin plate area, although decreasing with the distance from the lower edge. That great pressures are involved is also indicated by the relatively high water waves which are, at the upstream side, always induced by gate vibrations.

For the design of Tainter gates, the conclusion is that the axis of curvature should preferably coincide with the axis of rotation. A little higher may be permissible, but the paper of Imaichi *et al.*[20] indicates that at some rigidity and mass combinations this is not completely safe, probably due to the phase shift of forces related to wave radiation at the upstream side, a phenomenon which has been left out of the theory of Sections 2 and 3.

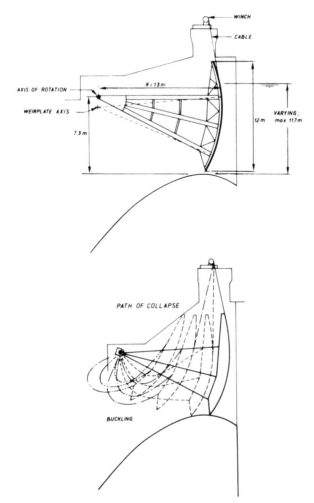

FIG. 14. Tainter gate vibrations leading to gate collapse (after Ishii et al.[21]).

4.1.2 Example 2

When a gate leaks (for instance side leakage, like Fig. 15) it may be the case that the flow itself introduces a throttling section at the upstream gate edge, and it has been shown in the preceding paragraphs that theoretically this leads to flow excitation; Kolkman[27] has experienced this in a hydraulic gate model. Reducing the gap at the upstream

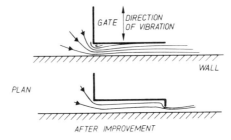

FIG. 15.   Dynamic instability related to small leak gaps.[27]

side had an adverse effect, but at the downstream side it appears to be effective.

4.1.3   Example 3

Both commonly used rubber seals shown in Fig. 16 tend to tighten under water pressure. They can provoke severe vibration when for some reason (deformation, wear, gate lifting) a small leakage gap occurs. The type of vibration is entirely comparable with the bath-tub plug vibration. The sensitivity to seal vibration follows from the instability indicator. Because the rubber is relatively pliant, the gap is intermittently completely closed and a pulsating pressure with great amplitude is generated in the water upstream as well as downstream of the gate. Even cavitation can be induced at the downstream side when the initial pressure is low. The pressure pulsations act on the gate plate as well, and important vibrations can be induced in the gate.

4.1.4   Example 4

In the case of Fig. 17, Abelev and Dolnikov[3] reported that top leakage introduced horizontal vibrations. They also presented a theoretical

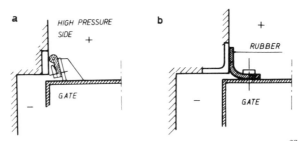

FIG. 16.   (a) Rubber 'music-note' seal and (b) flap seal.[27]

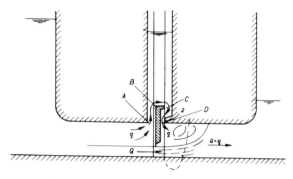

FIG. 17.   Top leakage at culvert gate.[3]

approach to the problem. The gate is especially unstable when the flow is throttled at the upstream side of a slit, as in Example 2. This means that throttling at points A and C is dangerous, but not at points B and D.

4.1.5   Example 5

At the Stoney gate of Fig. 18, Kolkman reported that downstream throttling of the leakage flow was not wanted, because this would

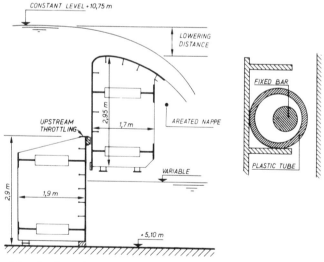

FIG. 18.   Leakage between upper and lower gates of a Stoney gate.[27]

result in a high horizontal load on the upper gate. A solution was finally found in the form of an upstream plastic tube seal which can roll during the gate movement. As long as there is a guarantee of sealing, the gate will be vibration free.

4.1.6 Example 6

Hydraulic model research on the edge shapes of Tainter gates (where prototype difficulties were encountered) was reported by Schmidgall.[52] There were vibrations caused by 'music-note' seals of prototypes of different Tainter gates (A_1 and B_1) and also caused by clamped-strip seals (C_1). It is of importance to find a universally applicable solution, because these gates offer great advantages and are widely used (Fig. 19).

The vibrations of A_1 and B_1 are directly explainable (instability indicator) and are somewhat similar to case A_3. C_1 appeared to have bad clamping of the rubber strip and horizontal movement of the strip also leads to a fluctuating gap. In C_3 a better clamping system was used. The sharp gate edges A_3, B_2, B_3 and C_2 proved to be vibration free in the hydraulic model, and those which have been applied in prototype (A_3, B_3) were also successful.

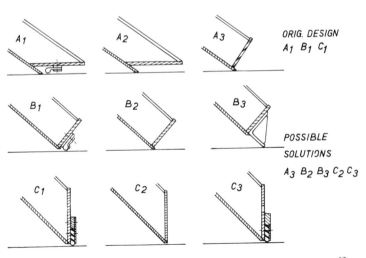

Fig. 19.   Lower-edge shapes of a Tainter gate (after Schmidgall[52]).

4.1.7 Example 7

The reversed Tainter gate of Fig. 20 needed a slidable top seal; a top seal with a protruding beam was designed, this solution being tested in a hydroelastic model. At small openings very strong vibrations occurred. The use of the instability indicator shows, when the gate tends to close, that at the downstream side a low pressure occurs which works on the upper lip in a downward direction. The solution decided on (Variant B) reduced the size of the protruding part of the lip and thereby reduced the clearance between gate plate and shaft wall. In the hydraulic model with a rigid seal the vibrations were eliminated. In the prototype some vibrations still occurred at small openings; so a rubber seal clamped along both sides might still have been better (Variant C).

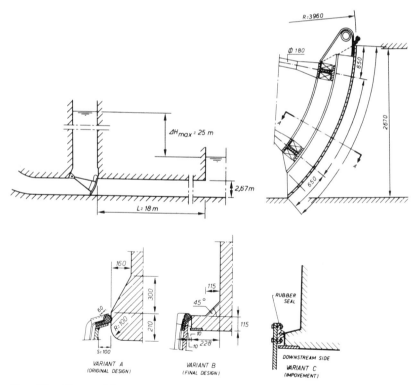

FIG. 20. Top seal for a reversed Tainter gate (after Kolkman[27]). (All dimensions in mm.)

4.1.8 Example 8

The example of 'horizontal' vibrations, like those occurring in the configuration of Fig. 21, is again predictable by means of the instability indicator. The inclined skin plate positions often occur (for instance in the reversed Tainter gate of Figs. 20 or 24), but difficulties are only encountered at stronger inclinations and when the edge also has a horizontal flexibility. A similar situation can arise at a vertical gate on an inclined bottom.

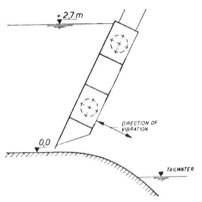

Fig. 21.   Gate with inclined skin plate (after Petrikat[48]).

4.1.9 Example 9

Figure 22a and b shows a configuration where the flow was throttled at the upstream side. With the new design, a cure of the vibration was obtained (Fig. 22b).

4.1.10 Example 10

The gate of Fig. 23 was reported to vibrate first vertically and then horizontally. The critical gate opening range was 0·4 to 1·2 times the beam thickness (0·8 was especially critical). Because this beam is sensitive to suction forces, the fluctuating-gap theory can explain the vertical vibrations; but in horizontal vibration the fluctuating discharge coefficient, which is related to unstable flow reattachment, is involved. The cure was found in the application of pieces of steel angle bar (see Fig. 23 'Cure'), 0·4 m long and spaced 1 m apart, to prevent synchronisation of the vortex street and to obtain alternating different critical gate positions.

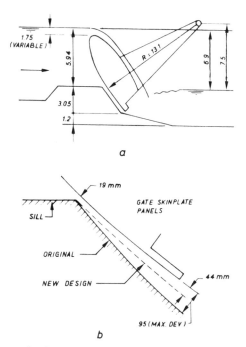

FIG. 22. Bottom slit shaping at a submersible Tainter gate (after Neilson *et al.*[41]).

4.1.11 Example 11

The example in Fig. 24 was found to have severe rotational vibrations of such large wave amplitudes that spattering of water occurred. The throttling of the flow clearly took place at the upstream gate edge and the case is comparable with the one shown in Fig. 15. A solution was later found by application of a mechanical damper which touches the bottom at small openings.

4.2 Examples Illustrating the Fluctuating Discharge Coefficient Theory

4.2.1 Example 1

The visor weir of Fig. 25 showed locally (at region A) horizontal plate vibrations when (at A) the opening was 0·45–0·55 m; this was clearly due to unstable flow separation, which can lead to a fluctuating discharge coefficient.

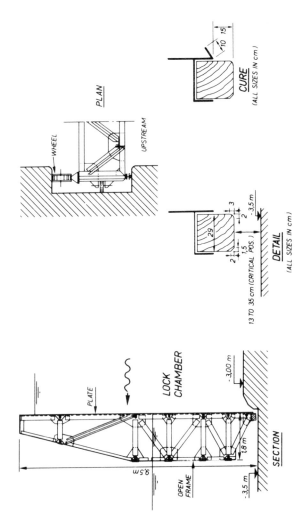

FIG. 23.   Lift gate in downstream lock head.[27]

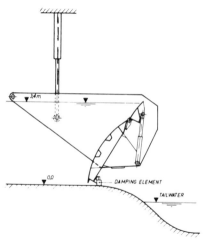

FIG. 24. Reversed Tainter gate with counter-curved plating (after Petrikat[48]).

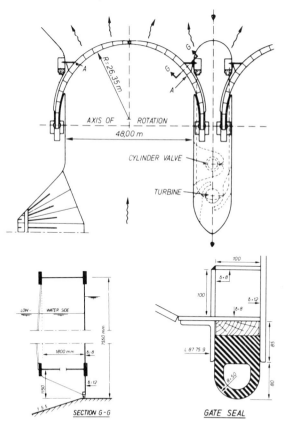

FIG. 25. Visor weir with semi-circular seal beam (after Kolkman[27]).

4.2.2 Example 2

In a laboratory set-up, where a 20-mm thick steel plate was clamped in a 1 m wide flume, unexpected horizontal plate vibrations occurred (waves at the upstream side are shown in Fig. 26a). This was with a rectangular gate edge (Fig. 26c) and a gap height at which instability occurs between separated flow and reattached flow, and also with a quarter-elliptic edge (Fig. 26b) where the flow separation is already unstable (except for small gate openings). The vibrations occurred at head differences of 0·2 m and greater.

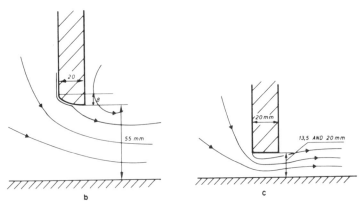

FIG. 26.   (a) Waves encountered in a laboratory experiment related to horizontal plate vibrations; (b) quarter-elliptic edge; (c) rectangular edge.

4.2.3 Example 3

The example shown in Fig. 27 was encountered in a scale model investigation. The local low pressure of the separation zone at $\theta = 40°$ and the adjacent unstable flow reattachment point make the gate sensitive to self-excitation. At the $\theta = 40°$ situation, the instability indicator is applicable: sudden raising of the gate tends to throttle the discharge and, by an increase of upstream pressure, the nappe is thrown far out and the separation zone with its low pressures increases in size. Moreover, the quantity of water in this separation zone tends to increase, but the lack of supply is another reason for low pressure. Another explanation of the mechanism can be that at a sudden rise of the gate some 'added mass flow', as illustrated in Fig. 8, moves to the left, which causes an uplift of the overflow nappe, thus reducing the discharge coefficient. The resulting extra pressure difference across the gate tends to raise the gate still more.

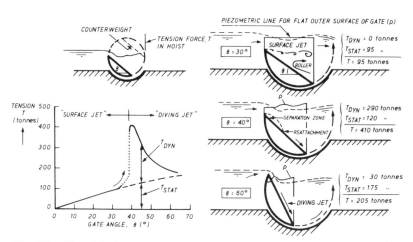

FIG. 27. Unstable flow pattern at Thames Barrier model (after Hardwick[14]).

4.3 Other Examples of Self-Exciting Vibrations

4.3.1 Example 1

In a scale model investigation of the gate shown in Fig. 28, it was found that vibrations were due to the fact that an initial upward gate movement caused a decrease of the force of the falling nappe on the lower girders, which is similar to the creation of an uplift force. This

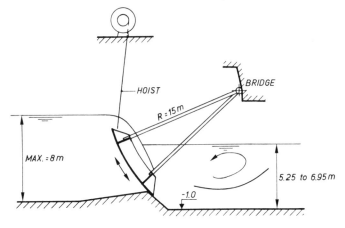

MOST CRITICAL SITUATIONS		
CREST	UPPER POOL	LOWER POOL
5.5 m	+ 7.7 m	+ 6.1 m
6.5 m	+ 6.8 m	+ 5.25 m

FIG. 28.   Submersible Tainter gate of Nakdong Barrage (after De Jong *et al.*[22]).

decrease is related to the horizontal distance between impact point and the point of rotation and to the varying water layer thickness above the girder. An improvement was found by adding flow spoilers at the gate crest (disturbance of the two-dimensional flow pattern). Aeration by nappe splitters had no effect.

4.3.2   Example 2

A series of collapses and damages of hollow cone jet valves are reported (Fig. 29), where the core vibrated in torsion and translation, while the inner vanes also vibrated. After thorough analysis of these accidents, Mercer[34] developed a rigidity parameter to be fulfilled to prevent vibrations. From the hydrodynamic point of view one may conclude that some potential instability of flow at the top of the central cone exists. Moreover, the vanes can behave unstably in the flow, similar to the production of tones by wind at a fixed edge (flute) or at the elastic lip of an accordion. In the latter case the instability indicator is valid: an initial upward bending of the lip causes a lift force.

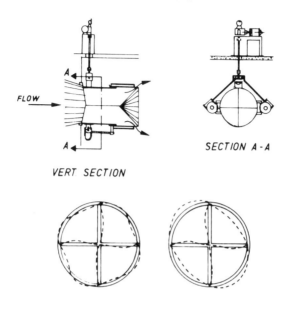

FLOW

A

A

VERT SECTION

SECTION A-A

VIBRATION MODES

FIG. 29.   Hollow cone jet valve (after Mercer[34]).

4.3.3   Example 3

It has been found in a scale model experiment that a roller gate with a sharp lower edge gets into severe horizontal vibration at a small opening height, when water levels are such that the upper wheel is just at the point of being unloaded. When a culvert gate is nearly or

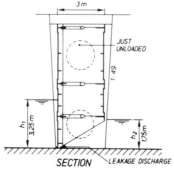

3 m

JUST
UNLOADED

1:49

h_1

3.25 m

h_2

1.75 m

SECTION   LEAKAGE DISCHARGE

FIG. 30.   Roller gate at the condition where the upper wheel gets unloaded
(after Kolkman[27]).

completely raised, a similar condition where the wheels are unloaded occurs, sometimes resulting in strong vibration. Although the excitation mechanisms may not always be the same, in the case of Fig. 30 the fluctuating discharge coefficient probably interferes. The unloaded upper wheel causes a zero rigidity for rotation and then any slight flow instability is enough to produce vibrations.

5   SELF-CONTROLLING GATE VIBRATIONS RELATED TO SHEAR LAYER INSTABILITIES

A cause of self-controlling vibrations may lie in shear layer instabilities in the region just behind the flow separation. It is a matter of design experience that unstable flow separation and/or reattachment cannot always be prevented. Figure 31 shows that a gate shape, which for a certain opening is well adapted to the form of the natural flow contraction (see Smetana, as cited in ref. 42), still gives rise to unstable flow separation for greater gate openings. For a rectangular profile, the most critical opening is at 65% of the edge plate thickness; at this opening it is the reattachment which is unstable.

One speaks of self-controlled vibrations when the magnitude of the excitation force is increased by the vibrations of the gate. In contrast to self-excitation, this increase is limited and has to be seen more as a shift of energy from turbulence excitation to the frequency range wherein a resonance vibration occurs. In Section 2, conditions of unstable separation or reattachment have been related to horizontal

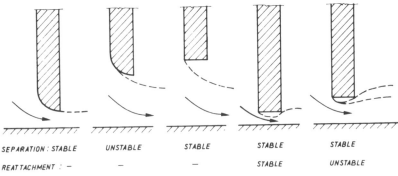

FIG. 31.   Flow conditions related to gate opening and edge shape.

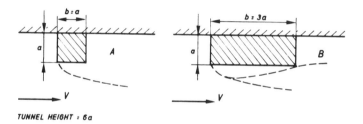

FIG. 32. Conditions at laboratory experiments of Naudascher and Locher.[39]

gate vibrations, because these conditions resulted in a sensitivity to a fluctuating discharge coefficient; but that is besides the self-control phenomenon. The shear layer (the transition zone between the jet, where the velocity is high, and the dead water zone where a rotating eddy may exist) induces dynamic pressures, firstly because in this layer the flow rotation of the high-velocity gradient changes into vortices whose size increases with distance, and secondly because, when flow separation and reattachment are not fully determined, there is a feedback between shear behaviour and the points where separation and reattachment occur. Figure 31 visualises the conditions of instability of flow separation and flow reattachment.

Naudascher and Locher[39] have published results of research where the flow excitation exerted on two geometries related to gates and also the effect of vertical vibration and cavitation on gates has been investigated. In the following, mainly the first part is summarised.

In situation A of Fig. 32 with $b/a = 1$, flow separation is stable and the flow reattachment is remote from the rib, while in situation B (with $b = 3a$) reattachment takes place at the gate and is easily disturbed by gate movement. It should be mentioned that for $b/a = 4 \cdot 5$ reattachment should be approximately stable. The conditions investigated are similar to those where a gate is nearly fully raised. V is defined as the oncoming velocity, the Strouhal number as $S = fa/V$ and the force coefficient as

$$C'_F = \sqrt{(\overline{F'^2})}/\tfrac{1}{2}\rho V^2 bL$$

where bL = area of the rib bottom.

Situation A: The dynamic excitation coefficient in vertical direction of the gate was measured and appeared to be $C'_F = 2\%$. To give an impression of the correlation of the excitation over the length of the rib (perpendicular to the drawing):

—when the measuring section, L, of the rib was small (of the order of b), C'_F was locally 4%, to be compared with the 2% found with a $6b$-long measuring section. The spectrum has no dominant frequencies; above $S = 0.015$ hardly any energy is present.

—when the rib was oscillated vertically (at amplitudes of 1% and 2%, respectively, of the rib height a), C'_F increased to 6% and nearly all energy was concentrated in the oscillation frequency (self-control).

Situation B: $C'_F = 5.5\%$ with a clear peak at $S = 0.022$. Vertical oscillation (again 1% and 2%) hardly affected the spectrum. The results indicate that, contrary to situation A, the tendency to strong flow oscillations is already fully triggered in this situation with a shear layer of limited length. When cavitation occurs, however, it is situation B which is the most affected. The results are still somewhat puzzling and do not yet fit into a generally applicable theory. In Section 2 it has been found that, for small gate openings, an unstable reattachment is easy to influence, but that is for horizontal vibrations. It might be that situation A is sensitive to self-excitation, because the effective blockage ratio of the tunnel is varied by the vibration, but this effect cannot, owing to the small initial blockage, be very important.

A second investigation by Martin *et al.*[33] concerned shear layer instabilities at the lower gate edge when the gate is in a low position. The configuration was similar to what is sometimes used as a high-head gate.

The rounded upstream edge was such that flow separation occurred, but the downstream lip could, at small gate openings, cause reattachment of flow. Gate openings, δ, from $0.25\,b$ to $4\,b$ were tested and e was varied from 0.2 to $0.6\,b$. It appeared that pressures measured at the gate bottom have a dynamic coefficient $C'_p = \sqrt{(\overline{p'^2})}/\frac{1}{2}\rho V^2 = 3\text{–}7\%$, where $V = q/0.61(\delta + e + r)$.

The range of gate openings was such that conditions with and without flow reattachment were met. Each test condition showed two dominant Strouhal numbers $S = fd/V = 0.33$ and 0.84; these varied only little with variations of δ and e. A theoretical analysis was also presented, where a sort of wavelength was defined as $\lambda = 0.5\ V/f$ ($f = $ dominant excitation frequency and $0.5\ V$ is the average velocity in

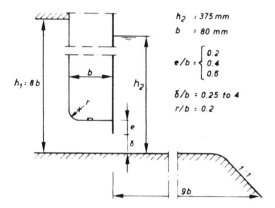

h_2 : 375 mm
b : 80 mm
e/b : $\begin{cases} 0.2 \\ 0.4 \\ 0.6 \end{cases}$
δ/b : 0.25 to 4
r/b : 0.2

$h_1 = 8b$

$9b$

Fig. 33. Gate geometry tested by Martin *et al.*[33]

the shear layer) and instability was predicted for $b = \lambda(n \pm \frac{1}{4})$. (The theory is in a way related to results found for instabilities of an overflow nappe (Section 7).) It was supposed that the vibration causes undulations in the shear layer so that the enclosed water volume tends to vary, which results in pressure variations. At the $(n \pm \frac{1}{4})$ conditions, maximum volume variations occur. The two measured dominant values of S coincide with $b = 0.75\ \lambda$ and $1.75\ \lambda$, and no other peaks were found in the spectrum of the pressure recordings. It is not clear why in the experiments the same dominant Strouhal numbers are also found when the flow at higher gate openings is not reattached at the gate edge.

A third investigation (Hardwick[15]) was for a rectangular, block-shaped gate in free-surface flow, which was forced into vertical oscillation (see Fig. 34). Water forces, the added mass effect of which was subtracted, were measured.

The gate opening was 67% of the gate thickness, b, which was the position of maximum instability of flow reattachment and at which maximum vibration amplitudes have been experienced by several authors. When S is expressed in terms of $S = fb/\sqrt{(2g\Delta H)}$, it appears from experiments that $S = 0.3$–0.5 is the most critical range. The excitation can be analysed and presented in two ways: (1) as if the force is purely periodic with a coefficient $C'_F = F/\frac{1}{2}\rho V^2 b$ (F = force amplitude per unit width of the gate) and (2) as if the excitation is expressed as a negative damping, c_w. Both C'_F and the dimensionless

94   P. A. KOLKMAN

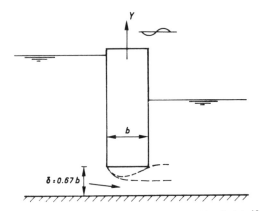

FIG. 34.   Conditions of experiments by Hardwick.[15]

damping $C_d = c_w/(\rho\sqrt{(2g\Delta H)}b \times \text{span})$ appear far from being constant;
they appear still to be a function of S and of the relative vibration
amplitude y_0/b. The C'_F increases with y_0/b (this indicates a certain
degree of self-control) till a 2–3% amplitude is reached. C_d decreases
with amplitude in the critical S range. This means that no definite
conclusion can be drawn about the excitation mechanism.

Concluding this section, it has to be stated that shear layer instabilities and the degree of self-control which is connected with them
are still difficult to quantify. For gate design it is still advisable to keep
resonance frequencies remote from dominant Strouhal numbers. Without scale model investigations it is not yet possible to quantify the
self-controlling gate vibrations. When possible, one should avoid
shapes at which unstable flow phenomena are likely to occur.

6   GATE SEAL DESIGN IN RELATION TO GATE VIBRATIONS

In many of the examples given in the previous sections, the shape of
the gate seal appears to be of great importance. In the older literature
on gate vibrations (the oldest systematic research was published in
1933 by Müller[36]), all the seals were hard wooden beams of a thickness
between 15 and 40 cm. They were non-elastic, so some leakage could
easily occur and, when there was erosion by suspended sand, the
leakage could increase still more. The basic shape was rectangular and
sometimes the corners were rounded or bevelled. No general shape

had been found which guaranteed under all circumstances a vibration-free design. Moreover, the sand erosion mentioned above could modify the shape of the edges.

With the development of rubber seals, designed in a great variety of shapes, the seal thickness was reduced. This has an advantage, because the area of attack of flow forces is also reduced. On the other hand, because Strouhal numbers remain of the same order of magnitude, excitation frequencies increase and can come nearer to the resonance frequencies and even higher vibration modes become involved. Also, more-elastic material can induce local vibrations, which can lead to a dynamic load on the whole gate.

The wooden side-seals of gates were generally designed so that gate support in the closed position was effected by the seals; and when the gate was a little opened, wheels took over and a small leakage gap occurred, a moment at which vibrations could arise (Fig. 23). With rubber side-seals it is now more common to let the seals slide; for instance, the seals shown in Fig. 16 will normally keep sealing. The water pressure keeps them tightened, even when the wall has certain surface irregularities. These seals are not suited for high heads because the friction increases too much, resulting in excessive wear. As long as the sealing shows no leakage, an important source of vibration is eliminated. When leakage exists, the seals of Fig. 16 induce vibrations.

In order to prevent wear, there are also more massive rubber seals with embedded slide strips of nylon or bronze; these slide seals remain partially compressed during the sliding, and sealing is less dependent on water pressure.

An important role in the development of sealing was played by Petrikat. He performed many prototype and model tests to study the effect of seal shape and elasticity on gate vibrations. In his early publications (see ref. 45), the theoretical approach was based on eqn. (1), presented in Section 2 with only the non-coupled excitation. At any leak gap or gate opening, an excitation is assumed of purely periodic character with a force amplitude (per unit width) of

$$\hat{F} = C_A \tfrac{1}{2}\rho V^2 b$$

where b represents the lip thickness. So

$$C_A = \hat{F}/\tfrac{1}{2}\rho V^2 b \qquad (33)$$

where $\hat{F} = $ force amplitude per unit width of the gate, and $C_A = $ excitation coefficient.

When in resonance, the equilibrium gate amplitude depends on the equilibrium between excitation and damping forces

$$(c + c_w)\dot{y} = \hat{F} \sin \omega t \tag{34}$$

By extensive research on the C_A values and $(c + c_w)$ values of many types of gates and gate seals in prototype and hydraulic model tests, better shapes were developed (see ref. 45). Later developments are presented in refs. 46, 47 and 48.

As has been described, for instance in Section 5 in the experiments of Hardwick,[15] C_A depends in reality on the value $S_n = f_n b / V$ and on the relative vibration amplitude y_0/b. This last parameter is also introduced in more recent publications of Petrikat (see, for instance, ref. 48). Although one can say that the concept of eqn. (33) is too simplified, the great number of experiences of Petrikat made it valuable for comparing different seal types. Other authors also have tried to use this approach, but no generally applicable information was obtained.

Modern seal design for the lower gate edge is often as sharp as possible (a steel plate without a rubber seal, or combined with a rubber strip fixed in the bottom, or a design like solution C_3 of Fig. 19).

At the gate top, the seal is subject to some sliding. A music-note seal tends to vibrate when a small leak gap occurs (Fig. 35, variant a), but when the gate is moved upwards, the pressure difference across the seal disappears. The critical range of gate positions can be reduced

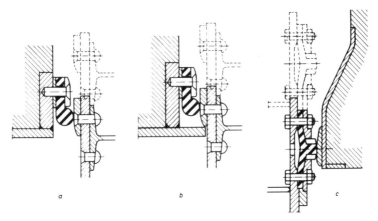

FIG. 35. Top seals of culvert gates; heads increase from a to c (after Petrikat[48]).

when the solution of variant b is used. For high-head gates, a seal clamped along both sides (variant c) gives better results, optionally in combination with the strip of variant b.

7   GATES WITH OVERFLOW

Several mechanisms exist in which a gate with overflow is in danger of developing self-excited vibration.

1. When the gate is rigid, an oscillating overflow nappe with an enclosed air cushion underneath produces a volume variation of the air cushion. This volume variation produces pressure fluctuations in the air cushion, which in their turn can be the cause of the oscillation of the nappe. This is a possible mechanism of self-excitation. For the theoretical approach see Schwarz,[53] Treiber[57] and Kolkman.[26] It appears that the mechamism can be partly described by theory and that, even when an (imaginary) energy dissipation or damping is introduced in the air cushion,[26] the system can maintain a harmonic oscillation. The determining parameter is the oscillation frequency (f) times the time (T) a particle of water needs for its fall. When $fT = (n + \frac{1}{4})$, maximum vibratory energy is produced by the flow $(n = 1, 2, 3, \text{etc.})$. The point where theory and experiment disagree is the necessary cushion rigidity. Experiments show that at a relatively high rigidity vibrations are still possible; this is not found by theory. The best remedy against these nappe oscillations, which can be the cause of a heavy pulsating gate load, is to ventilate the air cushion with nappe splitters. Another possibility to open the nappe is to apply a 'crenelated' gate crest with alternating parts at two different levels. Partenscky et al.[44] determined a maximum critical thickness of the overflow nappe of a rigid gate (up to about 5% of the fall height).

2. When the gate is elastic and begins to oscillate, the nappe gets into an oscillation too; this again results in air pressure fluctuations which can excite the gate. This is once again a mechanism of self-excitation. Theoretically it appears that the air volume varies due to both nappe oscillation and gate oscillation, but the latter is sometimes supposed to be small (see Homma et al.[17]). Experience shows that the critical nappe thickness (defined near the gate edge) can be greater than found for rigid gates by Partenscky

et al.[44] The author experienced a value at least two times greater than 5% of the fall height and Pulpitel[49] reported even 15%. The energy level above the gate crest is nearly twice the nappe thickness.

For the design of nappe splitters (see for instance Fig. 36) a V-shape is chosen to produce a gothic window-shaped ventilation hole in the nappe. A flat strip perpendicular to the nappe will

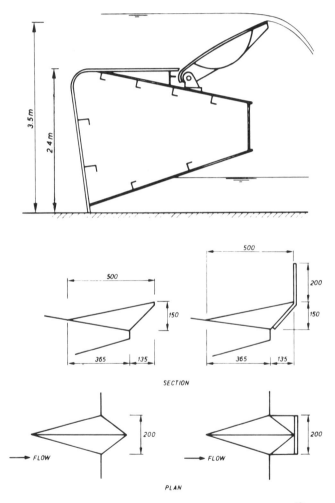

FIG. 36.   Flap gate with nappe splitters (after Ogihara[43]).

also work, but is more susceptible to accumulate ice and debris. The maximum allowable distance between the splitters is not found in the literature but is of the order of half the fall height of the nappe. When the spacing is greater, resonance phenomena in the air cushion can amplify the vibration. It is not always desirable to apply high splitters. In this case, another solution can be to make 'crenelations' at the gate crest, by which the nappe is split open at a point downstream of the crest. A second effect is that different parts of the gate now have different values of fT (because the falling time, T, differs), whereby the critical condition is spread out and weakens.

3. Even when the air cushion is ventilated, the nappe can develop oscillation due to boundary layer development in the air at both sides of the nappe (see Binnie[8] and De Somer[54]); and when the cushion is not sufficiently ventilated the air can transmit this oscillation to the gate.

Remark

Sometimes splitters are not wanted because of the accumulation of ice or floating debris behind them, or because they influence the discharge calibration of the gate. Minor[35] indicates that an air pipe is effective only to stabilise low-frequency nappe oscillations induced by air expulsion and suction at the bottom of the nappe; against nappe vibration, splitters are necessary. Ventilation for small gates can be achieved by means of ventilation slots in the abutments.

4. At greater nappe thickness and higher downstream water level, the air cushion under the overflow nappe is removed by the flow and the space is filled with low-pressure water. Figure 37 shows an example where heavy vibrations were met in such a condition.

   In the scale model it was found that a small amount of air supply was sufficient to prevent this condition. The cause of this self-excitation may be similar to the mechanism described in Section 2, where fluctuation in the discharge coefficient resulted in horizontal vibrations. The case of Fig. 27 may also be comparable to this one.

5. As has been mentioned in Section 1, overflow in combination with underflow (for instance in the Stoney gate of Fig. 18, or in a hook gate) results in a flow pattern with Von Kármán vortices, like behind a body in free flow. This phenomenon is partly suppressed when air can enter under the overflow nappe. More information is found in an early publication by Naudascher.[37]

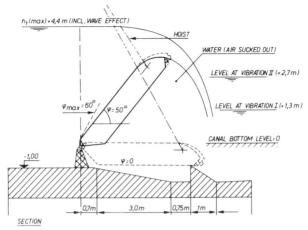

F‍IG. 37.   Flap gate without air cushion under the overflow nappe.[27]

8   THE PREVENTION OF GATE VIBRATIONS

In this short context it is not possible to give a great number of recipes for preventing vibrations, but from the foregoing examples and theories some basic elements for sound gate design can be summarised. For many cases it is still necessary to perform a hydroelastic scale model investigation (see Section 10), but even in such cases the preliminary design of the gate should be optimised beforehand.

The points 1 to 4 below are related to the hydraulic conditions and to the gate shape. For the other points the mechanical properties interfere.

Summarising:

1. Flow conditions must be well defined to prevent general flow instabilities, unstable flow separation or unstable flow reattachment. An example of good design is a Tainter gate on a spillway crest, with only the free undershot jet downstream.
2. Self-excitation must be prevented. It follows from the fluctuating-gap theory that suction forces are often an indication for self-excitation; a more refined way of detection is the use of the stability indicator in Section 2. For overflow gates ventilation is important. Suction forces can often be prevented by a correct shaping of the seal and a reduction of the seal size. For upper

seals of culvert gates, the suction can be reduced by the application of a metal strip which reduces the maximum leakage flow (Fig. 35b), although care must be taken to ensure that the configuration does not resemble too much the dangerous one of Fig. 15 which can lead to skin plate vibrations.

3. Dynamic loads by waves, unstable hydraulic jump, cavitation, partial aeration of culvert flow, etc., should be prevented or minimised.

4. Complete zero load on wheels and hoists should not occur, in order to prevent the interference of play.

5. Resonance frequencies should be above the dominant excitation frequencies.

6. A higher rigidity means, in general, an increase of safety for two reasons: firstly the resonance frequency increases, and secondly the fluctuation-gap theory shows that the negative hydrodynamic damping is then transformed into a negative instantaneous hydro-dynamic rigidity.

7. Higher mechanical damping is favourable. For smaller high-head gates this can be a reason for the application of sliding gates. Additional dampers are not attractive and should be considered only as a remedy when an unsound design has been executed.

In practice it will often turn out that gate design is a matter of compromise between many demands, and that it is difficult to come to a completely safe and yet economic design. This is the case because often the shape and hydraulic functioning, not only of the gate but of the whole hydraulic structure, are involved.

9   CAVITATION IN RELATION TO GATES

When noise or vibrations are observed at gates, it is often far from clear whether flow-induced vibration or cavitation is involved. Therefore, a short introduction is included on cavitation phenomena and their remedies. For detailed information on cavitation, see Knapp *et al.*[25] and, as a more recent addition, Hamitt.[13]

Nuisance resulting from cavitation at or near gates can consist of noise, vibration, hammering, wear at the edges of sealing parts, and damage to hoists and the wheels. These nuisances are mainly caused by the shocks induced during the collapse stage of cavitation bubbles or voids. Even when the collapsing voids are remote from the structure, the shocks are transmitted through the water to walls and gates.

The following stages can be recognised by the noise which is heard when the pressure is gradually lowered in a steel pipe including a valve or a nozzle, while the discharge remains constant:

1. Incipient cavitation: an extra noise as if sand is passing. In laboratory conditions the detection by microphones or pressure transducers is still more sensitive and hence incipient cavitation can be detected at an earlier stage. At a certain stage, the noise can decrease somewhat because some of the bubbles are gas-filled and damp out noise.
2. Developed cavitation: a noise as if gravel or pebbles are passing.

These two stages are both related to cavitation downstream of the gate, induced by the local low pressure zone and turbulence field behind the gate. When the pressure is further reduced, a third stage appears:

3. Choked flow: a low level noise (but it can induce a hammer effect at the stage of implosion). The discharge is limited, because the pressure downstream of the gate will not become lower than the vapour pressure, and a free jet is formed.

In pipe flow, another cause of the occurrence of voids is the separation of the water column related to non-stationary flow and pressure waves. The collapse of voids will produce heavy water hammer shocks.

Initial (incipient) cavitation occurs at locations where pressures are low, often in the core of vortices or eddies.

In a two-dimensional situation, vortices are related to the layer along the wall, and in gates to the shear layer above the contracted flow zone especially (see Fig. 38 where P_0 is located in the shear layer).

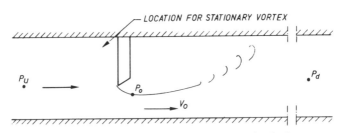

FIG. 38. Reference point for pressure and velocity.

In this case, the core of the vortices will generally not touch the culvert ceiling or the gate. When, however, a vertical side wall exists, the core (and hence the vacuum) can touch this wall directly. This can be the cause of severe wall erosion (see Kenn et al.[24]).

The above shear layer cavitation is of random character and vacuums move with the flow till they implode, and bubble expansions and implosions continuously take place.

Cavitation can also be induced by stationary vortices, resulting from an initial rotation in the flow (mostly due to wall friction) which is subsequently forced to change direction; these cavities have a more stable character. Near gates this can incidentally occur when the flow directly upstream of the gate is forced to dive underneath the gate (Fig. 38). The phenomenon is quite similar to vortices which suck in air at gates or culvert intakes in a free-surface flow. These relatively stable vortices can also be induced by gate slots. Because these cavities remain for a longer period, diffusion of dissolved gas takes place. And because of their stable character and the gas inside the cavity, implosions are not harmful. But when the vortex core with the cavity touches a wall, local erosion can still occur.

The determining factors for cavitation can be divided into flow parameters and physical parameters of the fluids involved, the vapour and the gas.

Flow parameters are the ambient pressure, the flow velocity (local and momentary pressure fluctuations depend on these parameters), the velocity distribution and the turbulence.

Physical parameters involved are evaporation and gas diffusion (which are related to temperature effects and produce heat themselves), the vapour pressure, the gas content (free and dissolved) and the surface tension. Only the flow parameters can be influenced by the design of the structure.

9.1 Definition and Order of Magnitude of the Thoma Number

To define the flow condition where cavitation is involved, the Thoma number or cavitation number has been introduced

$$\sigma = (p_0 - p_v)/\tfrac{1}{2}\rho V_0^2 \tag{35}$$

where p_0 and V_0 are the pressure and flow velocity, respectively, at arbitrarily chosen reference points and p_v is the vapour pressure.

When cavitation just starts (incipient cavitation), σ has the value σ_i. When the reference point coincides with the point where the bubble explosions are initiated, σ_i is found to be zero. This is not feasible, but there is an interest in choosing the reference point near the point where cavitation starts, because the value of σ_i will then remain low and σ_i values of different configurations will be more comparable.

At gates, the most dangerous cavitation is the one initiated in the shear layer behind the gate, and p_0 at this point and V_0 in the vena contracta are suitable as reference values (Fig. 38). Now σ_i is found to be of the order of $1\cdot2$–$2\cdot0$,[29] but it can be as low as 1 before cavitation reaches the developed stage. At a sudden widening of a circular pipe (and at small gate openings), σ_i values are lower (see Rouse[51]) and can reach the σ_i value of $0\cdot6$ which occurs when a circular jet flows into infinite water. The location chosen for p_0 and V_0 means a change of the location of the reference point when the gate position changes, but this can generally be neglected.

Because p_0 and V_0 are parameters which have, in practice, to be derived from the upstream and downstream parameters (by application of Bernoulli's law and using a contraction coefficient which in its turn follows from the head loss coefficient), Tullis[58] proposed the following definition of σ (see also Fig. 38)

$$\sigma = (p_d - p_v)/(p_u - p_d) \qquad (36)$$

His value for σ_i varies widely with the gate opening and varies also for different gate types. Another investigation of Tullis concerned scale effects, and he concluded that σ_i increases considerably with the gate size.[59] Definite conclusions about scale effects are difficult to reach, because only the intensity of shock waves at the wall is detected and hence the detection methods include scale effects. Also, with visual detection in laboratory tests, it is not possible to 'scale' the detection method correctly.

Other values of σ_i which are of importance are:

1. Cavitation due to wall roughness (Arndt[4])

$$\sigma_i = 16 C_F \qquad (37)$$

(C_F = friction factor of the wall).

2. Cavitation due to gate slots. Studies to establish gate slot shapes with better (lower) σ_i values have been presented by Ball[5] and Ethembabaoglu.[11] The study of Rosanov et al.[50] shows that, depending on the shape, σ_i varies between $0\cdot3$ and $2\cdot5$ (V_0 and p_0 are the values in the throughgoing flow).

3. Cavitation due to wall surface irregularities. Arndt[4] found a dependence of σ_i on the shape of the perturbation and on the relation (size)/(boundary layer thickness). For practical applications the test results of Ball[6] with two-dimensional steps and surface irregularities are often used to define the maximum acceptable wall roughness, but in his paper the relevant relation (size)/(boundary layer thickness) is not mentioned. For more experiences with damage in relation to surface irregularities, see Falvey.[12]

As far as the cavitation damage is concerned, when the value of σ becomes lower than σ_i, many authors have tried to establish relations between damage, σ values and material resistance. In fact the σ value is not the only relevant parameter; Kenn et al.[24] came to the conclusion that for concrete (in conditions where the axes of vortices in the shear layer are perpendicular to the wall), the water velocity must exceed 30 m/s before erosion becomes of importance. The author has also seen surface damage at somewhat lower velocities (of the order of 25 m/s).

9.2 Remedies for cavitation

Remedies for cavitation are, apart from repair and maintenance, possible in three different domains: improvement of flow (and pressure) conditions, aeration (to damp out shock effects and to increase pressure) and the choice of resistant materials. Hence the following improvements can be considered:

1. Prevention of conditions with low pressures, high velocities and high turbulence. One of the worst conditions, but sometimes inevitable in high head dams, occurs when a gate gets stuck and an emergency gate nearby has to be lowered. When the vena contracta of the decelerating jet of the upstream gate nearly touches the edge of the downstream gate, flow retardation takes place in two steps and the gate loss coefficient decreases. This results in a high velocity and a low pressure, while in addition the condition with a shear layer of limited length is highly turbulent. The cavitation involved will lead to very high dynamic pressures.[32]

2. Placing of the gate at the downstream end of the culvert or guaranteeing otherwise a free flow downstream of the gate. For gates which are in a regulating position for long periods this is

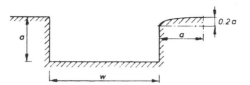

FIG. 39.   Slot with low σ_i value (after Ethembabaoglu[11]).

especially important; Fig. 29 shows the hollow cone jet valve often applied at high-head gates (many other solutions exist).

3. Leaving out gate slots, for instance by applying a Tainter gate or by filling up the slots of an emergency gate with filler blocks. Also, one can design gate slots such that low σ_i values are obtained (see Fig. 39).

4. When gates are fully submerged, application of deep culvert positions.

5. Application of wider culverts upstream of the gates; this reduces velocities and increases pressures in the approach culvert.

6. At fully submerged gates, a step-wise widening (in all directions) of the culvert just downstream of the gate can be applied. Cavitation then takes place further away from the walls, and the head loss at the gate increases; see ref. 10.

7. Application of sharp-edged gates.

8. Application of smooth walls.

9. Application of aeration pipes (they work only when average pressures are below atmospheric). When aeration takes place in the form of small bubbles, the cushioning effect damps out dynamic pressure peaks. At free-surface flow, aeration slots or offsets are applied; see ref. 7 and Fig. 40. Care has to be taken that the de-aeration takes place in a well-defined way, to avoid explosion-like expulsion and also to avoid (in a culvert network system) a changed or unstable flow distribution.

10. Application of a cavitation-resistant wall revetment. (Inox is a very good but costly revetment.) Concrete can have a top layer of fibre concrete.

11. Application of replaceable wall revetment and gate edges.

12. At smaller scale structures, gates with low cavitation risk can be applied. They are based on the principle that the energy loss is distributed over a certain length (by friction) or over the whole

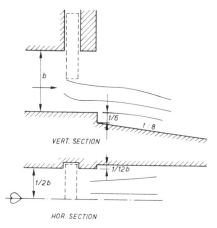

FIG. 40. Offsets for aeration; design rules (after Beichley *et al.*[7]).

gate area (by a great number of variable openings), and they can be made of appropriate materials.

For the calculation of the necessary depth location of a culvert, σ_i has to be known rather precisely. Laboratory experiments in low-pressure (cavitation) tunnels can be required. For the design of aeration slots, normal scale models on Froude similitude can serve to see whether indeed air is sucked in, but to see whether the air quantity is big enough for a safe design (a concentration of 6–8% is sometimes mentioned for a completely safe design) the model must be sufficiently large.

10 THE USE OF HYDROELASTIC SCALE MODELS

An important tool for the design of vibration-free gates is the hydro-elastic model. It can be with a single degree of freedom, multiple degrees of freedom or with an overall reproduction of elasticity. The last type is the most complete, but mainly suited for an overall check of the final design, because the design cannot easily be modified without simultaneously changing shape and rigidity. In the Netherlands all the projects with large-size gates have been checked in models with an overall reproduction of elasticity. In other countries, only the example of the Thames Barrier in England is known.[9] Often more than one model is used for the development of a gate design; in ref. 23 De Jong has published a research strategy for a gate design using different types of models, for which different scale effects could be expected.

Hydroelastic models have played an important role in the development of modern design of gates and seals, and a great deal of the contents of this chapter could not have been written without the experiences with such models. Their applicability has been increased due to fine machining, glueing and welding techniques, in combination with the application of plastic materials, miniaturised strain gauges and accelerometers suited for underwater use, and advanced techniques for data handling and analysis of spectra, spatial correlation and autocorrelation for the determination of natural modes and damping.

Figure 41 shows the hydroelastic model of the gates in the storm surge barrier across the Eastern Scheldt (Netherlands). In this investigation a fruitful interaction was obtained between a hydroelastic model and a finite-element computational model. The latter enabled a refined design of the hydroelastic model with continuous elasticity; after measurement of a number of local tensions in the scale model, the tensions in the whole gate could then be calculated. The model was used simultaneously for the research of flow-induced vibrations and to establish the response to wind wave loading, and the combination of both. Before the final design was reached, use was also made of a rigid

Fig. 41. Hydroelastic model of a gate, for research of wave impact loading and flow-induced vibrations.

model for wave-pressure measurements and of a single degree of freedom oscillator model (with, alternately, a horizontal or a vertical degree of freedom) to study the shape of the gate cross-section and of the seals.

In ref. 30 a review of the scaling rules and of the applicability and limitations of the different types of models is found. An extensive check (with prototype measurements) of a model with an overall reproduction of elasticity, concerning resonance frequencies, structural and hydrodynamic damping and flow-induced vibrations, is also presented. Haszpra performed a check with beam-in-flow models at different scales.[16]

REFERENCES

1. ABELEV, A. S. Investigations of the total pulsating hydrodynamic load acting on bottom outlet sliding gates and its scale modelling, 8*th IAHR Congress*, Montreal, 1959, paper 10A1.
2. ABELEV, A. S. Pulsations of hydrodynamic loads acting on bottom gates of hydraulic structures and their calculating methods, 10*th IAHR Congress*, London, 1963, paper 3.21.
3. ABELEV, A. S. and DOLNIKOV, L. L. Experimental investigations of self-excited vibrations of vertical lift gates. In ref. 18.
4. ARNDT, R. E. A. Cavitation in fluid machinery and hydraulic structures, *Ann. Rev. Fluid Mech.* (1981), 273–327.
5. BALL, J. W. Hydraulic characteristics of gate slots, *Proc. ASCE, J. Hydr. Div.*, **HY10, 85** (Oct. 1959), 81.
6. BALL, J. W. Cavitation from surface irregularities in high velocity, *Proc. ASCE, J. Hydr. Div.*, **HY9** (Sept. 1976), paper 12435, 1283–97.
7. BEICHLEY, G. L. and KING, D. L. Cavitation control by aeration of high velocity jets, *Proc. ASCE, J. Hydr. Div.*, **HY7** (July 1975), 829.
8. BINNIE, A. M. The stability of a falling sheet of water, *Proc. Roy. Soc. London, Series A*, **326** (Jan. 1972), 149–63.
9. CROW, D. A., KING, R. and PROSSER, M. J. Hydraulic model studies of the rising sector gate, hydrodynamic loads and vibration studies. In ref. 55.
10. DOMINY, F. E. Applied research in cavitation in hydraulic structures, *IAHR Congress*, Leningrad, 1965, paper 1.18.
11. ETHEMBABAOGLU, S. Some characteristics of static pressures in the vicinity of slots, 13*th IAHR Congress on Large Dams*, New Delhi, 1979, Question 50, R20.
12. FALVEY, H. T. Predicting cavitation in tunnel spillways, *Water, Power Dam Constr.* (Aug. 1982), 13.
13. HAMITT, F. G. *Cavitation and Multiphase Flow Phenomena*, McGraw-Hill Book Co., New York, 1980.

14. HARDWICK, J. D. Hydraulic model studies of the rising sector gate conducted at Imperial College. In ref. 55.
15. HARDWICK, J. D. Flow-induced vibration of vertical lift gate, *Proc. ASCE, J. Hydr. Div.*, **HY5** (May 1974), paper 10546.
16. HASZPRA, O. Verification of hydro elastic similitude criteria, *Proc. ASCE, J. Hydr. Div.*, **HY4** (April 1976), paper 12048.
17. HOMMA, M. and OGIHARA, K. Theoretical analysis of flap gate oscillation, *17th IAHR Congress*, Baden-Baden, 1977, vol. 4, paper C51.
18. NAUDASCHER, E. (Ed.) *Flow-Induced Structural Vibrations, IAHR/IUTAM Symp. Karlsruhe*, 1972, Springer Verlag, Berlin, 1974.
19. NAUDASCHER, E. and ROCKWELL, D. (Eds.) *Practical Experiences with Flow-Induced Vibrations, IAHR/IUTAM Symp. Karlsruhe*, 1979, Springer Verlag, Berlin, 1980.
20. IMAICHI, K. and ISHII, N. Instability of an idealized Tainter gate system without damping caused by surface waves on the back water of dam, *Bull. Japan. Soc. Mech. Engrs.*, **20** (146) (Aug. 1977), paper 146/9.
21. ISHII, N., IMAICHI, K. and HIROSE, A. Dynamic instability of Tainter gates. In ref. 19.
22. DE JONG, R. J. and JONGELING, T. H. G. Fluid elastic response study of the Nakdong barrage gates, *Int. Conf. on Flow-Induced Vibrations in Fluid Engineering*, BHRA, (Ed.), Reading, Sept., 1982.
23. DE JONG, R. J. Research strategy for the investigation of flow-induced vibrations of a grid gate, *IAHR Symposium, Section Hydr. Mach., Equipm.*, Amsterdam, 1983, paper 13.
24. KENN, M. J. and GARROD, A. D. *Cavitation Damage and the Tarbela Tunnel Collapse of* 1974, Instn. Civ. Engrs, Part I, No. 70, Febr., 1981.
25. KNAPP, R. T., DAILY, J. W. and HAMMIT, F. G. *Cavitation*, McGraw-Hill Book Co., Engineering Societies Monographs, 1970.
26. KOLKMAN, P. A. Instability of a vertical water-curtain closing an airchamber. In ref. 18.
27. KOLKMAN, P. A. Development of vibration-free gate design. In ref. 19.
28. KOLKMAN, P. A. Analysis of vibration measurements on an underflow type of gate, *10th Congress of IAHR*, London, 1963, paper 3.23.
29. KOLKMAN, P. A. *Cavitatie Inceptie Getallen bij Schuiven, Voorwerpen*. In: *Series Hydraulica bij Schutsluizen*, Note 7, Delft Technical University, Dept. of Civ. Eng., Hydraul. Struct. Branch, Nov., 1969.
30. KOLKMAN, P. A. Flow-induced gate vibrations, Thesis, Delft Univ. of Technology; Publ. No. 164, Delft Hydraulics Lab., 1976.
31. KOLKMAN, P. A. and VRIJER, A. Gate edge suction as a cause of self-exciting vertical vibrations, *17th IAHR Congress*, Baden-Baden 1977, paper C49; Delft Hydraulics Lab. Publ. 188.
32. LIEBL, A. High pressure sluice gates, *11th IAHR Congress on Large Dams*, Question 41, R42, Vol. II, 1973.
33. MARTIN, W. W., NAUDASCHER, E. and PADMNABHAN, M. Fluid-dynamic excitation involving flow instability, *Proc. ASCE, J. Hydr. Div.*, **HY6** (June 1975), paper 11361.
34. MERCER, A. G. Vane failures of hollow-cone valves, *IAHR Symposium on*

Hydraulic Machinery, Stockholm, 1970, paper G 4.
35. MINOR, H. E. *Schwingungen überströmter Wehre und ihre Beseitigung*, No. 35, Univ. of Stuttgart, Inst. für Wasserbau, Oct., 1975.
36. MÜLLER, O. Schwingungsuntersuchungen an unterströmten Wehren, *Mitt. Preuss. Versuchsanstalt für Wasserbau und Schiffahrt*, Berlin, 1933.
37. NAUDASCHER, E. Beitrag zur Untersuchung Schwingungserregenden Kräfte an gleichzeitig über- und unterströmten Wehrverschlüssen, *Technische Mitteilungen Krupp*, **17** (5) (1959).
38. NAUDASCHER, E. Hydrodynamische und Hydro-elastische Beanspruchung von Tiefschützen, *Der Stahlbau*, Nos. 7 and 9 (1964).
39. NAUDASCHER, E. and LOCHER, A. Flow-induced forces on protruding walls, *Proc. ASCE, J. Hydr. Div.*, **HY2** (Febr. 1974), paper 10347.
40. NAUDASCHER, E. and ROCKWELL, D. Practical experiences with flow-induced vibrations. In ref. 18.
41. NEILSON, F. M. and PICKETT, E. B. Corps of Engineers experiences with flow-induced vibrations. In ref. 19.
42. NOVAK, P. and ČÁBLEKA, J. *Models in Hydraulic Engineering*, Pitman, London, 1981.
43. OGIHARA, K. and UEDA, S. Flap gate oscillation. In ref. 19.
44. PARTENSCKY, H. W. and SAR KHLOEUNG, I. Oscillations de lames déversantes non-aérées, *12th IAHR Congress*, Seminar paper S6, Paris, 1971.
45. PETRIKAT, K. Schwingungserregungen an Stahlwasserbauten, *Der Stahlbau* (Sept. and Dec. 1955).
46. PETRIKAT, K. *Bestimmung der Schwingungserregenden Vertikalkräfte an Sohldichtungen von Hubschützen und Segmentwehrverschlüssen*, No. 21, Univ. of Stuttgart, Inst. für Wasserbau, Apr., 1972.
47. PETRIKAT, K. Structure vibrations of segment gates, *8th Symp. IAHR, Section Hydr. Mach., Equipm. and Cavitation*, Leningrad, 1976, paper 1.2.
48. PETRIKAT, K. Seal vibration. In ref. 19.
49. PULPITEL, L. Some experiences with curing flap gate vibrations. In ref. 19.
50. ROSANOV, N. P., MOYS, P. P., PASHKOV, N. N. and VOROBJOB, G. A. Research of vacuum characteristics of elements of hydrotechnical structures, *IAHR Congress*, Leningrad, 1965, paper 1.33.
51. ROUSE, H. Jet diffusion and cavitation, *J. Boston Soc. Civ. Engrs.*, **53** (3) (July 1966). 529–44.
52. SCHMIDGALL, T. Spillway gate vibrations on Arkansas river dams, *Proc. ASCE, J. Hydr. Div.*, **HY1** (Jan. 1972), paper 8676.
53. SCHWARZ, H. I. Nappe oscillation, *Proc. ASCE, J. Hydr. Div.*, **HY6** (Nov. 1964), paper 4138.
54. DE SOMER, M. *Discussion* [on papers mentioned in ref. 18], Univ. of Karlsruhe, 1972.
55. *Conf. on Thames Barrier Design*, London, Oct., 1977, Inst. of Civ. Engrs, London.
56. THANG, N. D. Added mass behaviour and its characteristics at sluice gates, *Int. BHRA Symp. on Flow-Induced Vibrations*, Reading, Sept., 1982, paper A2.

57. TREIBER, B. Theoretical study of nappe oscillation. In ref. 18.
58. TULLIS, J. P. and MARSCHNER, B. W. Review of cavitation research on valves, *Proc. ASCE, J. Hydr. Div.*, **HY1** (Jan. 1968).
59. TULLIS, J. P. Cavitation scale effects from valves, *Proc. ASCE, J. Hydr. Div.*, **HY7** (July 1973).
60. VRIJER, A. Stability of vertically movable gates. In ref. 19.
61. WEAVER, D. S. Flow-induced vibrations in valves operating at small openings. In ref. 19.

Chapter 3

AERATION AT HYDRAULIC STRUCTURES

K. HAINDL

Department of Hydromechanics and Applied Hydraulics, Water Research Institute, Prague, Czechoslovakia

1 ENTRAINMENT OF AIR IN HYDRAULIC STRUCTURES—CAUSES

Entrainment of air in flowing water at hydraulic structures is due to:

1. disintegration of the water jet in the ambient air;
2. high velocities of supercritical flow resulting in an air–water mixture in the chute or overfall spillway (air entrainment increases still further when translation or standing waves are produced);
3. hydraulic jump or local rollers occurring when a jet impinges on the water surface;
4. the suction effect of flowing water (e.g. from the space under an overflow jet);
5. steady flow transition phenomena in closed conduits (e.g. the hydraulic jump at the transition of free-surface supercritical flow or stratified flow into a pressurised flow, the ring jump at the transition of water flow in an annulus along the walls to full-section flow); and
6. the air layer above the flowing water being set in motion (e.g. in tailrace galleries of shaft spillways, bottom-outlets, etc.).

Air entrainment is also encountered wherever negative pressures occur in the flow, as long as there is a supply of air at this point.

Air entrainment at intake structures is often the result of vortices.[1,2]

Care must also be taken to release air from closed conduits where

this is necessary for safe operation. Air in the two-phase flow soon
concentrates at the top of the closed conduits in the form of air
cushions that can cause water hammer effects at sudden outspurts
and—in the case of dragging—undesirable pneumatic shocks.

So far, only mechanical aspects of air entrainment have been mentioned, but there are also chemical effects. When air bubbles get into
contact with water, oxygen starts to dissolve, which, especially when
water is discharged from the bottom layers of impounding reservoirs
poor in dissolved oxygen or devoid of oxygen due to eutrophication
processes, or in polluted rivers with high oxygen demands, has a
positive effect on water quality. Turbulence accelerates considerably
the mass transfer phenomena which can be utilised with advantage at
hydraulic structures.

Only some aeration problems can be solved on the basis of findings
of double-phase flow mechanics; the majority have to be solved by
means of experimental hydraulics and here model studies and full-scale
structures play an important role.[3] The results of experimental studies
may, of course, be limited and influenced by the equipment and
measuring techniques used, and most of these findings are likely to be
improved in future.

Mutual volumetric relations between the gaseous and liquid components, i.e. air and water, are expressed by volume concentration of the
gaseous component, gas–liquid discharge ratio or volume concentration of the liquid component.

Volume concentration of the gaseous phase in the liquid–gas mixture
is the ratio of the total volume of the gaseous component, V_a, and the
total volume of the mixture, V_m, where the volume of the liquid
component is $V = V_m - V_a$, thus

$$c = \frac{V_a}{V_a + V}$$

With identical velocities of the two components in the aerated water
zone we can substitute for the volumes V_a and V the (volume)
discharges of the gaseous and liquid components, i.e. air and water, Q_a
and Q. (Subscript 'a' refers in all symbols to the gaseous component.)
Then

$$c = \frac{Q_a}{Q_a + Q} \tag{1}$$

In aerated water the volume concentration of the liquid phase is usually called the 'water factor'

$$\omega = \frac{Q}{Q_a + Q} \tag{2}$$

The air–water discharge ratio is designated as

$$\beta = \frac{Q_a}{Q} \tag{3}$$

The interrelations are as follows:

$$\omega = 1 - c \qquad \omega = \frac{1}{1 + \beta}$$

$$\beta = \frac{c}{1 - c} \qquad \beta = \frac{1 - \omega}{\omega}$$

$$c = \frac{\beta}{1 + \beta} \qquad c = 1 - \omega$$

The water flow equation in the air–water mixture is

$$Q = \omega A v$$

The discharge of the gaseous component, Q_a, and hence also the air discharge ratio, β, depend on the pressure at the considered point. At a point with a pressure head x, this is

$$\beta = \varepsilon \beta_b \tag{4}$$

if β_b is the air–water discharge ratio at atmospheric pressure, where

$$\varepsilon = \frac{h_b}{h_b + x}$$

is a compression coefficient if isothermal pressure–volume change is assumed (h_b is the barometric pressure height). The specific mass of the mixture (at pressure head x) is

$$\rho_m = \frac{\rho Q + \rho_a Q_a}{Q + Q_a} = \frac{\rho}{1 + \beta}\left(1 + \beta \frac{\rho_a}{\rho}\right) \approx \frac{\rho}{1 + \beta} \tag{5}$$

where the second term in parentheses has a magnitude of the order of thousandths of the first term and can therefore be neglected.

Similarly the specific weight of the mixture can be expressed by

$$\gamma_m = \gamma \frac{1}{1 + \beta} = \gamma \omega \tag{5a}$$

2 AERATED FLOW IN OPEN CHANNELS

2.1 Characteristics of Aerated Water Flow and Aeration Rate

In channels with great slopes, aeration of the water flow is achieved by its agitation through turbulence. Aeration depends on the turbulence intensity as created by the turbulent boundary layer. Air starts to penetrate into the water flow when the discharge velocity exceeds a certain minimum (3 to 6 m/s) and when the turbulent boundary layer penetrates the whole flow depth at the critical point, which can be determined according to Bauer[4] from the relationship between the boundary layer thickness, δ, the distance from the entry, l, and the linear dimension of roughness

$$\frac{\delta}{l} = 0.0175 - 0.0025 \log \frac{l}{k} \tag{6}$$

The air bubbles diffused in the flow tend to follow its turbulent fluctuations and have the same mean velocity as the water enveloping them. Aeration first becomes evident along the channel walls where, due to increased turbulence, the air concentration is also greater than inside the flow. Likewise, piers in the channel or on the spillways contribute to increased aeration.

The first to deal with aerated water flow was Ehrenberger,[5] who verified laboratory results in the field. He was followed by a number of investigators.[6,7] A thorough laboratory investigation of the self-aerated supercritical flow was carried out by Straub and Anderson.[8] They divided the flow on a chute into an upper part, which included the ejected water drops in air, and a lower part, representing the turbulent flow layer where air bubbles were suspended. The air concentration increases from the bottom and approaches the value $c = 1$ of the free atmosphere. They expressed experimental results of the mean concentration in rough channels as a function of $\sin \delta'/q^{1/5}$, where δ' is the slope of the channel from the horizontal and q is the discharge per unit width. Anderson[9] later presented an experimental relationship for smooth channels using the parameter $\sin \delta'/q^{2/3}$. The relationship for rough channels can be expressed, in the range of the experiments, for q $(m^3/s/m)$, by

$$c = 0.7226 + 0.743 \log \left(\frac{\sin \delta'}{q^{1/5}} \right) \tag{7}$$

and for smooth channels by

$$c = 0{\cdot}5027\left(\frac{\sin \delta'}{q^{2/3}}\right)^{0{\cdot}385} \tag{8}$$

In engineering practice it seems advantageous to use the relationships of aeration to the Froude number derived from measurements on real structures. Thus Hall[10] expressed the aeration ratio by

$$\beta = K\,\mathrm{Fr}^2 \tag{9}$$

using the Froude number in the form

$$\mathrm{Fr}^2 = \frac{v^2}{gR}$$

and the hydraulic radius

$$R = \frac{q}{v + (2q/b)}$$

He obtained the coefficient K for a wooden channel, concrete channels and a concrete channel with numerous changes in direction

$$K = 0{\cdot}00355{:}\ 0{\cdot}0041{:}\ 0{\cdot}00535{:}\ 0{\cdot}0104$$

Hall's experimental channels were narrow chutes, i.e. with the width less than five times the depth (turbulence produced at the walls, the effect of which rapidly extends to the whole width of the chute, resulted in more intensive aeration than obtained in wide channels).

Yevjevich and Levin[11] completed Hall's relation by introducing

$$\psi = \frac{n}{R^{1/6}}\sqrt{g}$$

(where n is the Manning–Strickler coefficient for unaerated water) and a modification of the Coriolis coefficient

$$\alpha_a = \frac{\displaystyle\int_0^y \omega_x u^3\,\mathrm{d}y}{\omega v^3 y}$$

For the wooden Ehrenberger flume, they calculated $\alpha_a = 0{\cdot}94$, for the Mostarsko Blato chute with high channel roughness (stone pavement)

$\alpha_a = 1 \cdot 18$. They adjusted Hall's relation to

$$\beta = K' \mathrm{Fr}^2 \psi \alpha_a \qquad (10)$$

They found coefficient K' to have a relatively constant value of $0 \cdot 175$ with deviations of $\pm 10\%$.

Both authors show that water aeration depends on the roughness of the channel bed and walls and that friction losses in the aerated flow depend on water aeration (ω).

Assuming the validity of the Manning–Strickler equation, even at high supercritical velocities, the value of the experimentally investigated roughness coefficient, n, corresponding to the aerated flow, was always less than the value of the corresponding non-aerated flow in the same channel. Using their own and other tests, Yevjevich and Levin[11] proved a relationship between the coefficient n and the water factor near the bottom, ω_b (e.g. for the coefficient $\omega_b = 0 \cdot 4$, they obtained n for the aerated flow about 30% lower than for the non-aerated flow).

Figure 1 shows the distribution of the water factor along the vertical for the wooden Ehrenberger flume (curve a), for the Mostarsko Blato channel[11] with rough pavement (curve b) and for typical distributions in a rough and a smooth channel (curves c and d)—after Anderson[9]—with a 15° slope with the same water discharge. A corresponding form

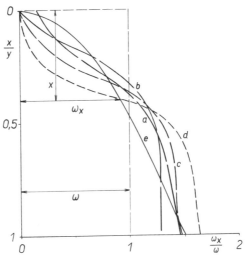

Fig. 1.   Distribution of the concentration of the liquid phase along the vertical in aerated open channel flow.

of concentration distribution (or water factor) in the vertical is shown in the experiments of Thandaveswara and Lakshmana Rao,[12] who also proved the relation between the aeration ratio and the Froude number.

The aeration of the water flow with supercritical velocities can be further increased when rollwaves are produced in the channel; then the aeration distribution in the vertical, the velocity distribution, etc., will also be different. Likewise, oscillating standing waves can also contribute to the intensity of aeration.[13]

Although the theoretical understanding of the aeration mechanism and its effect on the hydraulic parameters of the self-aerated flow are still far from satisfactory, most practical questions can be adequately answered.

2.2 Specific energy and equations of non-uniform aerated water flow

Assuming a parabolic distribution of the water factor in the vertical[13] (Fig. 1, curve e), the water factor in the depth, x, below the surface, will be

$$\omega_x = \tfrac{3}{2}\omega \frac{x^{1/2}}{y^{1/2}}$$

and the specific pressure will be

$$p = \int_0^x g\rho\omega_x \, dx = g\rho \int_0^x \tfrac{3}{2}\omega \frac{x^{1/2}}{y^{1/2}} \, dx = g\rho\omega \frac{x^{3/2}}{y^{1/2}}$$

The average value of the static part of energy will be

$$e = \frac{1}{y} \int_0^y \left(z + \frac{p}{\gamma}\right) dz = \frac{1}{y} \int_0^y \left(z + \omega \frac{x^{3/2}}{y^{1/2}}\right) dz = y\left(\frac{1}{2} + \frac{\omega}{2\cdot5}\right)$$

$(x = y - z; \ dz = -dx)$.

Substituting for $(\omega/2\cdot5)(\omega/m)$, where for the parabolic water factor distribution $m = 2\cdot5$, we can write

$$e = y\left(\frac{1}{2} + \frac{\omega}{m}\right) = yk$$

where

$$k = \frac{1}{2} + \frac{\omega}{m}$$

Since $\omega \leqq 1$, $\geqq 2$, then $k \leqq 1$.

For a rectangular (uniform) distribution of the water factor in the vertical $m = 2$, and for triangular distribution $m = 3$. For the distribution of the water factor in the vertical in the wooden flume (Fig. 1, curve a) $m = 2.45$ and the aeration distribution in the Mostarsko Blato channel with rough stone pavement (Fig. 1, curve b) m becomes 2.35. For a rough channel with 15% bottom slope according to Anderson's tests[9] (Fig. 1, curve c) $m = 2.47$, whereas for a smooth channel (Fig. 1, curve d) $m = 2.73$ with the same water discharges.

The equation for the specific energy in the aerated flow will thus have the form

$$E = ky + \frac{\alpha v^2}{2g} \tag{11}$$

The coefficient k expresses the aeration magnitude and distribution in the vertical. In the expression for the specific energy of the aerated water flow we did not consider the kinetic energy of air present in water, since it is practically negligible; similarly, the effect of transverse and longitudinal velocity pulsation was not taken into consideration. (The energy included in the pulsations is expressed in the head loss.)

We assume the relationships for uniform aerated flow to be also valid for non-uniform flow. Starting from the Bernoulli equation for two sections 1 and 2, distance dl, depths y_1, y_2, we get

$$E_1 + i \, dl = E_2 + dy_z$$

where dy_z signifies the head loss between the two profiles.

According to eqn. (11)

$$ky_1 + i \, dl + \frac{\alpha_1 v_1^2}{2g} = k_2 y_2 + \frac{\alpha_2 v_2^2}{2g} + dy_z \tag{11a}$$

Assuming that between these sections ω, k, m and α remain constant (although they can vary along the chute) eqn. (11a) changes to

$$i - \frac{k \, dy}{dl} = \frac{\alpha}{2g} \frac{dv^2}{dl} + \frac{dy_z}{dl} \tag{12}$$

Substituting for v^2 from the continuity equation in aerated flow

$$Q = \omega A v$$

and using Manning's equation gives after rearrangement

$$\frac{dy}{dl} = \frac{i - \dfrac{Q^2 n^2}{\omega^2 A^2 R^{4/3}}}{k - \dfrac{\alpha Q^2 b}{g A^3 \omega^2}} \tag{13}$$

or

$$dl = \frac{k - Fr^2}{i - \dfrac{Q^2 n^2}{\omega^2 A^2 R^{4/3}}} dy \tag{14}$$

Multiplying eqn. (14) with any value of a positive slope, i', for which the uniform discharge for a cross-section A would be

$$Q_{i'} = \omega_{i'} A \left(\frac{1}{n_{i'}} \cdot R^{2/3} \sqrt{i'} \right)$$

and designating

$$\frac{\omega}{\omega_{i'}} = r \quad \text{and} \quad \frac{n}{n_{i'}} = N$$

equation (14) changes to

$$i' \, dl = \frac{k - Fr^2}{\dfrac{i}{i'} \dfrac{Q^2}{Q_{i'}^2} \left(\dfrac{N}{r} \right)^2} dy \tag{15}$$

For the integration of eqn. (15), we substitute

$$Z = \frac{Q_{i'}}{Q} \frac{r}{N}$$

$$a = \frac{y_1 - y_2}{Z_1 - Z_2} = \frac{dy}{dZ}$$

and

$$Fr^2 = \frac{Fr_{i'}^2}{Z^2 N^2}$$

Equation (15) then can be written as

$$\frac{i'}{ak}\,dl = \frac{1-\dfrac{Fr_{i'}^2}{Z^2 N^2 k}}{\dfrac{i}{i'}-\dfrac{1}{Z^2}}\,dZ \tag{16}$$

For a bottom slope $i>0$, we put $i'=i$; then

$$\frac{i}{ak}\,dl = dZ - \left(1-\frac{Fr_i^2}{N^2 k}\right)\frac{dZ}{1-Z^2} \tag{17}$$

When integrating we consider the value Fr_i^2 as constant and equal to the mean value in the interval l_{1-2}. Integration of eqn. (17) results in

$$l_{1-2} = \frac{ak}{i}\left[Z_2 - Z_1 - \left(1-\frac{Fr_i^2}{N^2 k}\right)[B(Z_2)-B(Z_1)]\right] \tag{18}$$

where

$$B(Z) = \int \frac{dZ}{1-Z^2} + C$$

For the bed slope, $i=0$, we take as auxiliary slope, i', a random small value for which the uniform discharge, Q_i', would be in the region of subcritical flow; then $\omega_i'=1$ and n_i is constant.

Equation (16) for $i=0$ is converted to the form

$$dl = \frac{ak}{i'}\left(\frac{Fr_{i'}^2}{N^2 k} - Z^2\right) dZ \tag{19}$$

After integration in the interval l_{1-2}, assuming a constant $Fr_{i'}^2$ value as before, we get

$$l_{1-2} = \frac{ak}{i'}\left[\frac{Fr_{i'}^2}{N^2 k}(Z_2 - Z_1) - [f(Z_2)-f(Z_1)]\right] \tag{20}$$

where

$$f(Z) = \int Z^2\,dZ + C$$

The accuracy of the calculation of the retarded and accelerated aerated flow depends on the accurate determination of the hydraulic factors considered in the calculation, i.e. on the determination of the water factor ω, its distribution in the vertical, velocity distribution and on the validity of Manning's equation for high velocities.

If the channel bottom is artificially roughened, practically uniform flow with reasonable channel length can be achieved.

3 TRANSITION PHENOMENA

3.1 General Properties

A very frequent cause of air entrainment in hydraulic structures is steady flow transition phenomena, i.e. phenomena at the transition of a certain kind of double-phase flow to full profile flow in closed conduits.[14] One of them is the hydraulic jump in closed conduits[15]—a phenomenon at the transition of supercritical flow to full profile flow, or the transition phenomenon of a jet into pressure flow, or the ring jump[16] that is used with advantage in hydromechanical practice—the phenomenon at the transition of annular flow to full profile flow. To this group also belong other, similar, transition phenomena not defined in our classification. These transition phenomena occur in hydrotechnical practice in horizontal, inclined or vertical pipes (in the last case with the exception of the hydraulic jump in closed conduits); they are characterised by their ability to completely mix all fluid components to a mixed homogeneous flow. At the same time, the transition phenomena lead to dissipation of energy, the reduction of velocities and increase of pressure.

The transition phenomenon appears at the point where its dynamic head is in equilibrium with the pressure head downstream of it.[14] The equation for the dynamic height, e.g. in the case of a ring jump, is derived by means of the momentum equation between sections I and II (Fig. 2) resulting in

$$\varepsilon_2 = \frac{h_b}{h_b + h}$$

$$h = \left[\frac{4\alpha_1 Q v_1}{\pi D^2 g} - \frac{16\alpha_2 Q^2}{g\pi^2 D^4} (1 + \beta_b \varepsilon_2) - K \right] = \theta \qquad (21)$$

where h_b is the atmospheric pressure, h is the pressure height, K is the negative pressure in section I and α is the Boussinesque coefficient.

The expression θ on the right-hand side of eqn. (21) has the height dimension and expresses the kinetic values of the transition phenomenon (dynamic height of the transition phenomenon).

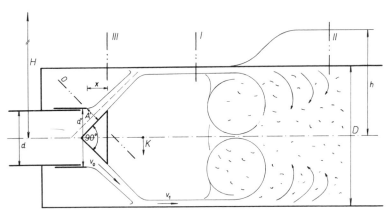

FIG. 2.   The ring jump.

3.2   The Ring Jump

The ring jump has been defined as a hydraulic phenomenon at the transition from annular flow to full profile flow.[14,16] Its dynamic head in horizontal conduits is given by eqn. (21) producing annular flow by the water streaming around a circular disc with the diameter $D-2Y$; i.e. with the width of the annulus Y, the discharge area in the section of the jet contraction is

$$A_o = \bar{\mu}\bar{A} = \bar{\mu}\pi Y(D-Y)$$

Writing

$$v_1 = \varphi v_o = \varphi\sqrt{(2g(H+K))}$$

the equation of the dynamic height can be expressed in the form

$$\theta = \frac{4\alpha_1\varphi Q^2}{g\pi^2 D^2\bar{\mu}Y(D-Y)} - \frac{16\alpha_2 Q^2}{g\pi^2 D^4}(1+\beta_b\varepsilon_2) - K \qquad (22)$$

A comprehensive experimental study of the quantity of air taken up by the ring jump from the space surrounded by the water annulus showed a relationship of the air–water discharge ratio that can be expressed by

$$\beta_b = a(\mathrm{Fr}_1 - 1)^b \qquad (23)$$

where Fr_1 is the Froude number of annular flow in section I in front of the jump in the form

$$Fr_1 = \frac{v_1}{\sqrt{(gy_1)}}$$

y_1 has very low values calculated from expression $A_1 = \pi D y_1$; hence

$$Fr_1 = \frac{\varphi^{3/2} Q \sqrt{(\pi D)}}{\sqrt{(g)[\bar{\mu} \pi Y (D-Y)]^{3/2}}} = \frac{\varphi^{3/2} \sqrt{2} \sqrt{\left(\dfrac{H+K}{D}\right)}}{\sqrt{\bar{\mu}} \sqrt{\left(\dfrac{Y}{D} - \left(1 - \dfrac{Y}{D}\right)\right)}} \qquad (24)$$

The constants a and b can be determined in this case for the position of the ring jump at a distance of $2D$ behind the disc, for $K = 0$ (or K very close to 0), by the values $a = 0.02$, $b = 0.86$. The negative pressure head K in the core of the annular flow is a function of the air–water discharge ratio, β.

The relationship between the air–water discharge ratio in the core of the annular flow, i.e.

$$\beta_1 = \varepsilon_1 \beta_b \left(\varepsilon_1 = \frac{h_b}{h_b + K} \right)$$

and the relative negative pressure

$$\frac{K}{H+K}$$

for constant Fr_1 values is shown in Fig. 3.

For a ring jump in a conduit, diameter D, and the annular flow created by the outflow from a fixed dispersion cone valve, diameter d (Fig. 2), $d' = d/\vartheta$ is the diameter of the valve sleeve; $m = x/d$ is the relative opening. The area of the outflow section perpendicular to the cone and passing through the edge of the valve sleeve is

$$A' = 2\pi \frac{x}{\sqrt{2}} \left(\frac{d'}{2} - \frac{x}{4} \right) = \frac{\sqrt{2}\,\pi d^2}{4\vartheta} m(2 - \vartheta m)$$

The outflow velocity is then

$$v_o = \frac{Q}{\varphi_o A'}$$

where the coefficient $\varphi_o < 1$ expresses the jet contraction in the outflow and includes also the effect of the deviation between the actual

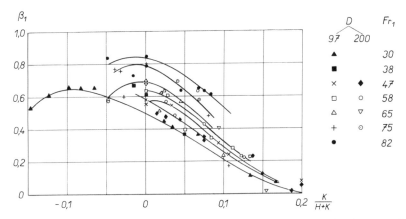

FIG. 3.   Air–water discharge ratio and relative negative pressure in the core of
an annular flow.

angle of the outflowing jet and the valve cone angle. Between the
sections 0 and I there occurs an energy loss expressed by the coefficient
$\varphi_1 < 1$, i.e. $v_1 = \varphi_1 v_0$. Putting $\varphi_1/\varphi_o = \varphi$, then

$$v_1 = \frac{4\varphi Q\vartheta}{\pi d^2 m (2-\vartheta m)\sqrt{2}}$$

and for the dynamic head of the ring jump we get

$$\theta = \frac{16\alpha_1 Q^2 \varphi\vartheta}{g\pi^2 D^2\sqrt{2} \cdot d^2 m(2-\vartheta m)} - \frac{16\alpha_2 Q^2}{g\pi^2 D^4}(1+\beta_b\varepsilon_2) - K \qquad (25)$$

When a smaller amount of air is brought to the space of annular flow
than that necessary for the establishment of equilibrium of the ring
jump for $K = 0$, the negative pressure head, K, increases; it can
theoretically increase only to the value $|K| = h_b$, as long as the kinetic
energy of the water jet is able to produce this negative pressure. At a
certain value of reduced $\beta(K)$ the hydrodynamic equilibrium of the
jump cannot be maintained, the vortex area is formed directly behind
the valve cone resulting in a submerged ring jump. If the pressure head
is less than the dynamic head, $h < \theta$, the ring jump shifts downstream
and the length of the annular flow increases whereby the value of
coefficient φ decreases and the dynamic height θ decreases. It must be
remembered that the possible length of annular flow corresponds to its
initial kinetic energy. The ring jump is produced in the profile where

$h = \theta$, or, if the mentioned equilibrium is not reached, annular flow (possibly deformed annular flow) appears in the whole conduit section concerned.

If the pressure height $h > \theta$, jump rollers form closely behind the valve cone and a submerged ring jump is produced. The initial assumptions are different from those of the unsubmerged ring jump (eqn. (25)). The submerged ring jump strips air and forces it into the pressure flow, as long as the pressure height does not exceed a certain value[14] $h \leqq h_o$. The air–water discharge ratio due to the submerged ring jump decreases with the increase of h from the value β of the unsubmerged ring jump to $\beta = 0$ at $h = h_o$.

Figure 4 shows the relationship between coefficient φ and the relative opening, m, for $d/D = 1/2$ and $d/D = 1/4$, with the unsubmerged ring jump at a distance of $2D$ behind the fixed-dispersion cone valve.

The air quantity taken up by the ring jump from the annular flow core is given by eqn. (23), where the Froude number is expressed in the form

$$\mathrm{Fr}_1 = \frac{\varphi^{3/2} \vartheta^{3/2} 8 Q \sqrt{D}}{d^3 [m(2 - \vartheta m)]^{3/2} \pi \sqrt{(2g)} . \sqrt[4]{2}} \tag{26}$$

The experimental values of $\beta = f(\mathrm{Fr}_1)$ at $K = 0$ (or only with a slight negative pressure) for the position of the ring jump at a distance $2D$ behind the cone valve and for $d/D = 1/2$ are plotted in Fig. 5. The constants a and b are in this case 0.03 and 0.86, respectively.

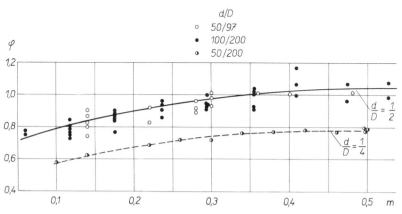

FIG. 4.   Energy losses in a cone dispersion valve.

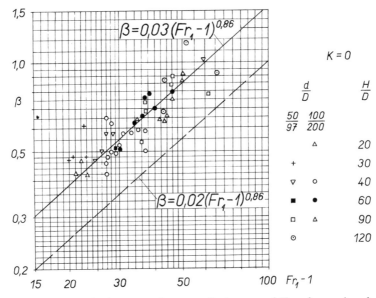

Fɪɢ. 5.   Relationship between air–water discharge and Froude number for a
ring jump.

With the ratio $d/D = 1/4$, the experimental values lie below this
straight line, but in its close vicinity.

When the space behind the valve is not aerated and the pressure
conduit behind it is shorter, air penetrates upstream behind the valve
periodically, and from there is again sucked off by the jump: pressure
surges occur and the flow regime is unstable.[17]

Air forced by the ring jump into the pressure flow behind it first
disperses through the whole flow section in the form of bubbles; due to
the ascending velocity of the bubbles it later gathers at the top of the
horizontal pipe where it forms air cushions dragged in the flow
direction. Let us define the length of the deaerated zone[18] in the
horizontal conduit as length of the pipe from the start of the full-
section flow behind the jump phenomenon to the point where all air
bubbles, dispersed behind the ring jump, reach the top of the conduit.
The air bubble that is at the ring jump at the bottom of the conduit,
due to its ascending velocity in turbulent flow, u_t, reaches the ceiling of
the conduit in the time $t = D/u_t$, covering a distance of

$$l_2 = v_2 \frac{D}{u_t}$$

We relate the ascending velocity in turbulent flow in the area of aerated water to the velocity of a single bubble in quiescent water, u

$$u_t = \eta u$$

On models of different size, air bubbles of the same size were observed behind the transition phenomenon in pipes as well as elsewhere (for normal water roughly with a diameter of 2–3 mm). For air bubbles with a diameter of 2–8 mm the ascending velocity was experimentally found to be the same, $u = 23$ cm/s (see, for example, refs. 19 & 20). The size of the air bubbles is affected by the chemical composlition of the water; Novak[21] gives, e.g. for tap water, for water with 0·3% dissolved $NaNO_2$ and 0·6% $NaNO_2$, a mean bubble size of 2·53, 1·72 and 1·57 mm, respectively (behind a hydraulic jump). The coefficient η, expressed by a certain mean value between section II (with high turbulence) up to the de-aeration section, is a ratio of the relative velocity v_2/u and relative length l_2/D from the equation

$$\frac{l_2}{D} = \frac{v_2}{\eta u} \qquad (27)$$

In Fig. 6 the relationship between the coefficient η and the Froude number, Fr_1, for the ring jump behind the outlet from the fixed-dispersion cone valve is shown as curve a; curve b refers to the ring jump formed by water flowing around a disc.

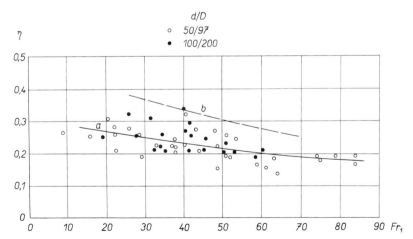

FIG. 6.   Ascending velocity coefficient and Froude number for aerated flow downstream of a ring jump.

3.3 Transition Phenomenon in a Vertical Conduit—Submergence of a Vertical Shaft†

Considering the transition phenomenon of flow in a vertical conduit (e.g. shaft spillway, etc., Fig. 7) with flow and dimensions establishing air transport by the descending vertical flow of the air–water mixture for uniform air transport (i.e. equal descending velocity of the two components) the volume flow of air in the whole descending flow of the mixture is $\beta_b \varepsilon$, where

$$\varepsilon = \frac{h_b}{h_b + x^+}$$

With uniform air transport, the volume concentration of the gaseous component in the mixture is expressed in the form

$$c = \frac{Q_a}{Q_a + Q} = \frac{\beta_b \varepsilon}{1 + \beta_b \varepsilon} = \frac{\beta_b h_b}{h_b + x^+ + h_b} = \frac{\bar{a}}{h_b + x^+ + \bar{a}}$$

where $\bar{a} = \beta_b h_b$.

The relationship between the height of the aerated water column and the pressure height in the differential form is

$$\mathrm{d}x = (1 - c)\, \mathrm{d}x_m$$

If at a certain point of the vertical descending flow in the air transport the pressure head is B (pressure $p = g\rho B$), then at the point situated x_m lower, the pressure head is $x + B$ according to the relationship

$$x_m = \int_0^{x_m} \mathrm{d}x_m = \int_0^x \frac{\mathrm{d}x}{1 - c} = \int_0^x \left(1 + \frac{\bar{a}}{h_b + x^+} \right) \mathrm{d}x = [x + \bar{a} \ln |h_b + x^+|]_0^x \tag{28}$$

where $x^+ = x + B$, i.e.

$$x_m = x + \bar{a} \ln \left| \frac{h_b + B + x}{h_b + B} \right|$$

Let us further consider the vertical descending flow of the air–water mixture with air transport and the transition phenomenon of the impinging jet (Fig. 7). The height of the whirling region of the

---

† Section 3.3 was written in cooperation with M. Haindl, Institute of Information Theory and Automation, Czechoslovak Academy of Sciences, Prague, Czechoslovakia.

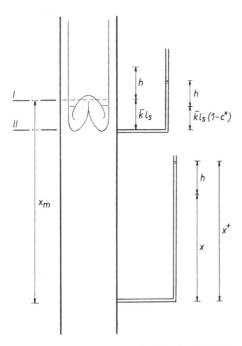

Fig. 7.   Transition of flow in a vertical shaft—definition sketch.

transition phenomenon is

$$B_1 = \bar{k}l_s$$

and the corresponding pressure height

$$B = \bar{k}l_s \frac{1}{1 + \beta_b \varepsilon^+} \tag{29}$$

The pressure head at depth x_n is $x + h$. Equation (28) is then integrated in the range B_1 to x_m resulting in

$$x_m = x + (B_1 - B) + \bar{a} \ln \left| \frac{h_b + h + x}{h_b + h + B} \right| \tag{30}$$

where

$$B_1 - B = \bar{k}l_s - \bar{k}l_s \frac{1}{1 + \beta_b \varepsilon^+} = \bar{k}l_s \frac{\beta_b \varepsilon^+}{1 + \beta_b \varepsilon^+} \tag{31}$$

In the case of the ring jump we can take

$$\bar{k}l_s \cong \frac{D}{2} \quad (D \text{ is diameter of the pipe})$$

then

$$B_1 - B \cong \frac{D}{2}\frac{\beta_b}{1+\beta_b} \tag{31a}$$

and

$$B \cong \frac{D}{2}\frac{1}{1+\beta_b} \tag{29a}$$

when we consider the region of the vortices $\varepsilon^+ \cong 1$.

The transition phenomenon of the impinging jet exerts throughout the aerated water column a dynamic increase in the pressure head, h, which is expressed at the point of the transition phenomenon at atmospheric pressure by means of the momentum equation in the form congruent with eqn. (21) for $K = 0$.

The coefficient of compression in the section behind the transition phenomenon is

$$\varepsilon_2 = \frac{h_b}{h_b + h + B} \tag{32}$$

The position of the transition of the falling jet into the full section flow can be determined in the following way.[22]

The velocity of the water jet at impact on the surface is given by $v_1 = \varphi\sqrt{(2gh_1)}$, where h_1 is the height of the water level in the reservoir above the aerated water column (Fig. 8) and φ is the velocity coefficient.

Using the Manning equation and expressing the hydraulic radius by

$$R = \frac{Q}{v_1 \pi D} = \frac{Q}{\pi D \varphi \sqrt{(2gh_1)}}$$

we get from

$$v_1 = \sqrt{\left(\frac{2gh_1}{1+\dfrac{n^2 h_1 2g}{R^{4/3}}}\right)} = \varphi\sqrt{(2gh_1)}$$

$$\varphi = \sqrt{\left(\frac{Q^{4/3}}{Q^{4/3} + n^2(\pi D)^{4/3}(2g)^{5/3}h_1^{5/3}\varphi^{4/3}}\right)} \tag{33}$$

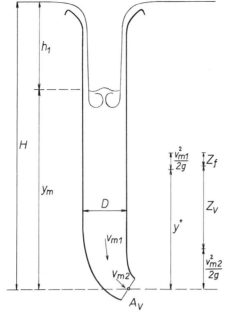

Fig. 8.   Transition of flow in a vertical shaft.

The height of the aerated water column above the outlet section of the shaft we denote y_m, and the corresponding pressure height, y^+ (Fig. 8). The relation between y_m and y^+ we get from

$$y_m = y^+ - h + (B_1 - B) + \bar{a} \ln \left| \frac{h_b + y^+}{h_b + h + B} \right| \tag{30a}$$

The height of the aerated water column above the outlet y_m corresponds to the pressure height y^+ in front of the shaft outlet that must overcome the pressure loss by friction in the submerged section, Z_f, the loss in the outlet, Z_v, and the corresponding difference of the velocity heights (Fig. 8), i.e.

$$y^+ = Z_f + Z_v + \frac{v_{m2}^2}{2g} - \frac{v_{m1}^2}{2g} \tag{34}$$

where

$$v_{m1} = \frac{4Q}{\pi D^2} (1 + \beta_b \varepsilon_{m1})$$

with

$$\varepsilon_{m1} = \frac{h_b}{h_b + y^+}$$

and

$$v_{m2} = \frac{Q}{A_v}(1 + \beta_b \varepsilon_{m2})$$

For the outflow into atmosphere, $\varepsilon_{m2} = 1$, and for the outflow into a tunnel, $\varepsilon_{m2} = h_b/(h_b + \frac{1}{2}z)$, where z is the depth (pressure head) at the beginning of the tunnel.

The quantity of air forced by the ring jump into the pressure flow behind it can be expressed by the experimental relation (23) where the Froude number with $y_1 = R$ can be expressed by

$$\text{Fr}_1 = \frac{\varphi^{3/2} 2^{3/4} h_1^{3/4} (\pi D)^{1/2}}{Q^{1/2}} g^{1/4} \tag{35}$$

Air uptake can be further achieved by a water jet falling freely in the shaft; the quantity of the entrained air depends on the thickness of the water jet and its disintegration.

To enable the discharge by free fall in the vertical shaft to pass into full flow in the shaft, the inlet part of the shaft must not be submerged i.e. the velocity of the freely falling jet, v_1, must be greater than the flow velocity in the full shaft. We can see that this condition is met when the right-hand side of eqn. (21) (with $K = 0$) is positive. Hence it is sufficient to limit the solution by the condition $h > 0$.

This condition must be met for the entire unsubmerged section of the shaft. The computation of the point in the shaft (h_1) where for a given discharge (Q) submergence occurs, or the computation of the discharge at which submergence occurs at a given point of the shaft, may be carried out on a computer or by a graphical–numerical procedure. This leads to the solution of a non-linear system of 24 equations, and therefore it is not possible to find the analytical expression $Q = f_1(h_1)$, or $h_1 = f_2(Q)$, and the task must be solved numerically by using eqns. (21) to (35).

3.4 The Hydraulic Jump in a Closed Conduit

The hydraulic jump in a closed conduit is a hydraulic phenomenon at the transition of supercritical flow to pressure flow. It frequently occurs in hydrotechnical practice, e.g. in tailrace galleries and covered canals with variable bed slopes, in inverted siphons, in supply conduits downstream of sluice or Tainter gates, etc. It is also a suitable means for kinetic energy dissipation, especially downstream of chutes with wave regimes, etc.[12]

For rectangular flow profiles of width b and height D with a supercritical flow depth y_1 and pressure height behind the jump h (Fig. 9), and using the momentum equation, we get an expression for the dynamic height of the jump[14,23]

$$\theta = \frac{1}{D}\left[\frac{\alpha_1 Q^2}{gb^2 y_1} - \frac{\alpha_2 Q^2}{gb^2 D}(1+\beta_b\varepsilon_2) + \frac{D^2}{2} + \frac{y_1^2}{2}\right] - K \qquad (36)$$

The hydraulic jump in a closed conduit is produced at $\theta > D$ for $\theta = h$. When $h < \theta$, the hydraulic jump is shifted downstream to the profile where the desired equilibrium is reached; when $h > \theta$ a submerged hydraulic jump occurs.

The surface roller of the jump strongly entrains air from the space in front of the jump and forces it into the pressure flow behind it.

Air entrainment by the hydraulic jump in a closed conduit has been studied by many authors. The first to deal with it were Kalinske and Robertson,[24] in circular pipes of diameter 150 mm, who within the range of their experiments ($Fr_1 = 1\cdot5$ to 30, where for y_1 the discharge area was divided by the width at the surface) found the constants in eqn. (23) to be $a = 0\cdot0066$ and $b = 1\cdot4$. This was verified by measurements on conduits with rectangular cross-section of 266×200 mm at atmospheric pressure in front of the hydraulic jump,[23,25] plotted in Fig. 10 together with additional data from experiments on larger models[26]

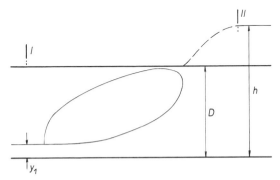

FIG. 9.   Hydraulic jump in a closed conduit.

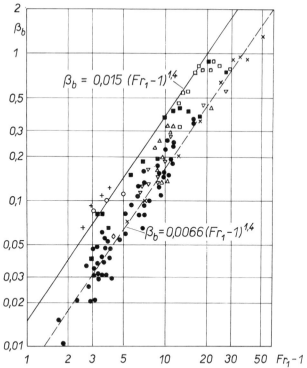

FIG. 10.   Plot of eqn. (23) for a hydraulic jump in closed conduits.

+	Denison	$9' \times 19'$	$2.74\ m \times 5.79\ m$
○	Hulah	$5' \times 6.5'$	$1.52\ m \times 1.98\ m$
▽	Norfork	$4' \times 6'$	$1.22\ m \times 1.83\ m$
■	Pine Flat	$5' \times 9'$	$1.52\ m \times 2.74\ m$
◇	Tygart	$5.67' \times 10'$	$1.73\ m \times 3.05\ m$
×	Ikari	$7.9' \times 7.9'$	$2.4\ m \times 2.4\ m$

Laboratory model:

△ }	Wisner	{ $25\ cm \times 25\ cm$
□ }		{ $50\ cm \times 50\ cm$
●	Haindl	$26.6\ cm \times 20\ cm$

supplemented by field measurements.[28,29] From this it can be seen that the entrainment capacity of the hydraulic jump in a closed conduit increases with the size of the pipe, and for the upper envelope of the field measurement data, the coefficient $a = 0.015$ in eqn. (23) should be used.

For the aeration zone length in the canal behind the hydraulic jump, expressed in eqn. (27), Haindl[23] derived from models of various sizes an experimental relationship for the coefficient

$$\eta = \frac{1}{K}\sqrt{\left(\frac{y_1}{D}\right)}$$

so that

$$l_2 = K\frac{Q}{ub}(1 + \beta\varepsilon_2)\sqrt{\left(\frac{D}{y_1}\right)} \tag{37}$$

where the value of the coefficient K increases with the flow velocity v_2 from $K = 0.75$ for $v_2 = 0.25$ m/s, and for $v_2 > 1.50$ m/s it reaches a constant value of $K = 1.55$.

With air accumulation at the top of the horizontal conduit (or a conduit with only a slight slope), when the air cushion is stopped by increased roughness (e.g. a joint), the air from the cushion can be withdrawn by the hydraulic jump in the conduit or can be removed by the splitting-off of smaller air cushions that are dragged along in the direction of the flow; or, finally, all of the air cushions can be dragged along the ceiling, accompanied by undesirable pneumatic shocks. The release of air cushions from the conduit causes water hammer effects that can reach considerable values. Serious defects in pressure galleries and structures are known to have been caused by these phenomena (e.g. ref. 30). This is why it is always better to avoid the dragging of air cushions by using deaeration chambers, formed by the ascending ceiling of the gallery or conduit and terminating in an air vent. For their dimensioning eqn. (37) can be applied. The hydraulic jump may also be used to withdraw air from the siphon top when put into operation.[31]

3.5 Transition Phenomenon of a Jet; Jet Fall

A jet also passes into full flow in a conduit (Fig. 11) under conditions of dynamic and pressure head equality as shown by eqn. (21). Air entrainment as well as dissipation of kinetic energy now causes rollers, enveloping the jet from the outside. Here the relative discharge of the entrained air can also be expressed by eqn. (23), where the Froude number is used in the form

$$\mathrm{Fr}_1 = \frac{v_1}{\sqrt{(gd_o)}}$$

where $d_o = $ jet diameter in *vena contracta* behind the nozzle.

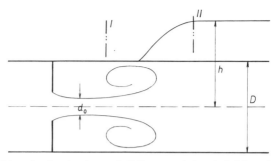

FIG. 11.   Jet flowing into a full flow conduit—definition sketch.

Experiments with the creation of a transition phenomenon in a horizontal conduit ($D = 200$ mm) at a distance of about $2D$ behind the outflow from the nozzle, with $K = 0$ in the range $Fr_1 = 7$–25, have shown that the constants in eqn. (23) are $a = 0.017$ and $b = 1.1768$. (With a longer jet it is difficult to achieve a transition phenomenon in a horizontal conduit.)

A falling jet very soon disintegrates and entrains air. Hoření,[32] in his model study of a horizontal projection of the jet, expresses the length L_o from the overfall edge measured along the jet axis to the point of its disintegration as a function of discharge per unit width in the overfall

$$L_o = 31.19 q^{0.319} \text{(cm, cm}^2/\text{s)} \tag{38}$$

He also showed that during the flight of the jet only a small part of its mechanical energy—about 12%—is lost due to friction with the ambient medium.

For a fully turbulent jet of circular section falling freely to the water surface in a pool, Elsawy and McKeogh[33] in their model study determined the disintegration length in the form

$$L_o = 48 Q^{0.33} \tag{39}$$

(somewhat greater than for a horizontally falling jet due to vertical shear forces).

The volume of entrained air, V_a, in the pool for a given initial Froude number, Fr_1, was found to increase with the height of the fall up to a certain limit, beyond which it remained constant. This value of V_a was determined by the expression

$$\frac{V_a}{d^3} = 1.2 \, Fr_1^{1.66} \tag{40}$$

where $Fr_1 = v_1/(gd)^{1/2}$, $v_1 = $ velocity at the outlet of the jet and $d = $ diameter of the jet.

During the fall of water through the shaft—where, for example, in the case of glory-hole spillways with spiral flow regime the water flow is concentrated in an annulus along the mantle of the shaft—air becomes entrained due to the jet disintegration in the annular flow; the sub-pressure produced in the air core causes an additional air flow through the shaft. The entrainment from the central air core into the annular water flow begins at the inception point where the turbulent boundary layer penetrates through the whole flow thickness. The position of the inception point can be calculated as for a high-speed open channel flow (see Section 2.1).

If during the fall of water in the shaft the outflow from the shaft is not submerged, so that no transition phenomenon is created, the total air entrainment in the shaft, Q_a, can be subdivided into air flow in the air core in the centre of the dropshaft, Q_{aC}, and the entrained air flow into the annular water layer, Q_{aE}

$$Q_a = Q_{aC} + Q_{aE}$$

Hack,[34,35] in his model study of water falling through a smooth and an artificially roughened shaft, determined the air–water discharge ratio in the annular layer, $\beta_E = Q_{aE}/Q$, by the relation

$$\beta_E = \beta_{EM}(1 - e^{(m\,Fr_0^{1/3} - Fr^{1/3})}) \tag{41}$$

where the Froude number, Fr, is related to the unaerated water, i.e. according to eqn. (35); Fr_0 is the Froude number at the inception point. The coefficient $m = 1 \cdot 8k/D + 0 \cdot 0108$ (k is the absolute roughness and D is the dropshaft diameter). Hack adopted the maximum possible air–water discharge ratio β_{EM} as 4.

For the total air entrainment, Hack proposed the empirical correlation

$$\beta = 0 \cdot 35 + 16 \cdot 09\left(\frac{\beta_E}{1 + \beta_E}\right)^{2 \cdot 88} \tag{42}$$

where $\beta = Q_a/Q$.

It is evident that in spillway shafts, secondary supply shafts, etc., very substantial amounts of air flow must be taken into consideration.

4 AERATION OF HYDRAULIC STRUCTURE
ELEMENTS—AIR VENTS

4.1 General

To avoid severe sub-atmospheric pressures in a conduit downstream of gates, the conduit must be connected to the atmosphere through an air vent located downstream of the constriction.

Adequate supply of air is important to minimise structural damage due to cavitation and vibration. The demand of air is given by the type of flow or by the hydraulic phenomena downstream of the constriction. Thus, downstream of a partly opened gate of an outlet conduit, a free water level flow may form along the entire outlet conduit. (It may appear as stratified flow, wavy or slug flow.) A foamy flow may form (the conduit section filled with almost-uniform air–water mixture but not yet flowing under pressure); at small openings of the gate, spray flow with numerous small droplets and entraining a relatively large quantity of air may occur. Flow with free water level may change its structure by a hydraulic jump with free water level at the transition of supercritical and subcritical flow, or by a hydraulic jump in a closed conduit at the transition from supercritical flow into flow under pressure.

The hydraulic jump in a closed conduit can also be pressed to the gate, and, due to submergence, its entraining capacity will decrease or the jump may not entrain any air at all, and only pressurised flow of water alone will occur. In tailrace tunnels of glory-hole spillways one must deal with an inflow of highly aerated water downstream of the inlet throttle. Here, aeration at the throttle is necessary, mainly when discharges are approaching the design discharge.[36] If not aerated, water adheres for a certain length to the tunnel ceiling, alternately detaching and adhering, whereas if the inlet throttle is aerated, free water level flow is produced behind the initial point of the jet spray. Now the magnitude of the sub-pressure corresponds to the rate of aeration and the flow type at the beginning of the tunnel.

The cross-sectional area of an air vent is determined from the air demand and air flow velocity, v_a.

The air flow velocity, if the difference in the pressure heads (pressure drop at the point of outflow of the air vent), Δh, is expressed in metres of water column, is

$$v_a = \varphi \sqrt{\left(\frac{\rho}{\rho_a}\right)} \sqrt{(2g\Delta h)} \cong 27\cdot8\sqrt{(2g\Delta h)} \qquad (43)$$

where ρ/ρ_a is the ratio of water and air mass and the term φ incorporates the total losses in the submerged air vent. Usually, $v_a < 40$ m/s, since a higher velocity causes undesirable noise in the air vent and considerable pressure drops at its outflow. An acceptable pressure drop is equal to the sum of the loss and velocity heads only for air vents where a steady water flow can be assumed or at least where the change in its flow velocity occurs only very slowly. However, in air vents or rapidly moving gates unsteady air flow and water hammer effects occur, accompanied by a pressure drop in the outflow of the air vent which has to be added to the normal head loss.

4.2 Aeration Behind Sluice Gates or Tainter Gates[3]

If a hydraulic jump in a closed conduit is produced in the vicinity of the gate, the air demand is determined by its aeration capacity (see Section 3.4) according to eqn. (23), where for y_1 we use the depth in *vena contracta*

$$y_1 = \bar{\alpha}z$$

where $z =$ the height of gate lift, $\bar{\alpha} =$ coefficient of contraction.

In order to ascertain for which gate opening the air demand is the highest, we put

$$\frac{dQ_a}{dz} = \frac{d(\beta Q)}{dz} = 0$$

If we neglect the very slight variability of v with lift z, we get (for the exponent $b = 1\cdot4$ in eqn. (23)) the maximum air demand for

$$\frac{v}{\sqrt{(\bar{\alpha}z)}} = \frac{10}{3} \tag{44}$$

Assuming $v = \varphi\sqrt{(2g(H+K))}$, then the gate lift corresponding to the maximum air demand is

$$z = 0\cdot18\frac{\varphi^2}{\bar{\alpha}}(H+K) \qquad (z < D) \tag{45}$$

For high pressure gates, the highest air demand occurs as a rule when the gate opening approaches its maximum (as long as the formation of the jump roller is still possible). The relation between the air demand due to air entrainment of a hydraulic jump in a closed conduit and the gate lift has a single maximum.

If the hydraulic jump in the closed conduit is formed at a certain distance downstream of the gate or in the outlet end of the conduit or tunnel below the downstream water level, an additional air entrainment in the supercritical flow upstream of the hydraulic jump will occur, resulting in a pre-entrained hydraulic jump. In this case the quantity of air consumed for the aeration of the supercritical flow zone must be added to the air demand of the hydraulic jump.[37]

The supercritical flow in a free-flowing conduit downstream of a partly opened gate is similar to the high velocity flow in steep open channels (see Section 2) and the air demand is given by the same laws. The transport in the layer between the transition surface and the conduit soffit which is caused by either surface drag or momentum transfer through water droplets, or both, must be added to the transport of air carried by the water flow. Air entrainment into supercritical flow causes a pressure drop in the air flow through the air layer and an increase in air flow velocity. Sharma[27] showed that the air velocity at the interface is much higher than the average velocity of water alone and that the air velocity distribution is far from logarithmic. It is known from general observation of two-phase flow that the velocity of the gas phase in wavy, slug or stratified flow is much higher than the average velocity of the liquid phase. This follows also from the experimental results of Ghetti.[38] Sharma[27] proposes for free-flowing conduits relationships between the average air flow and Froude number in the *vena contracta*, Fr_c, which he obtained as envelopes of his measurements of air demand in model and prototype. For spray flow he proposes

$$\beta = 0 \cdot 2 Fr_c \qquad (46)$$

and for free flow

$$\beta = 0 \cdot 09 Fr_c \qquad (47)$$

For air demand in the case of foamy flow, Wunderlich[39] derived the expression

$$\beta = \bar{r}\left(\frac{1}{A_c/A_t} - 1\right) \qquad (48)$$

where A_c = the area of flow at *vena contracta*, A_t = cross-sectional area of conduit and $\bar{r} = \bar{v}_a/\bar{v} < 1$ = ratio of average air and water velocities.

The conditions for the occurrence of foamy flow behind gates in conduits—adequate Froude number in *vena contracta* and the depth of flow in *vena contracta* comparable to the vertical dimension of the conduit—are rather limited in practical cases.

Sharma plotted the β values for free-flowing conduits from model as well as available field measurements as a function of A_c/A_t with Fr_c as parameter, and showed that curves for the different values of the Froude number could be joined asymptotically to the line represented by eqn. (48) with $\bar{r} = 1$.

Spray flow is primarily caused by gate slots. It may also occur at small gate openings without slots in rough conduits, and due to leakage through the seals. Thus it depends on many factors and it is not possible to determine theoretically for which possible opening of the gate the maximum air demand due to the spray flow will occur. The air-demand curve for free-flowing conduits in relation to the gate opening has thus two maxima, the first for spray flow and the second for free flow.

4.3 Outflow from a Fixed Dispersion Cone Valve into the Conduit

The dispersion cone valve is one of the most frequently used control valves of bottom outlets of dams. When placing this valve on the downstream face of the dam with free outflow, the water becomes strongly dispersed, and ice can form. It is therefore often advisable to situate the outlet with fixed dispersion cone valves rather than in the tailrace or in an outlet chamber at the downstream face of the dam. When the outlet from the valve discharges into a closed conduit where annular flow is created, it is always necessary to deliver air into the core of the annular flow.

The air vent is again dimensioned according to the hydraulic regime occurring in the tailrace.

If a ring jump forms in the tailrace the greatest air demand occurs at the greatest opening of the valve, as a rule for $m < 0.6$. The discharge through the fixed dispersion cone valve is expressed by

$$Q = \mu \frac{\pi d^2}{4} \sqrt{(2g(H + K))} \qquad (49)$$

where $\mu = f(m)$ is given by the manufacturers.

When a ring jump occurs, the relationships given in Section 3.2 hold true. The air demand for a ring jump not too far downstream of the valve is expressed by eqn. (23) with the given constants a and b. With greater lengths of annular flow the air demand grows due to jet disintegration in the annular layer. In a flow regime without a ring jump, when the water jet along the top of the tailrace falls down to the invert, the air demand is less.

The formation of a ring jump in the tailrace is advantageous for kinetic energy dissipation and oxygen saturation of the outflowing water.

4.4 Outflow from a Needle Valve into the Conduit

We shall not deal here with the aeration of different types of valves, but show in the example of a differential needle valve how air demand depends on the cavitation characteristics and hence on the shape of the valve.

Figure 12 shows the results of a differential 200-mm needle valve model study (valve inside a conduit) carried out by Žajdlík.[40,41] The cavitation numbers, σ, are plotted against the relative opening of the valve; σ_1 corresponds to the first stage of cavitation (manifesting itself

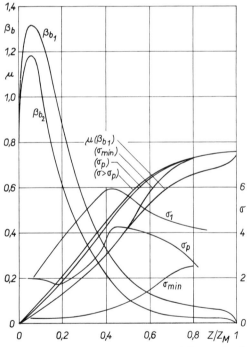

FIG. 12. Outflow from a needle valve into a conduit—cavitation numbers and air–water discharge ratios.

by the increase in noise and shocks in the valve), σ_p to the second stage of cavitation, when at the points of the greatest negative pressures the first vapour bubbles appear; σ_{min} are the minimum values of the cavitation number, where it is still possible to carry out measurements on the model. The plotted values of β_{b1} and β_{b2} are the maximum air–water discharge ratios for aeration through openings of 6 mm diameter, situated on the circumference of the narrowed cross-section behind the valve (1) and for aeration by an opening of 40 mm diameter from above (2) with cavitation coefficients σ_{min}. Values of the discharge coefficient μ (for $K = 0$ in eqn. (49)) for three cases and for aeration, β_{b1}, are also shown.

When the needle valve (or another similar valve) discharges with a concentrated water jet into the tailrace (diameter D), the air demand is given similarly to the preceding cases according to the flow regime in the conduit.

5 NATURAL DE-AERATION OF VERTICAL DESCENDING FLOW IN SHAFTS

In practice we also encounter the case of descending flow through vertical shafts, where in the upper part free fall of the water jet may occur. When the jet impinges on the surface of the submerged part, it creates mixed air–water flow in this part and it is necessary to exclude the transport of air through the conduit. This is, for example, the case of filling pressure systems, where the inlet or the intermediate part is formed by a vertical conduit or shaft and dragging of the stripped air through another part of the pressure system must be prevented (inverted siphon, pressure tunnel, etc.).

During the passage of the water–air mixture down a vertical conduit there exists a discharge velocity at which the zone of aerated water, with a certain air concentration in the water, reaches a limited length and, below the boundary of the aeration zone, there is flow of water only.

In such a case we speak about a zone of natural de-aeration.[42] Curtet and Djonin[43] found a relationship between the length of the aerated water zone, L_s; and the slip velocity of the air and water particles

$$v_g = \frac{Q}{A(1 - c_s)}$$

where c_s is the mean air volume concentration in the aeration zone. (The space concentration was measured by reading the levels of the water and air–water columns after sudden closure of the flow by a guillotine valve.) Dimensional analysis led the authors to the conclusion that for this case the Froude number in the form

$$\mathrm{Fr} = v_g/\sqrt{(gL_s)} = \text{constant} \tag{50}$$

For their experiments the constant was $\mathrm{Fr} = 0.06$.

In our experimental study we determined the mean volume concentration from the measured lengths of the aerated water zone, L_s, and the pressure below it, given by the relation

$$p = \varphi g y^+ = \varphi g [L_s(1 - c_s) + h] \tag{51}$$

where h is the dynamic height, given by eqn. (21), and y^+ is the pressure head. From eqns. (51) and (21) (with $K = 0$) we get

$$c_s = \frac{L_s - y^+}{L_s} + \frac{Q}{L_s g A}\left[\alpha_1 v_1 - \alpha_2 \frac{Q}{A}(1 + \beta_b \varepsilon_2)\right] \tag{52}$$

It can easily be shown[44] that in this case the mean air concentration is only given by the aeration zone length and the pressure value below it.

With low slip velocities in the upper part of the aeration zone, elongated bubbles (minimum diameter 5–8 mm) are formed which change continuously to spherical bubbles of about 3 mm diameter at the end of the zone. With greater slip velocities the elongated bubbles are formed approximately in the upper two-thirds of the zone and the lower third is filled with spherical bubbles.

The relationship between the aeration zone lengths and the slip velocity is illustrated in Fig. 13, which shows the results of the experimental study carried out on two models of an impinging axial circular water jet and a jet falling through a circular sector along the wall. The curve through the cluster of measured points corresponds, for lower v_g values (smaller L_s), to a parabola according to eqn. (50). After reaching a certain value of the slip velocity, $v_g = 0.18$ m/s, the de-aeration zone length suddenly increases. When this value is exceeded, the air is transported by the descending air–water downstream flow in the vertical pipe.

As mentioned in Section 3.2, the size of the air bubbles in the aerated water was found to be approximately the same on models of different sizes. That means that air bubbles in the zone of aerated

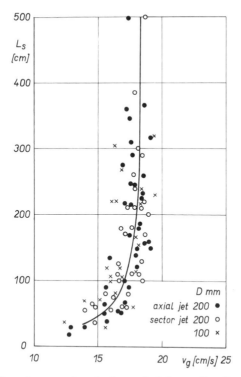

FIG. 13.   Aeration zone lengths in vertical descending flow in shafts.

water on structures of various sizes (even if slightly differing in size) behave identically. The length of the de-aeration zone depends on the slip velocity, v_g; i.e. with the same concentration, c_s, the deaeration zone lengths with identical apparent velocities, Q/A (the apparent velocity is equal to the discharge velocity downstream of the aeration zone), are equal in pipes of various sizes presuming an identical turbulence effect. With increasing lengths of the falling water jet, c_s slightly increases; in addition an increase of the mean concentration by air uptake with the dispersion of the falling water jet can be expected. With increasing c_s the value of the apparent velocity corresponding to the boundary value of v_g will be lower for a certain length of the deaeration zone, L_s, i.e. $Q/A = v_g (1 - c_s)$. With increased length of the falling water jet, i.e. increased kinetic energy of the jet impinging on the water cushion, a certain increase in the length of the transition phenomenon will occur.

With higher slip velocities than $v_g = 0 \cdot 18$ m/s, it is necessary to deal with downwards air transport through the vertical descending conduit (even if for the complete removal of the air still higher velocities may be necessary).

6 OXYGEN ENRICHMENT AT HYDRAULIC STRUCTURES

6.1 General
The dissolved oxygen content of water is one of the indicators of water quality. Polluted rivers have relatively low dissolved oxygen concentrations or high oxygen deficits. Due to eutrophication processes, the water in the bottom layers of impounding resevoirs is deprived of some or all of the oxygen, with oxygen deficit being at a maximum during the summer stagnation.

Every aeration of river water—by overfalls over weirs, in stilling basins or otherwise—is advantageous, as it usually means oxygen enrichment and improvement of the water quality.

The gas flow into the liquid can be generally expressed according to Fick's Law of diffusion by the equation

$$\frac{dM}{dt} = k_L A (C_s - C) \tag{53}$$

where dM/dt = mass flow of gas into the liquid (g/s), k_L = the liquid film coefficient (cm/s), A = gas–liquid interface area (cm^2), C = gas concentration in liquid (g/cm^3) and C_s = gas saturation concentration in liquid (g/cm^3)

By dividing by the volume V(cm^3) we get

$$\frac{dC}{dt} = k_L \frac{A}{V} (C_s - C) \tag{54}$$

and after integrating (assuming constant C_s, k_L and A/V) in the time interval (t_1 to t_2)

$$\ln \frac{C_s - C_1}{C_s - C_2} = k_L \frac{A}{V} (t_2 - t_1) \tag{55}$$

where

$$\frac{C_s - C_1}{C_s - C_2} = r \tag{56}$$

is called the deficit ratio.

With continuous saturation, where the liquid volume is $V = Qt$ and the volume of the gaseous component $V_a = \beta Qt$, the latter is present in the liquid–gas mixture in bubbles of spherical shape and diameter d_b; as the transfer area is the Nth multiple of the bubble surface and the gaseous component volume the Nth multiple of the bubble volume, then[21]

$$k_L = \ln \frac{C_s - C_1}{C_s - C_2} \frac{1}{(t_2 - t_1)} \frac{d_b}{6\beta} \tag{57}$$

Coefficient k_L is clearly a function of the gas diffusivity (a function of temperature T, the size of diffusing particles and the liquid viscosity ν) and of the turbulence or degree of mixing in the liquid medium. The latter effect proves to be most important in continuous mixing.

For continuous water oxygenation, the mass inflow of dissolved oxygen in water (mass per time unit) can be expressed by

$$Q_{O_2} = \kappa \beta Q C_p \tag{58}$$

where C_p = oxygen concentration in air and κ = oxygen utilisation rate.

The oxygen utilisation rate, κ, expresses the ratio of mass quantity of dissolved oxygen to the total quantity supplied, hence

$$\kappa = \frac{(C_2 - C_1)Qt}{C_p \beta Qt} \tag{59}$$

The oxygen utilisation rate is thus a function of the air–water discharge ratio, β: it further depends on the degree of turbulence during mixing and on the contact time of the two phases. It is also affected by the presence of oxidisable components in water.[45,46]

Since the maximum possible utilisation of oxygen is for $C_2 - C_1 = C_s$, the highest possible value of the oxygen utilisation rate is

$$\kappa_{max} = \frac{C_s}{C_p \beta} \tag{59a}$$

It is evident that for oxygenation purposes it is economically appropriate to mix only with low values of β. The mixing mode is the more appropriate the more the dependence of oxygen utilisation rate, $\kappa = f(\beta)$, approaches the relationship $\kappa_{max} = f(\beta)$.

6.2 Oxygen Uptake at the Outflow under a Gate with Hydraulic Jump, and at a Jet Falling into a Pool

The overfall over a dam (weir) or the outflow under a gate are the most frequently encountered instances of outflow from water reser-

voirs and in both instances air entrainment occurs and hence also
potential water oxygenation.

Both instances were systematically investigated by Novak et al.[47]
They expressed dissolved oxygen saturation by the deficit ratio related
to temperature at 15°C, r_{15}.

Based on an experimental study of an outflow under a gate with a
hydraulic jump downstream, they expressed the relation of the deficit
ratio, the Froude number, Fr_1, and the Reynolds number, Re, of the
flow upstream of the hydraulic jump by the relation

$$r_{15} - 1 = k_1 Fr_1^{2.1} Re^{0.75} \qquad (60)$$

where

$$Fr_1 = \frac{v_1}{\sqrt{(gy_1)}}, \qquad Re = \frac{Q}{bv} = \frac{q}{v}$$

They showed that the size of the air bubbles is a function of the
salinity of water (see Section 3.2) and hence the coefficient k obtained
for tap water, for water containing 0·3% $NaNO_2$ and 0·6% $NaNO_2$ is
$1·004 \times 10^{-6}$, $1·2445 \times 10^{-6}$ and $1·5502 \times 10^{-6}$, respectively. (The
range of their laboratory-scale measurements was $145 < q < 710\,cm^2/s$,
$2·8 < Fr_1 < 8·5$.)

For the deficit ratio in the case of a jet falling into a downstream
pool Novak et al. derived the relationship

$$r_{15} - 1 = k' Fr_J^{1.78} Re^{0.53} \qquad (61)$$

where the coefficient k' is given for tap water, for water containing
0·3% $NaNO_2$ and 0·6% $NaNO_2$ as $0·627 \times 10^{-4}$, $0·869 \times 10^{-4}$ and
$1·243 \times 10^{-4}$, respectively.

The given correlation was developed for an undisintegrated water jet
(eqn. (38)) with a downstream water depth equal to or greater than the
optimum depth X, i.e. when the air bubbles did not reach the bottom
of the pool and optimum contact time was ensured.

For the optimum depth X (cm), they present the relation

$$X = 0·433\,Re^{0.39}\,Fr_J^{0.24} \qquad (62)$$

The disintegration of a jet will result in different energy losses and the
creation of a significantly larger air–water interface (but not necessarily
larger oxygen uptake).

The Froude number is defined by

$$\mathrm{Fr}_J = \left(\frac{\pi\sqrt{(2gh_1^5)}}{Q}\right)^{1/4} = \left(\frac{gh_1^3}{2q_J^2}\right)^{0.25} \tag{63}$$

The form of the Froude number using the diameter of the jet d (or the discharge Q) is valid for a circular jet; for a jet with rectangular cross-section the form of the Froude number using the length of the fall h_1 and the discharge per unit jet perimeter at the point of impact $(q_J = r_{hy}\sqrt{(2gh_1)})$ applies (r_{hy} is the hydraulic radius at the point of impact). In eqn. (61), $\mathrm{Re} = q_J/\nu$ with the discharge q_J related to the unit jet perimeter at the point of impact. In the case of a wide rectangular jet (e.g. overfall over a long crest) the perimeter is approximately equal to one or two jet widths, according to whether the jet gets into contact with air on one or both sides (i.e. a jet over a spillway or a free-falling jet).

Rectangular spillway jets converge either very quickly to circular or diverge to flat rectangular shapes. The height of the fall, where the converging jets acquire a circular shape, is given by Burley[48] by the experimentally determined expression

$$h_1 = 431 b^{0.36} Q^{0.8} (h_1, b \text{ in metres, } Q \text{ in m}^3/\text{s}) \tag{64}$$

and as criterion for a diverging jet

$$\frac{z}{b} > 1 \cdot 288 \tag{65}$$

where $z =$ overfall height.

The given results can also be used for multiple jets or cascade weirs. If one circular jet for Froude number Fr_J is split into N jets of equal diameter, the resultant Froude number will be $\mathrm{Fr}_J \sqrt[4]{N}$. The advantage afforded is obvious, a higher Froude number can be attained for the same discharge and height of fall, therefore greater aeration is achieved.

Since a cascade weir may consist of a series of free overfalls with pools, it is necessary in the calculation of successive oxygen saturation on each single step of the cascade to use the successively changed oxygen saturations. By evaluating the specific oxygenation effects for the investigated oxygen saturation modes, Novak[21] shows that the free overfall and hydraulic jump are comparable while the latter has the advantage of requiring smaller tailwater depth.

The laboratory results (eqns. (60–65)) correlated well with field measurements ($h_1 < 8.5$ m) and resulted in oxygenation efficiencies between 0.91 and 0.16 kg O_2/kWh with about 50% of initial deficit.

The preceding values are on the whole competitive when compared with commercial aerators, i.e. turbine and surface aerators.

6.3 Oxygenation by Steady Flow Transition Phenomena, Oxygen Uptake in Outflows from Bottom Outlets and Turbines

One of the most important factors affecting the mass transfer and oxygenation of water is turbulence during mixing, i.e. intense internal mixing. These properties are exhibited in an open channel, e.g. by the hydraulic jump—see Section 6.2 and work by Leutheusser et al.[49]—and in a closed conduit by steady flow transition phenomena that show a similar character. These transition phenomena in conduits—see Section 3—obviously have even higher transfer characteristics because of the sufficient length of contact time of air bubbles with water, whilst maintaining high turbulence of flow.

In saturation by means of transition phenomena, the specific discharge is given by eqn. (57) and the oxygen utilisation rate, κ, is indirectly proportional to the air–water discharge ratio, β. The relationship $\kappa = f(\beta)$ has always a similar character to the relationship $\kappa_{max} = f(\beta)$ (eqn. (59a) and it approaches it more or less for low input saturations (C_1). When the ring jump is used, the curves $\kappa = f(\beta)$ are very close to the curve $\kappa_{max} = f(\beta)$.

Normal water contact times of approximately 5 s are sufficient to achieve an output saturation (C_2) approaching saturation concentration.[45] As the κ values increase with decreasing β and the quantity of the entrained air and hence also β increases with the head, low head values are sufficient for an effective saturation. In dam outlets the heads are usually considerably greater than adequate heads for the complete oxygen saturation of water, but the higher values of β have a useful effect on other chemical and physico-chemical processes that are taking place.

Since in dam outlets both the discharge and the head on the valve are variable, the dynamic height of the transition phenomenon is also variable. To achieve equilibrium of the dynamic and pressure heads, which determines the origin of the transition phenomenon, a descending tail channel behind the outflow from the valve (gate) was designed in such a way that a transition phenomenon was always produced in it.[50] This is shown in the design of the aeration outlets in Fig. 14. With

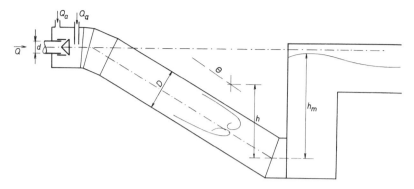

FIG. 14.   Dam outlet discharging into a tailrace conduit.

height of the water–air mixture in the ascending flow x_m, the pressure head, x, can be derived similarly for the descending flow (see Section 3.3, eqn. (28)) with the final values $x_m = h_m$ and $x = h$.

Figure 15 shows an application of the above principle for an outlet discharging into a stilling basin.

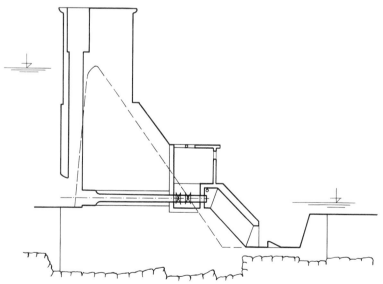

FIG. 15.   Dam outlet discharging into a modified stilling basin.

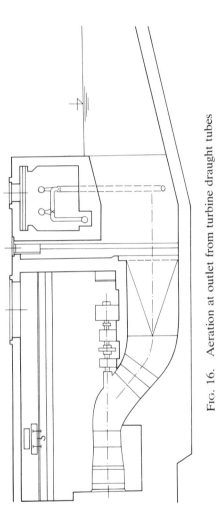

FIG. 16. Aeration at outlet from turbine draught tubes

Results of oxygenation achieved by these means are consistently in the region $10–13 \, g/m^3 \, (O_2)$.[51]

For comparison, the oxygenation effect produced by the outlet of a dam—where air entrainment occurred in the hollow core of the jet behind a Johnson valve, by dispersion of the jet during its fall as well as in the hydraulic jump in the stilling basin—was found to be an increase from $0·8 \, g/m^3 \, O_2$ to $5·6 \, g/m^3 \, O_2$, i.e. the total effect was about one-half compared with that of the specially designed aeration outlets.

By making use of transition phenomena in the design of the bottom outlets, not only is effective oxygenation of the outflowing water achieved but also good dissipation of its kinetic energy.

The situation at dams with power generation, where the oxygen-deficient water is discharged through the turbines, is more complicated. It is, for example, possible to put aeration into sub-pressure points of the turbines, but this usually results in a decrease of the turbine output. Aeration outlets using the formation of transition phenomena and discharging into the outlets from draught tubes of turbines (according to Fig. 16) seem therefore to be appropriate. These auxiliary aeration outlets are used in the case of potential oxygen deficits in the river (mainly in the period of summer stagnation).

The oxygenation effect can—in comparison with commercial aerators, i.e. turbine and surface aerators—be very high.

Similarly, oxygen saturation of navigable waterways can be increased in navigation locks. The improvement of the oxygen balance in the lock with direct filling can be achieved by discharging auxiliary aeration outlets into the stilling basin of the lock. The author's solution for a lock on the Oder is described in ref. 52.

If oxygenation in rivers is necessary, other means may also be used, e.g. the creation of an artificial bubble curtain produced by passing compressed air through a porous filter, perforated pipe, etc. (technical parameters are given, for example, by Markofsky and Kobus[53]). Another means is the use of mechanical aerators, used either as surface aerators or submerged turbine aerators.

In new structures we can use the suggested solutions for avoiding negative ecological impacts; even in existing structures it is usually possible to achieve the required effect by relatively minor measures. In any case, it is the duty of the hydraulic engineer to take into account in his design the whole complex of possible effects of the structure on the environment.

REFERENCES

1. CHANG, E. Review of literature on drain vortices in cylindrical tanks, *BHRA-Fluid Engineering* (March 1976), TN 1342.
2. DHILLON, G. S. *Vortex formation at pipe intakes and its prediction*, Report No. 6, Central Board of Irrigation and Power, New Delhi, January 1980.
3. NOVAK, P. and ČÁBELKA, J. *Models in Hydraulic Engineering—Physical Principles and Design Applications*, Pitman & Sons, London, 1981, 480 pp.
4. BAUER, W. J. Turbulent boundary layer on steep slopes, *Proc. ASCE*, **79** (281) (1953).
5. EHRENBERGER, R. Wasserbewegung in steilen Rinnen mit besonderer Berücksichtigung der Selbstbelüftung, *Österreichischer Ingenieur u. Architektenverein* (15/16 and 17/18) (1926).
6. *Aerated flow in open channels*, Progress Report, Task Committee on Air Entrainment in Open Channels, *J. Hyd. Div. ASCE*, **87** (HY 3) (May 1961), Part 1, 73–86.
7. Air entrainment by flowing water, Part IV, *Proc. IAHR*, Minneapolis, 1953, 403–533.
8. STRAUB, L. G. and ANDERSON, A. G. Experiments on self-aerated flow in open channels, *Proc. ASCE*, **84** (HY 7) (December 1958).
9. ANDERSON, A. G. Influence of channel roughness on the aeration of high-velocity, open channel flow, *Proc. IAHR*, Leningrad 1965, Vol. 1 No. 1, 37.
10. HALL, S. L. Open channel flow at high velocities, *Transactions ASCE*, **108** (1943), 1393.
11. YEVJEVICH, V. and LEVIN, L. Entrainment of air in flowing water and technical problems connected with it, *Proc. IAHR*, Minneapolis, 1953, 439–54.
12. THANDAVESWARA, B. S. and LAKSHMANA RAO, N. S. Developing zone characteristics in aerated flows, *J. Hydr. Div. ASCE*, **HY 3** (March 1978) 385–96.
13. HAINDL, K. and LÍSKOVEC, L. *Nadkritické proudění ve vodním stavitelství* (*Supercritical Flow in Hydraulic Engineering*), Práce a studie VÚV (Water Research Institute), Prague, 1973.
14. HAINDL, K. *Prstencový skok a přechodové jevy proudění* (*Ring Jump and Steady Flow Transition Phenomena*), Academia, Prague, 1975.
15. HAINDL, K. Hydraulic jump in closed conduits, *Proc. IAHR Congress*, Lisbon, 1957, D-32.
16. HAINDL, K. Transfer of air by the ring jump of water, *Proc. IAHR Congress*, Paris, 1971, A-44.
17. HAINDL, K.: L'instabilité de l'écoulement à la sortie d'une vanne conique débitant dans un canal couvert, *Comptes Rendus, VII ièmes Journées de l'Hydraulique*, Lille, 1964.
18. HAINDL, K. Zone lengths of air emulsion in water downstream of the ring jump in pipes, *Proc. IAHR Congress*, Kyoto, 1969, B 2, 9–20.
19. BENFRATELLO, G. Moto di una bolla d'aria entro un liquido in quiete, *Memorie e Studi dell Inst. di Idr. e Constr. Idraul.*, Milan, 1953.

20. HABERMAN, W. L. and MORTON, R. K. Experimental study of bubbles moving in liquids, *Proc. ASCE*, **LXXX** (1954), No. 387.
21. NOVAK, P. Luftaufnahme und Sauerstoffeintrag an Wehren und Verschlüssen, *Symposium on Artificial Oxygen Uptake in Rivers, Darmstadt, June, 1979*, DVWK, Publication No. 49, Bonn, 1980.
22. HAINDL, K. and HAINDL, M. *Zahlcení šachtového přelivu (Submerging of a Glory-hole Spillway)*, Vodní hospodářství, 1982, No. A 11.
23. HAINDL, K. *Teorie vodního skoku v potrubí a její aplikace v praxi (Theory of the Hydraulic Jump in Closed Conduits and its Use in Practice)*, Práce a studie VÚV (Water Research Institute), Prague, 1958, No. 98.
24. KALINSKE, A. A. and ROBERTSON, J. M. Closed conduit flow, *Trans. ASCE*, **CVIII** (1943), No. 2205.
25. HAINDL, K. and SOTORNÍK, V. Quantity of air drawn into a conduit by the hydraulic jump and its measurement by gamma-radiation, *Proc. IAHR Congress*, Lisbon, 1957, D-31.
26. WISNER, P. Sur le rôle du critère de Froude dans l'étude de l'entrainement de l'air par les courants a grande vitesse, *Comptes Rendus AIHR Congrès* Leningrad, 1965.
27. SHARMA, H. R. Air entrainment in high head gated conduits, *J. Hydr. Div. ASCE*, **102** (HY 11) (Nov. 1976), 1629–46.
28. CAMPBELL, F. B. and GUITON, B. Air demand in gated outlet works, *Proc. IAHR Congress*, Minneapolis, 1953, 529–33.
29. JUKIO, M. and ILGININ, S. N. Air demand in conduits partly filled with flowing water, *Proc. IAHR Congress*, Montreal, 1959.
30. BUNATIAN, L. B. K voprosu o pričinach avarii diukerov (About causes of inverted siphon failures), *Trudy Arm. NIIGiM*, No. 1, 1952.
31. CASTELEYN, I. A. and KOLKMAN, P. A. Air entrainment in siphons. Results of tests in two scale models and an attempt at extrapolation, *Proc. IAHR Congress*, Baden-Baden, 1977, A 63.
32. HOŘENÍ, P. *Studie rozpadu volného vodního paprsku ve vzduchu (Disintegration of a Free Jet of Water in Air)*, Práce a studie VÚV (Water Research Institute), Prague, 1956, No. 93.
33. ELSAWY, E. M. and McKEOGH, E. J. Study of self aerated flow with regard to modelling criteria, *Proc. IAHR Congress*, Baden-Baden, 1977, Ab 60, 475–82.
34. HACK, H. P. *Lufteinzug in Fallschächten mit ringförmiger Strömung durch turbulente Diffusion*, Bericht der VAW der Techn. Universität München, 1977, No. 36.
35. HACK, H. P. Air entrainment in dropshafts with annular flow by turbulent diffusion, *Proc. IAHR Congress*, Baden-Baden, 1977, Ab 64, 507–14.
36. HAINDL, K., DOLEŽAL, L. and KRÁL, J. Příspěvek k hydraulice šachtového přepadu (Contribution to the hydraulics of a glory-hole spillway), *Vodohospodarsky časopis* (1962) (3), 288–314; (4), 370–81.
37. HAINDL, K. Příspěvek k řešení zavzdušovacích potrubí (Contribution to air-vent solution), *Strojírenství* (1957), no. 11.
38. GHETTI, A. Elementi per lo studio idraulico degli organi di scarico profondo da serbatoi, desunti da ricerche sperimentali, *L'Energie Elettrica* (1959) (9), 801–16.

39. Wunderlich, W. Die Grundablässe an Talsperren, *Die Wasserwirtschaft* (1963), 70–75, 106–14.
40. Žajdlík, M. The effect of needle valve profile on its hydrodynamic and cavitation characteristics, *Proc. IAHR Symposium*, Rome, 1972, D 3.
41. Žajdlík, M. *Hydraulické poměry a dynamické účinky vodného prúdu na kuželový uzáver* (*Hydraulic and dynamic relations of a water jet on differential needle valve*), Research Report B-PU-84, VÚVH (Inst. of Water Management), Bratislava, 1969.
42. Haindl, K. and Ramešová, L. Modelling of zones of natural de-aeration, *Proc. IAHR Congress*, Baden-Baden, 1977, A 66, 523–33.
43. Curtet, R. and Djonin, K. Etude d'un écoulement mixte air-eau vertical descendant, *Houille Blanche* (1967), No. 5.
44. Haindl, K. and Ramešová, L. *Dvoufázové proudění kapalina–plyn* (*Double-phase flow liquid–gas*), Research Report VÚV (Water Research Institute), Prague, 1975, No. III-6-9/10.
45. Haindl, K., Jursíková, M. and Žáček, L. Oxygen transfer into water during ring-jump mixing, *Proc. IAHR Congress*, Cagliari, 1979, Ba 22.
46. Haindl, K., Nachtmann, T. and Žáček, L. *Dvoufázové proudění kapalina–plyn* (*Double-phase flow liquid–gas*), Research Report VÚV (Water Research Institute), Prague, 1980, No. III-7-6/2.
47. Avery, S. T. and Novak, P. Oxygen transfer at hydraulic structures, *J. Hydr. Div. ASCE*, **HY 11** (November 1978), 1521–40.
48. Burley, G. H. The effect of jet shape on oxygen transfer at free overfall rectangular weirs and the prototype study of oxygen transfer at hydraulic jumps, M.Sc. Thesis, University of Newcastle-upon-Tyne, 1978.
49. Leutheusser, H. J., Resch, F. J. and Alemu, S. Water quality enhancement through hydraulic aeration, *Proc. IAHR Congress*, Istanbul, 1973, B 22, 167–75.
50. Haindl, K. Suitable solution of bottom outlets of dams and oxidation outlets for the improvement of water quality in rivers, *Proc. IAHR Congress*, Istanbul, 1973, B 24, 187–94.
51. Haindl, K. and Jursíková, M. Zlepšení kyslíkové bilance toku pod přehradou užitím aeračních výpustí (Enhancement of the oxygen balance downstream of a dam by using aeration outlets), *Proc. Symposium, Czech. National Com. ICOLD*, Banská Bystrica, 1979.
52. Čábelka, J. *Směry rozvoje vodní dopravy a vodních cest v ČSSR* (*Trends in Development of Water Transport and Inland Waterways in Czechoslovakia*), Práce SF ČVUT (Technical University—Civil Eng. Faculty), Prague, March, 1981, Ed. V 3/1981, 115–212.
53. Markofsky, M. and Kobus, H. On the modelling of artificial reoxygenation, *Proc. IAHR Congress*, Baden-Baden, 1977, A, 459–66.

Chapter 4

SPILLWAYS OF HIGH DAMS

J. J. CASSIDY and R. A. ELDER
Bechtel Civil & Minerals, Inc., San Francisco, California, USA

1 INTRODUCTION

The function of the spillway for any dam is to safely convey flood flows past the dam without unacceptable damage. The high velocities and large levels of energy involved in flow over spillways make their design of considerable importance. The consequences of a high dam failing are normally much more severe than those for a low dam for equal reservoir capacity. Proper design of the spillway requires that its capacity should be adequate, that flow through the spillway be smooth enough to ensure performance as designed, that flow distribution should not induce downstream problems, that the structure be free of damaging cavitation, and that control gates (if used) operate as required without damaging vibration. This chapter deals with the hydraulic aspects of the design of spillways for high dams and is not concerned with hydrologic processes that may be considered in establishing the design flow. In addition, the chapter does not discuss the design or functions of stilling basins required for energy dissipation at the downstream ends of spillways. For the purposes of this chapter flip buckets are considered to be energy dissipators and are not treated.

The type of spillway to be used for a high dam is dictated by the type of dam, the peak rate of flow that must be passed by the spillway, the required operating functions of the project, and topographic and geologic conditions at the site. Figure 1 illustrates several spillway types often used. An uncontrolled overflow crest has always been recognised as the safest type of spillway crest. In general, earth and rockfill dams should utilise uncontrolled overflow spillway crests

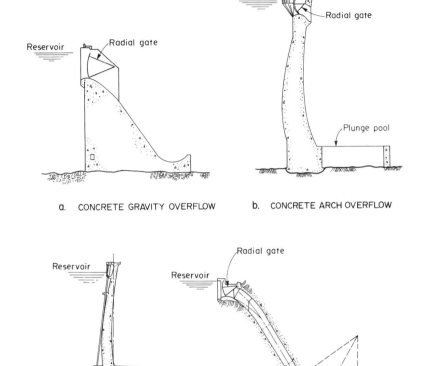

a. CONCRETE GRAVITY OVERFLOW   b. CONCRETE ARCH OVERFLOW

c. ORIFICE   d. TUNNEL

FIG. 1.   Common spillway types.

whenever possible because of the serious consequences resulting from
overtopping the dam as a result of a malfunction of gates during a
critical period. Uncontrolled overflow crests are frequently used on
chute-type spillways and on the overflow sections of thin arch dams;
the possibility of their plugging by trash should always be considered.
Thin arch dams frequently incorporate orifices controlled by fixed-
wheel or radial gates alone or in conjunction with overflow spillways.
Tunnel spillways usually incorporate a portion of one or more of the

diversion tunnels. In addition, a side-channel overflow spillway entrance has been used on a number of tunnel-type spillways. This type can produce an undesirable flow condition in the chute and should only be used where topographic conditions dictate its economic value, and then only after careful model testing.

The successful design of a spillway requires proper attention to several specific aspects: approach conditions; crest-gate selection and crest and pier design; chute conditions, including training-wall heights and potential floor erosion; possible problems attendant with long term operations; and as an adjunct to all of the foregoing, the proper use of physical model tests.

The end result of a successful design must be a spillway which will not cause the dam to overtop nor the crest to be breached and a design which delivers flow to the stilling basin or flip bucket such that these structures can be satisfactorily operated.

2 APPROACH AND CREST DESIGN CONSIDERATIONS

2.1 Approach Conditions

The approaching flow to a spillway can have a strong effect upon the flow pattern in the spillway chute. A badly distributed velocity of approach can result in a significantly diminished discharge coefficient for the crest. Poor approach conditions can also cause crest gate vibrations. In addition, undesirable approach conditions can generate strong waves that propagate through the spillway chute upsetting the balanced distribution of flow entering the stilling basin. Thus, for spillways for high dams it is always advisable to perform a model study to evaluate the effect of approach conditions upon flow further down the spillway unless the approach is symmetrical and unobstructed.

2.2 Crest Design

Design considerations associated with the overfall spillway crest include selection of the crest shape, selection of type and size of gates (if the crest is to be controlled), and the proper design of piers and abutments. Proper design of the crest will insure that flow is distributed well in the chute (and in the stilling basin) and that objectionable wave heights are not propagated downstream.

In practice, spillway crests are shaped according to the lower surface of the nappe produced by flow over a sharp-crested weir. General coordinates of such shapes are published in many references.[1,11,21] The shape chosen will dictate the pressures which are experienced on the surface of the crest as well as the discharge coefficient applicable for flow over the crest. The US Army Corps of Engineers has developed coordinates for several different geometric conditions including vertical and sloping upstream faces and vertical faces offset in the upstream direction. Coordinates given include the effects of upstream velocity of approach. If the head for which the spillway profile is shaped is termed the design head, H_0, operation at heads above the design head will produce pressures lower than atmospheric on most of the crest and an increase in the discharge coefficient. For operation at design head (using the US Army Corps of Engineers crest) the discharge coefficient, C_0, for use in the following equation

$$Q = C_0 L H^{3/2} \tag{1}$$

where Q is discharge in m^3/s, L is length of spillway crest in metres and H is the head on the crest in metres is approximately 2·20. If the head on the crest is increased to $1·33H_0$ the discharge coefficient will be approximately 2·30, a 4·5% increase in efficiency. The minimum pressure head on the crest, which occurs near the upstream tangent point, falls from atmospheric to approximately $-0·8H_0$. Obviously, pressure should not be allowed to approach the vapour pressure. A conservative minimum pressure is -5 m of water.

Prototype studies made by the US Army Corps of Engineers on Chief Joseph Dam, for a head of 14·1 m (1·11 H_0), showed no indication of pressure fluctuations which might produce concern. Locher made a detailed study of transient pressures on a model crest and also found no tendency for pressure fluctuations, other than those logically occurring in a turbulent boundary layer.[31]

Abecasis studied the flow over crest shapes at heads higher than design heads using an enclosed flume in which the pressure above the free surface could be lowered to produce lower than atmospheric pressure.[2] Thus, he was able to develop incipient cavitation conditions on the model crest. His studies showed that potential for cavitation on the crest does not occur unless the head on the crest becomes substantially greater than $1·5H_0$.

2.3 Gates

Crest-mounted gates for flow control have included radial gates, drum gates, vertical-lift gates and flap (bascule) gates. The radial and vertical lift gates are underflow gates while the drum and flap gates are overflow types.

The most common control gate utilised is the radial gate because it is generally the cheapest, the most easily installed, the easiest to seal and relatively failure safe. Bascule, or flap gates, are utilised in situations where debris or ice must be passed frequently and in general for heads on the spillway crest less than 6 m. The bascule or flap gate has the disadvantage of requiring large turning moments to maintain the gate in closed position. Thus, bascule gates are much more limited in height than radial gates. Drum gates have not been utilised in recent years but Grand Coulee Dam (1941) and Norris Dam (1936) in the United States utilised drum gates successfully. The drum gate can be fully automatic and operates through utilisation of the upstream head in the reservoir. The level of the water in the gate float wells can be adjusted to set the desired gate position. Vertical lift gates are seldom used on overflow crests of high dams but have often been used to control orifice spillways. They are utilised where sufficient space is not available for the use of radial gates.

Figure 2 illustrates the different types of gates commonly used on spillways. For various reasons, attempts have been made to make gate operation at least partially automatic. Automatic operation varies from that incorporated in the design of drum gates to specially designed floats to operate radial gates without power. Automatic operation, however, should be adopted only where maintenance is regular, inspection is frequent and close monitoring is possible during flood seasons.

Spillway controls for tunnel-type spillways have included radial gates, flap gates, and especially designed ring gates such as those used on the 'morning glory' entrance of Hungry Horse Dam in the United States. The gating of a 'morning glory' spillway entrance can present serious difficulties because the disturbance to flows created by non-symmetrically operated gates may create waves which are capable of producing unsteady oscillations between closed-conduit and open-channel flow in the tunnel downstream.

Gate-vibration problems are generally associated with flow past the gate lip or vortices acting at the face of the gate. If the lip is designed so that separation of the discharging nappe moves from the upstream to the downstream side of the lip, a fluctuating force acts on the gate. If the frequency of the fluctuating force is in resonance with the gate-supporting mechanism, amplitudes of vibration can become large

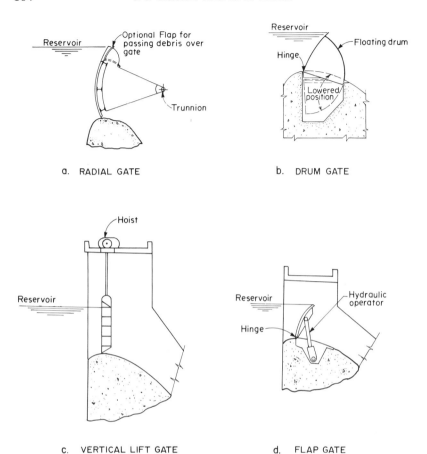

a. RADIAL GATE   b. DRUM GATE

c. VERTICAL LIFT GATE   d. FLAP GATE

Fig. 2.   Common types of gates.

enough to damage the gate or its operator, or simply prevent use of the
gate. Such vibration problems can occur with both radial gates and
vertical-lift gates. When the gates are cable-suspended the possibility
of amplitude amplification is greater.

2.4 Pier Design

Care must be taken when placing gates on spillway crests to ensure
that the approach flows do not create objectionable conditions at the
gates or in the chute downstream from the gates. Large separation

zones in the area immediately upstream from the gates, as can be caused by the flow approaching along the spillway face on either side (see Fig. 3a), can create large vortices. Those vortices may in turn cause the gate to vibrate, greatly reduce the flow through the gate, or create large waves in the chute which in turn can cause a major disturbance to the flow in the downstream chute. Interior piers, especially if very wide, can cause similar problems.

These problems can be minimised by modifications such as those shown on Fig. 3b. It should be emphasised that a very large intermediate pier, due to the effect of its wake, can create a downstream problem for which no simple solution exists. It is best to keep intermediate piers as narrow as strength requirements will allow.

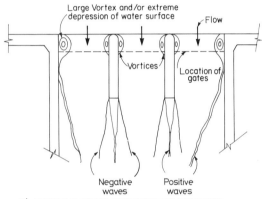

a.) EFFECTS OF SHARP ABUTMENTS AND THICK PIERS

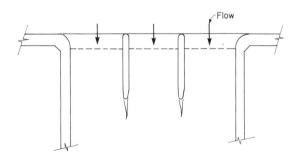

b.) CONFIGURATION WITH ROUNDED ABUTMENTS AND THINNER PIERS

FIG. 3.   Effects of spillway design on entrance conditions.

3   CHUTE AND TUNNEL DESIGN CONSIDERATIONS

3.1   Prototype Experience

Chute or tunnel spillways for high dams almost always experience velocities greater than 30 m/s. At these high velocities, erosion of poorly constructed concrete surfaces will occur. If the concrete used on the spillway is relatively weak, erosion can occur simply because of the high shear forces exerted by the flow or because of pressure fluctuations developed as a result of minor irregularities on the flow surface.

The serious problem most commonly encountered is that of cavitation pitting. Whenever velocities exceed 20 m/s, cavitation can generally be expected where projections or depressions exist on the flow surface. One of the early cases of damage due to cavitation was reported for Grand Coulee Dam[13] completed in 1941. Cavitation resulted from flow over a sloping surface generated by the exit of an outlet conduit intersecting the spillway surface. The slope away from the flow was 16:1 and the velocity was in excess of 30 m/s. To alleviate the cavitation condition, a system was devised to entrain air in the flow. This approach was found to be effective in preventing damage.

Yellowtail Dam (USA), a tunnel-type spillway, experienced serious cavitation damage in the horizontal section and lesser damage in the upper inclined portions.[4] The Yellowtail tunnel, which is 9·8 m in diameter, experienced flows up to 510 m³/s and was subjected to velocities possibly as high as 53 m/s. Erosion in the tunnel included large holes in the horizontal portion, immediately below a 55° vertical bend, with depth as great as 2·4 m and as wide as 5·9 m. Cavitation may have been triggered by loss of small epoxy mortar patches in the bend 6·4 mm deep.

Hoover Dam (USA), another tunnel-type spillway, experienced severe cavitation damage in and just below its 50° vertical bend upon its initial and only operation in 1945.[5] The 15·9-m diameter tunnel was subjected to discharges as high as 1075 m³/s and velocities as high as 45 m/s. The spillway had operated for four months at an average discharge of approximately 328 m³/s. Damage consisted of erosion of the concrete tunnel lining and underlying rock to a depth of 13·7 m and a length of 35 m. Cavitation was triggered by a bulge in the invert concrete immediately upstream from the bend, due to deflections of the forms during construction.

The spillway for the Reza Shah Kebir Project (Iran) experienced serious cavitation erosion problems in 1977. The chute-type spillway, designed for a flow of $16\,000\,m^3/s$, is divided into three separate chutes. During the first year of operation, cavitation damage was discovered upstream of all the spillway flip buckets; velocities in the chute in the entrance of the bucket were approximately 45 m/s. Damage included a large hole which progressed completely through the 1·5-m thick concrete chute floor and continued for 1 m into the underlying rock. A significant part of the later damage may have been caused by large pieces of the concrete being torn loose once cavitation pitting had become extensive. The failure has been attributed to deviations in the concrete surface in the chute amounting to as much as 10 cm vertically in 3 m horizontally. Less cavitation damage occurred downstream from bug holes and showed typical cavitation shadow patterns.

Keban spillway (Turkey) has also experienced significant cavitation damage downstream of transverse joints in spillway chutes.[6] The spillway, designed for a discharge of $1700\,m^3/s$, is controlled by six radial gates, each 24 m high by 16 m wide. Spillway discharge is divided into three channels and terminates in flip buckets. During 1976, flows of approximately $1\,000\,m^3/s$ were passed over the spillway and subsequently cavitation damage was discovered downstream from several transverse joints in the spillway chute floor. The holes produced by cavitation extended a substantial distance across the spillway chute and were as much as 0·4 m deep with some reinforcing bars torn out by the flow. The cause of the cavitation was found to be improperly constructed transverse joints.

In a study of Supkhun Dam (Korea) extensive cavitation damage was discovered and attributed to improperly constructed joints, protruding reinforcing bars, and irregularities in the surface which had not been smoothed prior to spillway operation.[7]

Bratsk Dam is Russia also experienced significant cavitation damage during operation.[7] Bratsk Dam, which is an overflow concrete structure approximately 104 m high, experienced damage approximately 70 m below the crest of the dam. The damage included several holes, with the largest being approximately 7·5 m by 10·5 m by 1·2 m deep. Cavitation was attributed to projecting reinforcing and structural steel and irregularities produced by improper joints in forms used during construction. Cavitation was not experienced where projections were less than 40 mm. No information was given relative to velocities of flow, but calculation indicates that velocities should have been in excess of 30 m/s. Aeration ramps were constructed on the spillway and were reported to be successful in alleviating cavitation damage in future tests.

In their study the Committee on Hydraulics for Dams of the International Congress on Large Dams solicited and received operating histories of 116 large dams.[8] The reports covered 123 spillways of which 84 were gated and 36 were uncontrolled. The remaining three apparently had both gated and uncontrolled sections on the spillway. The spillways ranged in capacity from less than 500 m^3/s to more than 10 000 m^3/s and in maximum velocities from less than 20 m/s to more than 40 m/s. Seventy-one of those reported had operated in excess of 100 days. Of the 71, 52 reported no damage, nine reported slight erosion (less than 2 cm deep), two reported moderate damage (2 to 10 cm deep) and eight serious erosion (more than 10 cm deep). Table 1 presents statistics on the spillway damage in terms of velocity and unit discharge. The survey indicated that aeration of flow had been provided in nine of the spillways. These nine spillways included four

TABLE 1
SUMMARY OF SPILLWAY EROSION CASES REPORTED TO ICOLD

Range of spillway capacity $(m^3/s/m)$	Number of cases of erosion in range				Total number of spillways reported
	No erosion	Slight erosion	Moderate erosion	Serious erosion	
>200	1	0	0	2	3
100–200	7	4	1	1	13
50–100	20	0	1	3	24
10–50	19	4	0	1	24
<10	5	1	0	1	7

Range of maximum velocity (m/s)	Number of cases of erosion in range				Total number of spillways reported
	No erosion	Slight erosion	Moderate erosion	Serious erosion	
>40	0	2	1	3	6
30–40	3	1	0	2	6
20–30	5	0	1	0	6
<20	14	2	0	1	17

overflow spillways on concrete dams, three tunnel spillways, one chute spillway, and one spillway controlled with flap gates. Six of the nine aerated spillways apparently suffered cavitation damage in spite of the aeration, two with serious damage. It is impossible to draw significant conclusions about effects of aeration from the study by the ICOLD Committee. Cavitation was apparently successfully controlled in nearly all cases by careful repair work and the use of epoxy and fibrous concrete patches further emphasised the importance of proper control in placing and/or finishing concrete surfaces to prevent serious cavitation damage. It should also be noted that cavitation damage can occur during small discharges. None of the survey results indicated that aeration devices had been added subsequent to the discovery of cavitation damage.

Guri Dam, completed in 1968, on the Caroni River in Venezuela incorporated three chute-type spillways, terminating in flip buckets. Operation occurs each year at discharges in the range of 10 000 m³/s. Since completion in 1968 as much as 6 m of the flip-bucket lips has been eroded away by cavitation. Aeration of the flow in one chute was provided by constructing a 0·75-m high aeration ramp (2·47 m long) near the top of the chute. The spillway was operated for one year with no further progression of damage to the flip bucket. Aeration slots have since been constructed on the first chute to be raised in the process of raising Guri Dam by 50 m. The slot produces air concentrations of approximately 40% immediately below the slot. This new chute has now operated for 100 days at 10 000 m³/s without cavitation damage.[22]

It should be pointed out that several very high dams have spillways which have operated for significant lengths of time without objectionable cavitation damage. The tunnel spillway on Fontana Dam in the United States has had a nearly trouble free operational life and has operated for several thousand hours.[9] Fontana's spillway has a tunnel 10·4 m in diameter and is subjected to velocities as high as 48 m/s. Particular efforts were made by the Tennessee Valley Authority during construction to maintain close tolerances in the spillway surface alignment and to provide quality concrete for construction.

Mica Dam is an example of a chute spillway for a high dam that has operated without objectionable cavitation damage.[10] After 49 days of initial operation at flows as high as 2100 m³/s, minor cavitation damage was discovered downstream of several defective construction joints. The damaged areas were removed and replaced with epoxy concrete.

The original imperfect joint was ground smooth and subsequent operation has not produced further damage.

3.2 Control of Cavitation

Experience has shown that high velocities over the concrete surfaces of spillways can produce damaging cavitation. Local bulges in forms or improper forming or finishing of concrete can result in local surface deviations which produce local zones of low pressure. If the low pressures reach the vapour pressure, cavitation will occur. The provision of high strength concrete in areas subjected to high velocity will aid in preventing damage but if cavitation takes place damage will occur.

Determining whether or not cavitation will occur at a particular velocity may be necessary during design or after construction when grinding or repair of surface deviations may be necessary to prevent damage. Accurate estimation of the velocity will be necessary, requiring proper values of absolute roughness. Elder reported values of 0·78 mm to 1·09 mm for the 5·5-m diameter Appalachia Tunnel.[12] This value probably represents the smoothest surface obtainable without

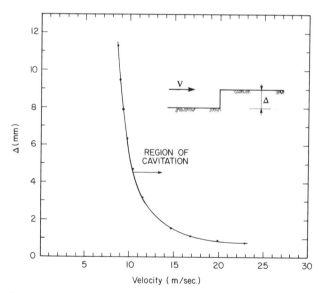

FIG. 4.   Incipient cavitation for flow over offsets into flow (from data by Ball[14]).

steel troweling of the finished surface. With good estimates of absolute roughness, velocities near the spillway surface can be calculated through hydraulic analysis and application of boundary-layer theory.[1]

The potential for cavitation as a result of flow over a surface deviation has been analysed by Ball[3,13] and Johnson.[30] Their results for abrupt and sloping offsets into and away from the flow are shown in Figs. 4, 5 and 6. It is of interest to note from Fig. 5 that at a velocity of 30 m/s, cavitation will take place downstream of a contraction joint which is offset away from the flow only 3 mm. Comprehensive studies, similar to those of Ball and Johnson but covering a great many

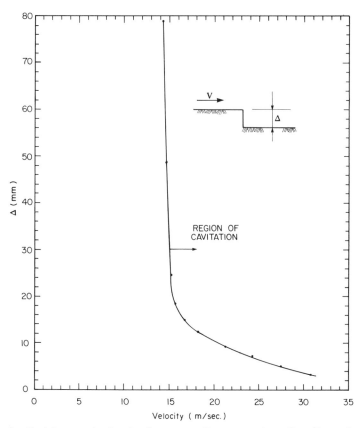

FIG. 5.   Incipient cavitation for flow over offsets away from flow (from data by Johnson[30]).

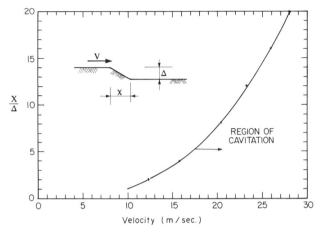

FIG. 6.   Incipient cavitation at offsets sloping away from flow (from data by Ball[3]).

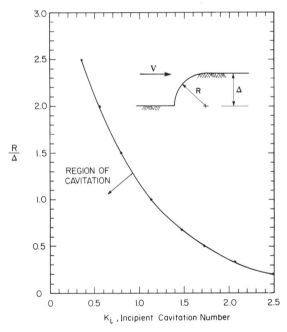

FIG. 7.   Incipient cavitation for a rounded offset (from data by Wang and Chou[15]).

geometric shapes of surface deformations, have been reported by
Wang and Chou.[15] Figures 7 and 8 show their results for sloping and
rounded offsets into the flow. Their results are presented in terms of
the incipient cavitation number K_i:

$$K_i = \frac{(H_a + H + H_r - H_v)}{V_0^2/2g} \qquad (2)$$

where H_a = atmospheric pressure head, H = static head due to water,
H_v = vapour pressure head, g = acceleration due to gravity, H_r = head
due to centrifugal pressure and V_0 = velocity near the top of the
deformation.

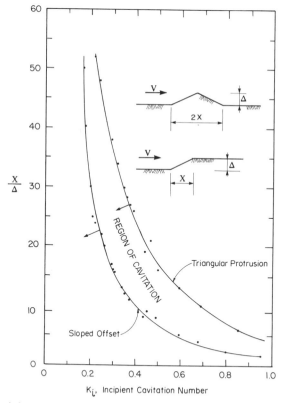

FIG. 8. Incipient cavitation for sloped protrusions (from data by Wang and
Chou[15]).

The centrifugal pressure is calculated as:

$$H_r = V_0^2/gR \tag{3}$$

where R = the vertical radius of curvature for the spillway surface. An algebraic sign must be included with H_r since a negative pressure arises as a result of a convex surface and a positive value for a concave surface.

Including the term H_r provides a pressure head approximation of greater accuracy than that obtained by the traditional one-dimensional hydraulic approach.

Arndt has shown that cavitation can occur on uniformly rough surfaces.[16] He studied triangular grooves in particular and found that the incipient cavitation index for such a surface could be written as:

$$K_i = 4f \tag{4}$$

where f is the Darcy-Weisbach resistance coefficient.

Aeration of spillway flows is being utilised increasingly to prevent damage due to cavitation pitting during high velocity operation. Without aeration, as the flow enters a low pressure area, a vapour pocket or bubble will occur if the pressure reaches the vapour pressure of the water. As the bubble moves downstream it will collapse upon entering a higher pressure area, with an extremely high pressure rise occurring over a very small area. The introduction of a compressible fluid (air) into the water in concentrations of 6–8% apparently 'cushions' the bubble collapse and the resultant pitting can be essentially eliminated. Attempts have been made to introduce air on spillways to reduce potential for cavitation damage since at least 1941.[19]

Slots or ramps to entrain air in rapid flows have been reported to have been successfully used on Yellowtail Dam,[4] Guri Dam,[22] Foz do Areia Dam,[17,18,23] Bratsk Dam,[7] and Nurek Dam.[19] The design of such slots has for the most part been used to alleviate particular observed cavitation problems and specific model studies for each problem produced a unique design of an air-entrainment appurtenance for that application. Attention is now being given to generalising designs for air entrainment devices to prevent cavitation damage on spillways in the design stage. Designs for air entrainment slots or ramps must address as a minimum: when is a slot required to prevent cavitation damage; where should the first slot be located; at what rate will there be entrainment; and what spacing must be provided between successive slots in order to maintain adequate (but not excessive) air entrainment? Figures 4, 5, 6, 7, 8 and eqn. (4) by Arndt provide a basis for this analysis. Falvey indicates that tunnel spillways of the US Bureau of Reclamation having cavitation indices of 0·20 or greater have not suffered cavitation damage[25] but some having cavitation indices less than 0·20 have often experienced cavitation damage. Thus, to determine the location of the first slot, velocities and cavitation indices should be computed along the length of the spillway. The first air slot must then be located upstream from the point at which incipient cavitation is apparent.

Several recent studies have been conducted to analyse the rate at which air is entrained by ramps or air slots.[15,17,18,19,22,23] The rate at which air is entrained is dependent on the following variables at least: geometry, flow velocity, surface tension and the air conduit geometry. Geometry of the slot or ramp is undoubtedly of first importance. Figure 9 illustrates the geometry of typical aeration slots and ramps.

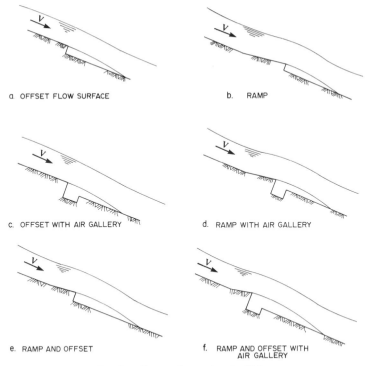

a. OFFSET FLOW SURFACE   b. RAMP

c. OFFSET WITH AIR GALLERY   d. RAMP WITH AIR GALLERY

e. RAMP AND OFFSET   f. RAMP AND OFFSET WITH
                                      AIR GALLERY

FIG. 9.   Types of aeration facilities.

Zaqustin *et al.* have recently scheduled laboratory and prototype studies on Guri Dam which hopefully will provide documented answers to the preceding design questions.[22] Currently, good starting points for design are provided in the papers by Falvey,[20,25] de S. Pinto and Neidert,[23] Zaqustin *et al.*[22] and Galerpin *et al.*[7]

3.3 Waves

Both open spillway chutes and tunnels flow as open channels and are subject to the same considerations with regard to waves. However, large waves formed in tunnel-type spillways are the more dangerous since they can reach the roof of the tunnel and cause the tunnel to flow as a closed conduit. Unstable transition from flow at partial depths to pressure flow can produce serious effects such as the entrapment of large pockets of air. The escape of those large pockets of air, and the subsequent forces developed by re-entering water, can produce dangerously high forces within the tunnel and related structures.

Shock waves may be generated by any displacement in supercritical flow. Thus, strong negative waves develop at the downstream end of thick piers. These propagate outward toward the chute walls with a wave celerity C as shown in Fig. 3. Particular care in the design of the spillway crest and the walls and floor immediately downstream will greatly alleviate the propagation of shock waves across the chute. For long spillways it is economically tempting to contract the channel in the downstream direction. Figure 10 shows curved and straight-crest arrangements which provide an efficient method by which the chute can be contracted. Flow along the wall creates a negative wave at the beginning of the uniform chute width. A positive wave is generated along the centre line of the contracting flow and propagates outward toward the walls. With careful design the positive wave can effectively counteract the negative wave along AB and CD (Fig. 10), and produce a smooth flow pattern in the downstream chute. As shown in Fig. 10, the angle between standing wave and the velocity vector is given by

$$\alpha = \sin^{-1}(C/V) \qquad (5)$$

Prototype studies by the US Army Corps of Engineers on Fort Randall Dam, indicate that use of a value of V equal to twice the average velocity in the chute gave a value of α in better agreement with that observed in the prototype.

The celerity of the wave can be approximately determined by

$$C = \sqrt{(gy)} \qquad (6)$$

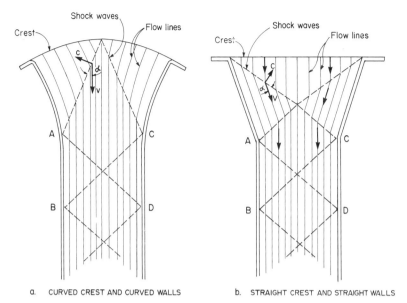

a. CURVED CREST AND CURVED WALLS   b. STRAIGHT CREST AND STRAIGHT WALLS

FIG. 10.   Wave patterns produced by spillway contraction.

where g is acceleration due to gravity and y is the depth of flow. Equation (6) is applicable only when the wave is small compared to the depth of flow, a condition which should be maintained in analytical design considerations. For large waves, significant energy losses are involved and physical model studies must be used for detailed design.

With the aid of a model study, Anastasi and Soubrier designed the chute spillway for Smokovo Dam in Greece.[26] The floor of the contraction was lowered locally to produce negative waves counteracting positive shock waves generated by lateral contraction and raised to produce positive waves to counteract negative waves produced by lateral expansions. Although the concept is not new, their example is of significant interest. Final design of the contraction was substantially different than the original concept developed theoretically by the authors, verifying that a physical model study is still necessary to produce a satisfactory design.

3.4   Air Entrainment

Wall heights in a spillway channel must provide sufficient freeboard to allow for possible shock waves, uncertainty in computed depth due to incorrect resistance coefficients, and bulking due to air entrainment. Air may be entrained in spillway flows by disturbances such as shock waves behind piers, by vortices generated by flow past gate slots, and intentionally by air slots or ramps. In general, air will be entrained in spillway flows once the turbulent boundary layer grows to the free surface, but air entrainment will not take place unless the flow occurs with a sufficiently high level of turbulent energy.[27] Falvey has reviewed the concentration of air, m, arising in a chute spillway and proposed the expression

$$m = 0 \cdot 05 \, \text{Fr} - \frac{(\sin \theta)^{1/2} W}{63 \text{Fr}} \qquad (7)$$

where Fr = Froude number ($V/\sqrt{(gD)}$), W = Weber number ($V/\sqrt{(\sigma/D\rho)}$), D = depth of flow, g = acceleration due to gravity, σ = surface tension, ρ = density of water, and θ = angle of inclination of the chute.

Equation (7) is limited to air concentrations not greater than 0·6. Bulked depth, D_B, of aerated flow can be expressed in terms of unaerated depth, D, and concentration as

$$D_B = D\left(\frac{1}{1-m}\right) \qquad (8)$$

However, aerated flow with air concentrations greater than 0·25 tends to flow at greater velocities than unaerated flow. Thus, eqn. (8) will provide a conservative estimate of flow depth in aerated flow.

Incorporation of air slots will add to the complexity of air entrainment considerations. Air slot design and operation was considered more fully in Section 3.2.

4   OPERATION STUDIES

No spillway design is complete until an operation study has been made and a proper operating manual has been prepared. In making such a study, attention must be focused on the two prime objectives of the spillway: to ensure that the dam will not be overtopped or the crest breached; and to deliver the discharge in a satisfactory manner to the energy dissipator or flip bucket. If an uncontrolled crest is used, the operation manual becomes essentially a maintenance manual.

With a gated spillway, extreme care must be taken to ensure that proper opening sequences are developed for the gates in order to guard against asymmetrical flows where multiple gates, but a common chute, are involved. Improper gate operation can lead to improper approach conditions, with resultant gate vibration; to undesirable flow patterns in the high-velocity chute with resultant wall overtopping and/or localised cavitation potential; and to improper flow distributions entering the energy dissipator or flip bucket.

In addition, the operation study must ensure that the stipulated maintenance procedures are capable of guaranteeing gate operation whenever required. A must in this case is periodic operation of each and every gate, not only to test the operating machinery but also to keep the seals from bonding to the seal plates.

5 MODEL STUDIES

With the present state-of-the-art, physical model studies are a necessity, not only for high-dam energy dissipators but also for the spillway approach and spillway proper. The spillway model may or may not include the dissipators but it must include sufficient approach topography so that the effect of the topography on approach flow is reproduced. If the dissipator is not included, the model should be designed and tested such that flow conditions at the entrance to the dissipator model can be specified.

In testing, approach flow problems should be studied first. After the major approach problems are resolved and a satisfactory approach flow is achieved, effects of piers, contraction, chute wall heights and flow distribution in the chute must be considered. Potential cavitation problems can also be studied, but eventually all problems must be resolved simultaneously; each has a mutual reaction with the others. Finally, the models should be used to develop the required gate-operating programme. During this phase, effects of possible gate malfunction must be evaluated in terms of potential for damage to the structure. Model scales of 1:50 to 1:100 are common for detailed spillway studies.

Separate model studies will be required for detailed design of air-entrainment slots or ramps in order to finalise geometric dimensions. It is of critical importance in the design of these air-entrainment devices that air flow to the device is adequate to prevent the slot filling with water during large flows. If the slot does fill with water, high velocities in the prototype will create pressures low enough within the slot to produce potentially serious cavitation damage. Air entrainment in the flow is a function of turbulence and spray created at the downstream side of the device, phenomena which cannot be accurately reproduced in a scale model. Vischer *et al.*[28] and de S. Pinto and Neidert[23] have shown that a model scale of 1:15 provides an accurate estimate of air entrainment in the prototype. In such models it will be extremely important to accurately model the pressure gradient in the air conduit system which will require separate scaling of that system. Novak and Čábelka[32] provide some guidelines for the design of air conduit systems as well as for energy dissipation coefficients on spillways based on detailed model studies.

REFERENCES

1. US ARMY CORPS OF ENGINEERS, *Hydraulic Design Criteria*, Waterways Experiment Station, Vicksburg, Mississippi, 1966.
2. ABECASIS, F. M. The behaviour of spillway crests under flow higher than design flow, *Proceedings, International Congress, IAHR*, Baden Baden, 1973.
3. BALL, J. W. *Cavitation damage caused by surface irregularities subjected to high velocities.* Distributed at the ASCE Hydraulics Division Specialty Conference, Seattle, August 1975.
4. COLGATE, D. C., BORDEN, R. C., LEGAS, L. and SELANDER, C. E. *Documentation of operation, damage, repair, and testing of Yellowtail Dam spillway*, Report No. HYD-483, US Bureau of Reclamation, Denver, August 1964.
5. WARNOCK, J. E. Cavitation in hydraulic structures, a symposium; experiences of the Bureau of Reclamation, *ASCE Transactions*, **112** (1947), 43–58.
6. AKSOY, S. and ETHEMBAGOGLU, S. Cavitation damage at the discharge channels of Keban Dam, *Proceedings of the 13th International Congress on Large Dams*, New Delhi, 1979, Vol. III, p. 369.
7. GALERPIN, R. A., OSKOLOKOV, A. G., SEMENKOV, V. M. and TSEDROV, G. N. *Cavitation in Hydraulic Structures* (translation from Russian), Energiya, Moscow, 1977.
8. *Hydraulics for Dams*, Draft Report of ICOLD Committee on Hydraulics for Dams, Comite Francais des Grand Barrages, Paris, April 1980.
9. *Fontana Project Hydraulic Model Studies*, Technical Monograph No. 68, TVA, Knoxville, 1953.
10. HUTCHINSON, H. A. J., DAVIES, J. P. and JONES, C. R. Operation of outlets, spillway, and intakes. Symposium on Mica Project, Planning Design and Construction, Vol. 40. In: *Proceedings, American Power Conference*, Chicago, 1978.
11. US ARMY CORPS OF ENGINEERS, *Hydraulic Design of Spillways*, EM

1110-2-1603, Office of the Chief of Engineers, Washington, D.C., March 31, 1965.

12. ELDER, R. A. Friction measurements in the Appalachia Tunnel, *ASCE Transactions* (1958) Paper No. 2961, p. 1249.

13. BALL, J. W. Cavitation from surface irregularities in high velocity flow, *ASCE Journal of Hydraulics Division*, **112** (HY9) (September 1976), 1283–97.

14. BALL, J. W. Construction finishes and high velocity flow, *ASCE Journal of the Construction Division*, **89** (CO2) (September 1963), 91–110.

15. WANG, X.-R. and CHOU, L.-T. The method of calculation of controlling (or treatment) criteria for the spillway surface irregularities, 13*th International Congress on Large Dams*, New Delhi, 1979, p. 977.

16. ARNDT, R. E. A. and IPPEN, A. T. *Cavitation near surfaces of distributed roughness*, Hydrodynamics Report No. 104, Mass. Institute of Technology, June 1967.

17. de S. PINTO, N. L., NEIDERT, S. H. and OTA, J. J. Aeration of high velocity flows; part one, *Water Power and Dam Construction*, **34**(2) (February 1982), 34–8.

18. de S. PINTO, N. L., Aeration of high velocity flows; part two, *Water Power and Dam Construction*, **34**(3) (March 1982), 42–4.

19. SEMENKOV, U. S. and LENTJAEV, L. D. Spillway dams with aeration of the flow over spillways, *XI Congress on Large Dams*, Madrid, 1973.

20. FALVEY, H. T. Predicting cavitation in tunnel spillways, *Water Power and Dam Construction*, **34**(8) (August 1982), 13–15.

21. DAVIS, V. C. and SORENSON, K. E. *Handbook of Applied Hydraulics*, McGraw-Hill Publishing Co., New York, 1969.

22. ZAQUSTIN, K., MANTELLINI, T. and EASTILLEJO, N. Some experience on the relationship between a model and prototype for flow aeration in spillways, *Proceedings International Conference on Modelling of Civil Engineering Structures*, Coventry, September 1982.

23. de S. PINTO, N. L. and NEIDERT, S. H. Model prototype conformity in aerated spillway flow, *Proceedings International Conference on Modelling of Civil Engineering Structures*, Coventry, September 1982.

24. PETERKA, A. J. Effects of entrained air on cavitation pitting, *Proceedings IAHR Congress*, University of Minnesota, Minneapolis, 1955.

25. FALVEY, H. T. *Cavitation in Spillways*; *Part II, Aeration Groove Design for Cavitation Protection*, US Bureau of Reclamation, Denver, Septemer 1982.

26. ANASTASI, G. and SOUBRIER, G. Essais sur modele hydraulique et etudes d'evacuateurs par rapport aux conditiones de restitution; II, l'elimination des ondes de choc dans les evacuateurs a contraction de coursier, *Proceedings ICOLD 13th Congress on Large Dams*, New Delhi, 1979.

27. FALVEY, H. T. *Air–Water Flow in Hydraulic Structures*, Engineering Monograph No. 41, US Department of the Interior, Water and Power Resources Service, Denver, December 1980.

28. VISCHER, D., VOLKART, P. and SIEGENTHALER, A. Hydraulic modeling of air slots in open chute spillways, *International Conference on the Hydraulic Modeling of Civil Engineering Structures*, Coventry, September 1982.

29. ECCHER, L. and SIEGENTHALER, A. Spillway aeration of the San Raque

project, *Water Power and Dam Construction,* **34**(9) (September 1982), 37–41.

30. JOHNSON, V. E. Mechanics of cavitation, *ASCE Journal of the Hydraulics Division,* **89** (HY3) (May 1963), 251–75.

31. LOCHER, F. A. *Some characteristics of pressure fluctuations on low-agee crest spillways relevant to flow-induced structural vibrations,* IIHR Report No. 130, Iowa Institute for Hydraulic Research, University of Iowa, Iowa City, February 1971.

32. NOVAK, P. and ČÁBELKA, J. *Models in Hydraulic Engineering: Physical Principles and Design Applications,* Pitman, London, 1981.

Chapter 5

ENERGY DISSIPATION AT HIGH DAMS

F. A. Locher and S. T. Hsu

Bechtel Civil & Minerals, Inc., San Francisco, California, USA

NOTATION

B	thickness of two-dimensional jet
b	width of channel or basin
C	coefficient, eqn. (9)
C_D	drag coefficient
$\sqrt{(C_D'^2)}$	rms drag coefficient
C_f	resistance coefficient for boundary layer
C_p'	$\sqrt{(p'^2)}/(\frac{1}{2}\rho V_1^2)$ rms pressure coefficient
D	diameter of jet
d	depth of flow, eqns. (3) and (4), also particle diameter, eqn. (9)
d_s	depth of scour
d_{tw}	depth of tailwater
d_{90}	particle size for which 90% of the sample is smaller
Fr	Froude number
F_B	drag force, blocks
$\sqrt{(F_B'^2)}$	rms drag force
F_D	drag force on sill
$\sqrt{(F_D'^2)}$	rms drag force on sill
F_2	hydrostatic force $= \gamma y^2 b/2$
g	acceleration of gravity
H	gross head from reservoir level to tailwater level
h	height of chute blocks, baffle blocks or sill
h_{cr}	critical depth, eqn. (10)
k	air resistance coefficient, eqn. (10)
L_0	throw distance for a jet without air resistance, eqn. (6)

L_1 throw distance for a jet with air resistance, eqn. (8)
$\sqrt{(p'^2)}$ rms pressure flucutations
q discharge per unit width
Re Reynolds number
R flip bucket radius
s spacing between baffle blocks
t_{max} maximum depth of erosion, eqn. (10)
V velocity of flow
V_0 velocity of jet leaving a flip bucket
V_1 velocity of supercritical flow upstream from a hydraulic jump
V_m mean velocity
w width of baffle blocks; also exponent, eqn. (9)
x coordinate in the direction of flow; also exponent, eqn. (9)
y depth, coordinate perpendicular to x, also exponent, eqn. (9)
y_1 depth of supercritical flow upstream from a hydraulic jump
y_2 sequent depth, $y_2/y_1 = \frac{1}{2}[\sqrt{(1 + 8Fr_1^2)} - 1]$
α flip bucket angle with the horizontal, also parameter, eqn. (8)
α_1 scour hole parameter
α_2 scour hole parameter
β coefficient, eqn. (5)
γ specific weight of fluid, also parameter, eqn. (8)
η blockage = $w/(w + s)$
θ angle between the tangent to a jet trajectory and the horizontal
ρ fluid density

1 INTRODUCTION

Of the twenty-five highest dams in the world as listed in a 1982 article,[54] all but two will have been completed after 1960. The magnitude of the energy that must be dissipated accompanying this trend in the construction of larger and higher dams almost defies the imagination. For example, the maximum combined energy dissipated below Tarbela's service and auxiliary spillways could be 40 000 MW, which is about 20 times the planned generating capacity at the site or, equivalently, exceeds the capacity of more than 35 large nuclear power units.

Flow velocities of 30 to 40 m/s are now commonplace; since problems of cavitation, erosion, scour and turbulence all increase with various powers of the velocity, the potential for major difficulties is indeed acute. No type of dissipator is immune to problems. Examples include the erosion of the plunge pool at Tarbela's service spillway,[46] the damage to the stilling basins of Tarbela's tunnel nos. 3 and 4,[45] the cavitation erosion of the flip bucket at Guri, Stage I,[23] and the damage to the chute and baffle blocks at Pit 6 and 7.[86]

The trend in the type of energy dissipators used at high dams is toward flip buckets, ski-jump spillways or high-capacity mid- and bottom-outlets, because these schemes usually provide the most economical solution. Other trends in hydraulic design of dissipators include the use of aeration to control cavitation (Chapters 3 and 4), the incorporation of large dispersion blocks to increase the efficiency of energy dissipation from jets, the development of cavitation-resistant polymerised concretes, and the use of electronic instrumentation both in the field and laboratory to measure the characteristics of fluctuating pressures and forces which have become so important in today's high-head structures.

The practical design of stilling basins and energy dissipators is an area in which an enormous amount of study has been done. There are very few standard designs that have been developed, in part because the type of dissipator that is used is so site specific. Selection of a final design is an iterative process involving many factors, including the general layout of the project, together with economic, geologic and topographic constraints to name only a few. Consequently, a great deal of creativity and effort is often required to produce a satisfactory design, and as a brief review of the literature shows, the range of solutions is limited only by the engineer's imagination and the owner's pocketbook.

In this chapter, the discussion of energy dissipators will be divided into five categories:

1. hydraulic jump basins;
2. roller buckets;
3. flip buckets;
4. plunge pools; and
5. dissipators for pressure conduits.

The salient features of each of these types will be reviewed, results of recent basic and applied research will be summarised, and problems in practice will be illustrated with examples of prototype operating experience. Since a model study is mandatory for the design of dissipators at high-head dams, some of the principal considerations in performing model studies for energy dissipators will also be discussed.

2 HYDRAULIC JUMP BASINS

2.1 Conventional Basins

If energy dissipators are an area that has been well studied, then hydraulic jump basins are surely the most studied of all types of energy dissipators. Standard designs for basins with a horizontal apron were presented by the US Bureau of Reclamation (USBR).[68] Basin II (Fig. 1) can be used for heads $H < 60$ m and specific discharges $q < 46$ m³/s/m without recourse to a model study; Basin III (Fig. 2) can be used safely for velocities $V < 18.2$ m/s and $q < 18.6$ m³/s/m without recourse to a model study. There is a great temptation to use Basin III in preference to Basin II because Basin III is much shorter. However, the baffle blocks are positioned well toward the front of the jump and are therefore exposed to the incoming high velocity flow. This in turn will lead to cavitation problems at high-head dams. For high-head applications, appropriate positioning of the baffle blocks can lead to significant reductions in basin length, as compared to Basin II. This is illustrated by the basin at Ramganda Dam which was designed for

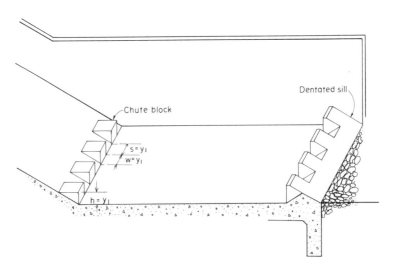

FIG. 1. Hydraulic jump basin, USBR Type II.

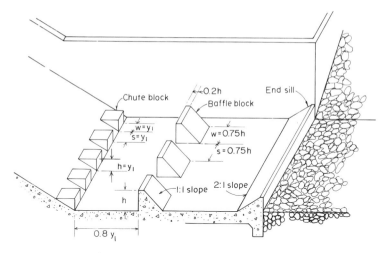

Fig. 2.   Hydraulic jump basin, USBR Type III.

$V = 42$ m/s and $q = 63 \cdot 5$ m³/s/m (ref. 30) and uses standard USBR baffle blocks. These conditions greatly exceeded the recommended USBR limits and therefore a very thorough investigation in a model study was required. In general, however, the use of baffle blocks in energy dissipators for high dams should be discouraged.

Basin designs on positive slopes have been presented by the USBR.[68] Basins with adverse slopes have also been used successfully, although slopes greater than 4% tend to result in a bucket-like behaviour rather than hydraulic jump action.[79] Ohashi[64] presents an example of a hydraulic jump basin with an adverse slope, together with a set of relationships for design.

Spatial hydraulic jump basins involve either a sudden change in width or a sudden drop in floor elevation to stabilise the jump (Figs. 3(a) and (b)). Several examples of practical designs of basins with a change in width were presented by Herbrand and Knauss,[33] and some design guides were presented by Torres.[93]

For dissipation in narrow, restricted valleys, a basin using a jump combined with side inflow has been used at Saucelle for heads of about 83 m and at lower heads for Castro (Fig. 4), San Pedro and Montefurado Dams in Spain.[31] Recent examples of stilling basins at high-head dams include Ramganda, Bhakra, Libby, Dworshak and Saiany Dams, the principal characteristics of which are listed in Table 1.

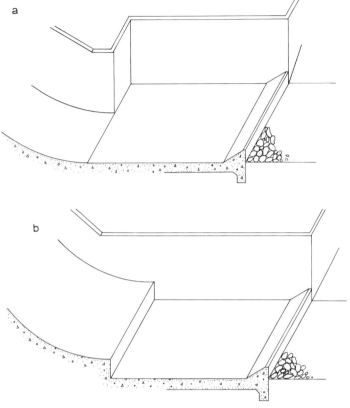

FIG. 3.   Spatial hydraulic jump basin. (a) Change in width, (b) change in depth.

2.2 Multiple Basins

Stepped basins may be a solution where erodability of the surrounding slopes or downstream river bed precludes the use of a flip bucket, e.g. Bolgenach;[34] double basins have also been used where foundation conditions such as a high ground water table or the cost of excavation makes it impossible to obtain the required tailwater, e.g. Sidi Saad,[56] Pusiosa-Ialomita,[62] Polyphyton,[34] and Mangla Dam.

Cascade spillways are, in fact, a series of stepped basins, and have been designed with and without appurtenances such as baffle blocks and end sills. One of the largest cascade spillways was recently completed for LG-2 in Canada; the design discharge is 15 300 m³/s, the

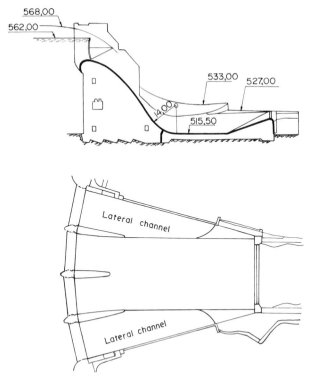

FIG. 4.   Stilling basin for Castro Dam (after ref. 31).

chute is 122 m wide and 1500 m long, and the drop from headwater to tailwater is about 135 m. The scale of the project is so large that line drawings do not convey the enormity of the undertaking, and the reader is referred to ref. 4 for photographs and details. Design parameters for cascade spillways were presented by Essery and Horner.[27]

2.3   Fundamental and Applied Research

2.3.1   Basic Research

The hydraulic jump continues to be the subject of numerous laboratory studies. Rajaratnam's 1967 review[72] listed 93 references; the list has surely doubled since then. One of the difficulties in comparing results from so many studies is the lack of a standard notation. In this

TABLE 1

CHARACTERISTICS OF SOME RECENT STILLING BASINS

Dam	Country	Gross head reservoir to stilling basin (m)	Width of basin b (m)	Design discharge Q (m³/s)	Unit discharge q (m³/s/m)	Reference
Bhakra	India	178	79·3	8212	108	66
Dworshak	USA	207	34·7	4248[a]	32·6[a] (122)	74
Libby	USA	118	35·4	4106[b]	40[b] (116)	74
Nezahualcoytl (Malpaso)	Mexico	118	50	6000	120	16
Pit 6 and 7	USA	53·3, 67	33·5	2265	67·6	86
Pit 6 (modified)	USA	54·9	33·5	2831	84·5	67
Ramganda	India	114	120	7620	63·5	30
Saiany	USSR	242	100[c]	13 600	140	108
Tarbela	Pakistan	122	35	2840	81	45

[a] Basin designed for a standard project flood of 1133 m³/s.
[b] Sweep out flow at $Q = 1416$ m³/s.
[c] Data estimated from figures in the reference.

chapter the notation used for discussion of hydraulic jumps is shown on Fig. 5. The approaching supercritical flow depth, velocity and Froude number are y_1, V_1, and $Fr_1 = \sqrt{(gy_1)}$, respectively. The sequent depth for a free hydraulic jump, y_2, is given by the relationship $y_2/y_1 = \frac{1}{2}(\sqrt{(1+8Fr_1^2)}-1)$. Tailwater depths other than the sequent depth, y_2, such as for submerged or forced jumps are denoted by the quantity d_{tw}; the length of the roller for a free or forced jump is L_r and for submerged jumps is L_{rs}. The origin of the x-coordinate is the beginning of the jump and X_B is the distance that baffle blocks or sills are located from the beginning of the jump. Other quantities will be defined where they first appear and in the Notation.

Perhaps one of the most interesting series of studies of the hydraulic jump has been summarised by Resch et al.,[75] who point out that the characteristics of the jump are influenced by the velocity distribution of the approaching supercritical flow. Two cases were presented, one with an essentially potential flow profile (referred to as undeveloped flow),

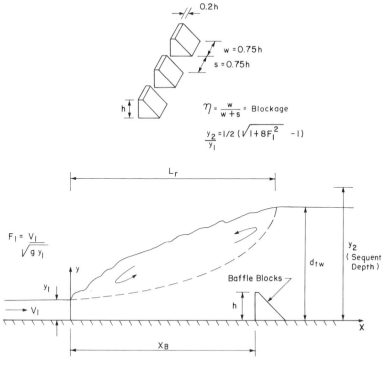

FIG. 5. Definition sketch.

and the second, with a fully developed profile in which the boundary layer has reached the free surface. Figure 6 presents the results of measurements of the streamlines for undeveloped and developed velocity profiles for a Froude number $Fr_1 = 6$. In general, for a given Froude number, hydraulic jumps with fully developed velocity profiles

1. were longer than jumps with nearly one-dimensional velocity profiles, the roller extended further downstream, and the streamline pattern showed fundamental differences in the mean structure of the flow in the jump;
2. had higher intensities of turbulence than jumps with undeveloped flow profiles, with higher intensities persisting further downstream;
3. resulted in jumps with lower sequent depths than jumps with

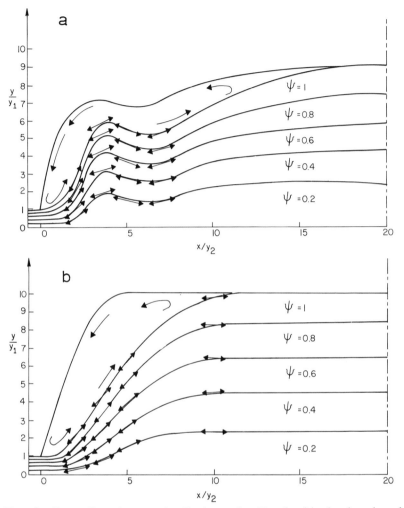

FIG. 6. Streamlines in a hydraulic jump for Fr = 6 with developed and undeveloped inflow conditions (after ref. 75). (a) Developed inflow, (b) undeveloped inflow.

undeveloped flow profiles, a logical consequence of the higher turbulence intensities and energy dissipation.

These results point out a scale effect in hydraulic models of spillways and stilling basins due to Reynolds number effects. It is well known that reduced-scale models of spillways must be very smooth. This means that the boundary-layer thickness in the model is much less than that in the prototype. Calculations should be made to evaluate these differences. In long chutes, for example, the velocity profile in the prototype will be fully developed, while in the model, the velocity profile will be undeveloped. Consequently, the hydraulic jump in the model would not be similar to that in the prototype as illustrated by the results shown in Fig. 6. Since a jump with an undeveloped profile requires a little higher tailwater than a jump with a developed profile, the model results will, in general, be conservative. Differences in the turbulence characteristics downstream from these two types of jumps may not be of much practical significance, but Resch *et al*'s results certainly point out a potential pitfall in model–prototype correlations as well as in comparison of turbulence and pressure fluctuation data among investigators of hydraulic jump phenomena.

2.3.2 Fluctuating Pressures on Slabs and in Energy Dissipators

Pressure fluctuations are another area in which some care must be exercised in interpreting experimental data. As long as the fluctuations are not Reynolds-number dependent, scaling according to the Froude criterion is satisfactory. However, measurement of pressure fluctuations along spillway chutes or in flip buckets in a model cannot be expected to scale according to the Froude criterion because the fluctuations are a boundary layer phenomenon and the boundary layer depends on the Reynolds number. The use of boundary layer trips is one possible solution to this problem.[42] Studies of fluctuating forces on baffle blocks, sills and other stilling basin appurtenances are generally not Reynolds-number dependent because of the non-streamlined shapes used in most hydraulic structures.

Damage caused by fluctuating pressures and forces is often spectacular. Turbulence in the stilling basin at Nezahualcoytl (Malpaso) Dam in Mexico, for example, resulted in displacement and transport of floor slabs $12 \, m \times 12 \, m \times 2 \, m$ that weighed 720 tons. The basin floor was damaged extensively and about 46% of the floor had to be reconstructed. Laboratory studies[16] showed that the slabs could be lifted vertically as a consequence of differential pressure fluctuations between the upper and lower surfaces of the slab. An extensive series of measurements of cross-correlation and spectra of the pressure fluctuations on slabs in stilling basins was reported in ref. (81).

Numerous investigators[15,40,57,60] have made general studies of pressure fluctuations under free and submerged hydraulic jumps. The root

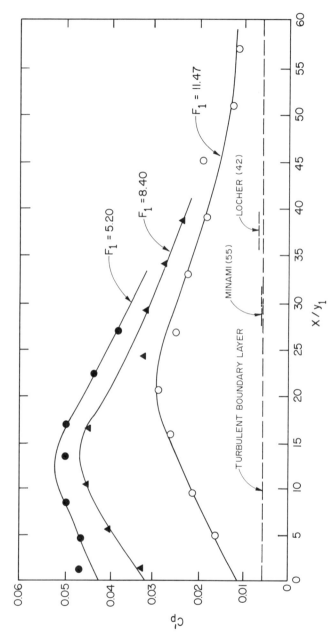

FIG. 7.   Pressure fluctuations under a free hydraulic jump (after ref. 1).

mean square (rms) pressure fluctuations $\sqrt{(\overline{p'^2})}$ have been measured as a function of distance, x, from the beginning of the jump, and the Froude number of the approach flow, $\mathrm{Fr} = V_1/\sqrt{(gy_1)}$. The rms pressure fluctuations are expressed in the dimensionless form $C'_p = \sqrt{(\overline{p'^2})}/(\tfrac{1}{2}\rho V_1^2)$. Akbari et al.[1] present measurements of pressure fluctuations on the floor under free hydraulic jumps for Froude numbers between 6·2 and 11·5 as shown in Fig. 7. Their data are in good agreement with those of Narasimhan and Bhargava,[57] Vasiliev[99] and Schiebe and Bowers.[83] The available data that are in good agreement show that for Froude numbers greater than 4, the maximum value of C'_p is about 0·05. The trend in the data indicates that as the Froude number increases, the maximum value of C'_p decreases and the location of the maximum rms pressure fluctuation moves further downstream from the toe of the jump. The location of this maximum is coincident with that of the maximum turbulence intensities ($1 \leqslant x/y_2 \leqslant 2$) measured by Rouse et al.[78]

Figure 8(a) presents results from Narasimhan and Bhargava[57] for pressure fluctuations under submerged jumps. They chose the length of the roller, L_{rs}, to normalise their data because the length of the separation zone, L_{rs}, is often used as an appropriate length scale in separated flows. Values of d_{tw}/y_2 and L_{rs}/y_1 computed from data given by Rajaratnam[72] are also shown to permit comparison with other data normalised with the more commonly used parameter, y_1.

Figure 8(b) shows a comparison of Narasimhan and Bhargava's data and Narayanan's data[60] for submerged jumps with data for free jumps. For a given Froude number, submergence of a jump decreases the peak value of the rms pressure fluctuations, but the increase in the length of the roller for a submerged jump as compared to a free jump results in higher rms pressures further downstream. As the submergence increases, the values of C'_p tend to first increase and then decrease, although the maximum values of C'_p never become greater than those for a free jump. This result is related to the changes in geometry of the free shear layer and roller as well as the free surface fluctuations as the submergence changes. These data show that as a jump is submerged, there is greater potential for erosion downstream from the jump. For submerged jumps, C'_p varied from 0·021 to 0·033 for $1·4 \leqslant d_{tw}/y_2 \leqslant 3·2$ and Froude numbers between 2 and 6 (Fig. 8(a)).

The magnitude of pressure fluctuations on the basin floor is influenced by the presence of baffle blocks and sills. An indication of the increase in the pressure fluctuations possible is given by Akbari et al.,[1]

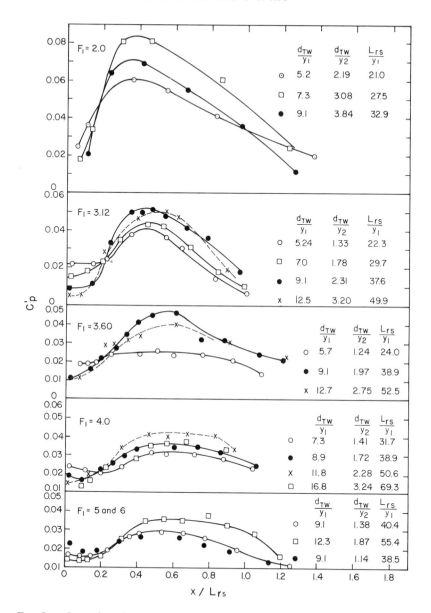

FIG. 8a.   Intensity of pressure fluctuations on the channel bottom for various submergences of a hydraulic jump.

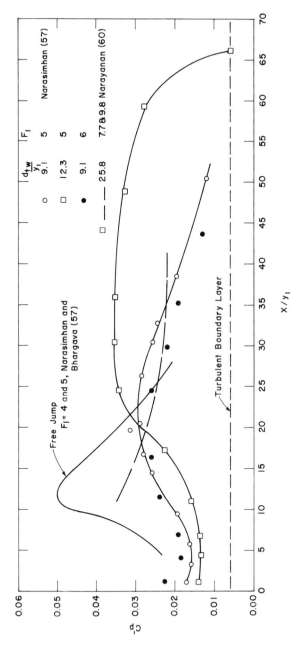

FIG. 8b.   Comparison of streamwise variation of pressure fluctuations in free and submerged jumps.

who measured C_p' as the position of a sill was varied ($13 \leqslant X_B/y_1 \leqslant 41$) within the jump. The maximum rms pressure fluctuations on the floor were obtained when the sill was located in the region of maximum pressure fluctuations for a free jump. For $h/y_1 = 2 \cdot 3$, $X_B/y_1 = 14$, and $Fr_1 = 7$, the maximum value of C_p' was about $0 \cdot 085$, or $1 \cdot 7$ times the maximum values obtained in a free jump.

Spectra of the pressure fluctuations obtained in the region of the maximum turbulence intensity show a tendency toward a dominant frequency similar to that observed in re-attaching flows. As x/y_1 increases, the tendency toward a dominant frequency in the spectra disappears.[60]

Enough information seems to be available to permit designers to account for the maximum fluctuating forces on floors of basins without chute blocks or baffle piers. Measurements with pressure transducers provide conservative results in estimating the fluctuating forces because the pressure fluctuations at a given distance, x, from the beginning of the jump are not highly correlated in either the lateral or longitudinal direction. Methods to account for the correlation of the pressure fluctuations in computing forces on stilling basin floors have been presented by Ramos[73] and Spoljaric.[85]

The maximum value of C_p' for free jumps is about an order of magnitude greater than C_p' for boundary-layer pressure fluctuations. Measurements by Locher[42] and Minami[55] show that the pressure fluctuations on spillways and slabs in regions not influenced by effects of gate piers or hydraulic jumps are essentially boundary-layer pressure fluctuations as shown on Fig. 7. Minami measured the prototype pressure fluctuations and velocity distribution on a spillway slab that served as the roof of the powerhouse at Shin-Nariwa Dam. Results of Minami's work were used by Stutz *et al.*[87] in the design of the powerhouse roof for Karakaya Dam which also acts as the spillway flip bucket. The results show that for velocities near 50 m/s, the rms pressure fluctuations are only in the order of 5 to 6 m of water.

Although the random nature of the boundary-layer pressure fluctuations alone does not ensure against response at the natural frequency of a structure, the combination of high structural mass, rigidity and the low level of the fluctuations on the roof slab in comparison with the mean pressure implies that vibration will not usually be a problem. Thin slabs would, of course, provide the potential for individual panel vibration.[89]

2.3.3 Mean and Fluctuating Forces on Baffle Blocks

The importance of determining the mean and fluctuating component of the forces acting on baffle blocks is well illustrated by the experience at Pit 6 and 7, two concrete gravity dams located on the Pit River in Northern California, USA. The dams are 56 m and 69·5 m high respectively, and the stilling basins were identical; each basin was 33·5 m wide and designed for $q = 67·6$ m^3/s/m. The basins were equipped with armoured chute blocks, and 10 large armoured baffle blocks as illustrated in Fig. 9. After peak discharges of about 2070 m^3/s, it was observed that six of the 10 baffle blocks at Pit 7 had been removed from the basin, four of the baffle blocks at Pit 6 were missing and some of the armouring on the chute blocks had been removed.

Details of the repairs as described by Strassburger[86] included replacement of some of the baffle blocks with a welded steel enclosure constructed of 50·8-mm thick steel plate with the same shape as the original baffle blocks. The units were anchored into bedrock by means of transverse beams and rock bolts, and were backfilled with concrete and pressure-grouted. Flood flows in 1974 removed two of these large

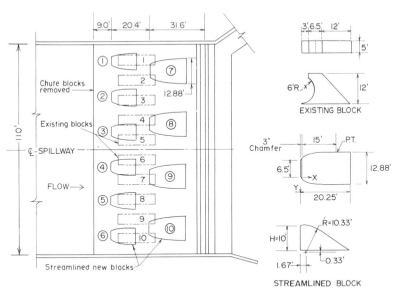

FIG. 9. Stilling basin for Pit 6 and 7, before and after modifications (after ref. 67). All dimensions in feet.

heavily armoured units from the basin at Pit 6. The fundamental cause of the failure was fluctuating lateral forces which rocked the units from side to side until they broke off and were washed out of the basin.

At Pit 6 the solution was to provide cavitation-free baffle blocks of a design developed by H. Thomas.[92] Since the drag of these blocks is less than that of a sharp-edged block with the same projected frontal area, the width of the cavitation-free blocks is larger than the original blocks. This significantly improves the stability against fluctuating lateral loads. To obtain satisfactory performance with regard to sweep-out of the flow and scour downstream from the basin, two rows of these blocks were provided, as shown in Fig. 9. The chute blocks were eliminated. Fluctuating forces were measured as described by Pennino and Larsen.[67] At Pit 7, the basin was changed from a hydraulic jump basin to a flip bucket, a solution not feasible at Pit 6 because of a bend in the river immediately downstream from the dam.

An extensive study of the mean forces on baffle blocks in unsubmerged jumps was conducted by Basco and Adams,[10] who measured the mean force on a row of baffle blocks. The drag force was investigated according to the functional relationship

$$\frac{F_B}{F_2} = f\left(Fr, \frac{X_B}{y_2}, \frac{h}{y_1}, \frac{w}{h}, \eta, Re, shape\right) \tag{1}$$

where F_B is the total drag force exerted by the blocks on the fluid, $F_2 = \gamma y_2^2 b/2$, b is the hydrostatic force, y_2 the sequent depth for a free hydraulic jump, $\eta = w/(w + s)$ is the blockage, Re is the Reynolds number and X_B and h are as defined as shown in Fig. 5.

In a subsequent paper, Basco[11] presented results for the optimum baffle block height and location as a function of Froude number for standard USBR baffle blocks. The range of parameters covered in these studies was $3 \leq Fr \leq 10$, $0 \cdot 344 \leq \eta \leq 0 \cdot 649$, $0 \cdot 3 \leq h/y_1 \leq 9$ and $0 \leq X_B/y_2 \leq 4$. The optimum design was admittedly subjective. Basco divided the observations of the water-surface profile into four regions: I, the jump profile was similar to a free jump; II, a boil with depth 10 to 15% greater than the tailwater depth occurred, excellent roller action was present and downstream wave heights were normal; III, the tendency to form a second jump was evident, with a diving jet behind the blocks being reflected from the floor to the surface, forming excessively high waves downstream; and IV, the jump was close to moving downstream from the baffles. Delineation of these four regions for a Froude number of 6 is shown on Fig. 10.

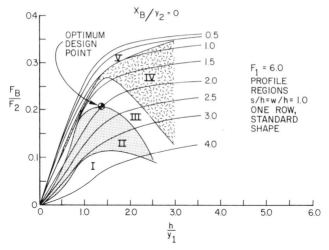

FIG. 10.   Regions of hydraulic jump performance for Fr = 6 (after ref. 11).

The principal conclusions of these studies were:

1. The optimum blockage was 50%, which coincides with recommendations for the USBR Type III basin.
2. A second row of baffle blocks resulted in about a 5 to 10% increase in F_B/F_2 for jumps in Region II. Thus, unless a second row improves the velocity distribution and decreases erosion downstream (such was the case with Pit 6), the additional basin length required to accommodate the second row of blocks does not seem warranted. One row of baffle blocks is adequate provided that there is sufficient tailwater. This is also in agreement with previous work on standard USBR blocks.[68]
3. The optimum geometry for d_{tw}/y_1, h/y_1 and block location X_B/y_2 is as shown on Fig. 11.

Figure 11 also compares Basco's results with Corps of Engineers recommendations for design,[95a] the USBR recommendations for the Type III Basin and data from 20 Corps of Engineers Projects as summarised in ref. 8. The USBR and Basco's block heights are in good agreement; both recommendations would have resulted in higher baffle blocks than at many Corps Projects. The baffle blocks would also be located further downstream than in a USBR basin. The most significant difference is in the tailwater requirements. Both Basco and the

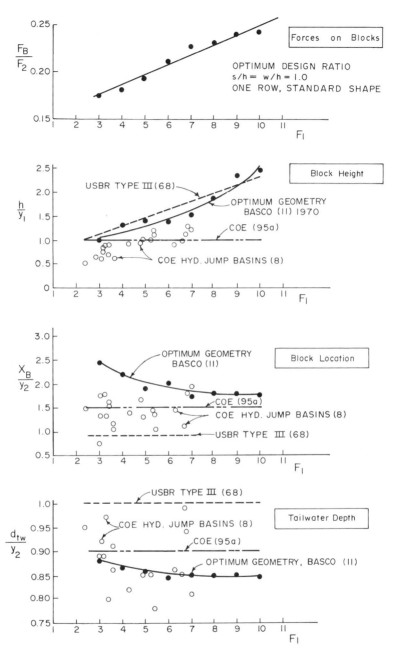

FIG. 11. Optimum block geometry and force ratio for hydraulic jump basins with no submergence. Comparison with Corps of Engineers and USBR criteria.

Corps recommend a tailwater depth less than y_2, which is also consistent with past Corps designs for forced jump basins. Clearly the USBR[68] recommendations for the Type II or III basin are quite conservative and result in a slightly submerged jump. The Type II or III basin is also a conservative design with respect to fluctuating forces and pressures, since both of these quantities decrease with submergence. This is a prudent course of action when recommending standard or preliminary designs that do not require model tests. Since any major structure will require model testing, some economy can probably be effected in the final design.

Ranga-Raju *et al.*[71] re-analysed Basco and Adams'[10] data and included data from Murahari (unpublished) who used rectangular blocks, as well as data from Gomasta.[29] There was general agreement among all three data sets, although the rectangular blocks seemed to result in less drag than standard USBR blocks. Ranga-Raju *et al.* attempted to collapse all of Basco and Adams' data on to one curve. The scatter was rather large, especially in the region of optimum design, $9 \leqslant X_B/y_1 \leqslant 24$. For determination of F_B/F_2 and computation of d_{tw}/y_2, the use of the original data presented in ref. 9 is probably the best approach. For the optimum geometry, the data shown in Fig. 11 are sufficient for design.

The mean and fluctuating forces on a single standard USBR baffle block were studied by Gomasta *et al.*,[29] in the form

$$C_D, \frac{\sqrt{(\overline{C_D'^2})}}{C_D} = \phi_{1,2}\left(\text{Fr}, \frac{X_B}{y_1}, \frac{h}{y_1}, \eta\right) \qquad (2)$$

where $C_D = F_B/(\frac{1}{2}\rho V_1^2 h)$ and F_B is the drag force per unit width on the block. The range of parameters studied was $4\cdot3 \leqslant \text{Fr} \leqslant 11\cdot5$, $1\cdot45 \leqslant h/y_1 \leqslant 4\cdot4$ and $0\cdot375 \leqslant \eta \leqslant 0\cdot73$. The mean forces were in good agreement with those of Basco and Adams.[10] The maximum rms values of the fluctuating drag force occurred for $11 \leqslant X_B/y_1 \leqslant 16$. Some of Gomasta's data was re-worked into the form F_B/F_2 and $\sqrt{(\overline{F_B'^2})}/F_2$ by Tyagi *et al.*,[95] where F_B is the force per unit width and $F_2 = \gamma y_2^2/2$. These results indicate that the maximum value of $\sqrt{(\overline{F_B'^2})}/F_2$ for $\eta = 0\cdot5$ and $\text{Fr}_1 = 7$ is about $0\cdot3$. This value is of the same order as F_B/F_2, which indicates that the rms drag force fluctuations are about the same as the mean drag force itself!

Pressure fluctuations at points on the front, sides, top and back of a standard USBR baffle block were reported by Lopardo *et al.*[43] The block was located in a basin $0\cdot8y_2$ from the toe of the spillway according to USBR recommended proportions for Basin III. There were no chute blocks used in Lopardo's tests. Effects of tailwater level on the pressure fluctuations were significant; pressure fluctuations on the sides of the block increased significantly with a decrease in tailwater, just as do the pressure fluctuations on the floor of the basin. As might be expected, a dominant frequency in the pressure fluctuations along the side of the blocks caused by flow separation from the block was also observed.

For standard USBR-shaped blocks, the height to width ratio of 1·33 undoubtedly provides sufficient stability as evidenced by its successful prototype performance. Non-standard baffle blocks are sometimes used to create enough drag force to significantly lower tailwater requirements for a basin, which usually results in high, narrow blocks. The original Pit 6 and 7 blocks with a height to width ratio of 2·4 are a good example, as are the blocks for the Silver Jack basin.[22] Since the failure of the Pit 6 and 7 blocks was caused by fluctuating lateral forces, it is clear that non-standard blocks with large height to width ratios should be studied not only to determine mean forces and pressures but also for effects of both fluctuating lateral and longitudinal forces.

2.3.4   Chute Blocks

A study to determine the pressure distribution on chute blocks and to evaluate the effects of chute blocks on energy dissipation was conducted by Suryavanshi et al.[88] They concluded that chute blocks contributed little to the energy dissipation in a hydraulic jump basin, and that the presence of chute blocks increased the depth of scour downstream from the basin. The measured pressure distribution indicated that the risk of cavitation is too great for chute blocks to be used with confidence at high dams. The experience cited earlier for Pit 6 and 7 as well as other prototype experience also indicates that chute blocks are unnecessary and even disadvantageous, provided that sufficient tailwater ($1·05y_2$ for a Type II or y_2 for a Type III basin) is available.

For cases with minimum tailwater, such as might occur during extreme flood events or during the rise of a major flood when the rise in tailwater lags steady-state conditions, chute blocks do assist in keeping the jump in the basin; the basin walls can therefore be lower. The basin performance may be judged adequate for such conditions where some damage is acceptable. Whether it is more economical to accept damage to the chute blocks in return for less excavation to provide the requisite tailwater is a matter of weighing potential risks and economics. The authors favour basins without chute blocks as a general rule, and for high dams, the use of chute blocks definitely should be discouraged.

2.3.5 Forces on Sills

Mean and fluctuating forces on sills have been studied extensively; typical work includes that of McCorquodale,[51] Karki,[38] Narayanan and Schizas,[58,59] and Akbari et al.[1] Particular cases may require special studies. For example, an extensive investigation was conducted by Ohashi[64] of mean forces and fluctuating pressures on a sill that acts as an end sill in a hydrualic jump basin at low to intermediate flows and as a flow deflector and flip bucket when the flow sweeps out of the basin. A model was also constructed to study the potential vibration problems associated with the sill. Another study of an end sill to deflect the flow in a confined area was reported by Anastasi et al.[2]

The principal results of studies on two-dimensional sills show that the maximum force occurs when the oncoming supercritical flow impinges on the sill with the drag coefficient $C_D = F_D/(\frac{1}{2}\rho V_1^2 hb)$ varying between $0 \cdot 3$ and $0 \cdot 45$, depending on the ratio of the height of the sill to the depth of the oncoming flow, h/y_1. The maximum value of the fluctuating force coefficient, $\sqrt{(F_D'^2)}/(\frac{1}{2}\rho V_1^2 hb)$, occurs when the toe of the jump is located over the sill and varies between $0 \cdot 03$ and $0 \cdot 05$, for $1 \leqslant h/y_1 \leqslant 3$. Data are also available for conditions with the sill located at various positions within the jump.[1,59]

2.3.6 Problems in Practice

In general, practical problems with hydraulic jump stilling basins fall into two categories: (1) those associated with cavitation and the dynamic forces on the basin floors and appurtenances; and (2) operational problems.

The difficulties associated with the lateral forces on high, narrow baffle blocks and with cavitation on the chute blocks at Pit 6 and 7[86] have been discussed previously. The cavitation damage on the Bluestone and Bonneville baffle blocks has been well documented.[18,21] With $X_B/y_2 = 0 \cdot 19$ and $0 \cdot 67$, respectively ($X_B/y_1 = 1 \cdot 7$ and $2 \cdot 3$) it is clear that the damage occurred because the blocks were located too close to the toe of the jump, where high incoming velocities and pressure fluctuations resulted in cavitation. Basco's recommendations,[9,11] together with the pressure and force fluctuation data now available, should make possible preliminary designs that are less cavitation-prone. Large, narrow baffle blocks will obviously have to be model-studied.

Forces on basin floors and walls can lead to failure, as discussed for Malpaso Dam; fluctuating forces in combination with improper cleaning of the rock surface and a thin slab resulted in extensive damage at Holjes[25a] for a flow of about one-third the design discharge. Data to estimate the magnitude of the fluctuations are available for preliminary design.[1,16,57,60,81]

Operational problems are illustrated by the recent experience at Libby and Dworshak Dams.[74] At Dworshak, unbalanced operation of the spillway gates resulted in eddies at the end of the stilling basin bringing material into the basin. Subsequent ball-milling action resulted in abrasion and removal of about $1530\,m^3$ of concrete. Model tests showed that once the material was in the basin, it could not be swept out. At Libby Dam, $1330\,m^3$ of concrete was removed by ball-milling action. Again, material was transported from the tailrace into the basin by unbalanced spillway operation. Large, balanced flows could sweep the material out, but such flows were infrequent.

Other examples of damage caused by material in the basin include Jupia and Ilha Solteria,[19] where changes in gate operation resulted in severe regressive erosion, at Strmec[28] where mis-operation resulted in removal of rock weighing 30 tons and undermining of the basin wall, at Anderson Ranch[36] where debris from the surrounding hillside fell into the basin, and at Bhakra[66] where flows during construction pulled debris from downstream into the basin. Damage to basins with baffle blocks can be especially severe because of ball milling action in the eddies behind the blocks.

On existing structures, the installation of humps at the basin outlet has been effective in preventing eddy formation;[65] for flared wall basins, uniform flow distribution is absolutely necessary. The importance of a careful model study of the potential for material to be transported into the basin is apparent.

3 ROLLER BUCKET DISSIPATORS

Design data for plain and slotted roller bucket dissipators illustrated in Figs. 12(a) and (b) were presented by Peterka.[68] The bucket at Grand Coulee Dam is the most noteworthy example of a plain roller bucket;

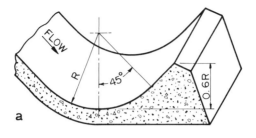

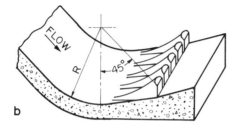

FIG. 12. Plain and slotted roller buckets.

the slotted bucket, which has served as an inspiration for dispersion blocks at Al-Ibtissam,[12] is illustrated by the Angostora dissipator. Roller buckets have not enjoyed great popularity, in part because they require substantially higher tailwater for satisfactory performance than standard hydraulic jump basins. In addition, solid bucket dissipators require symmetrical gate operation to prevent side rollers that bring material into the bucket. Subsequent ball-milling action in the bucket has resulted in damage to several installations. The principal advantage of a roller bucket is that it provides positive protection against undermining of the structure. In cases such as at Grand Coulee, where erosion downstream from the structure was a major consideration, a roller bucket may provide the best overall design.

4 FLIP BUCKETS

4.1 Application

When geologic and topographic conditions permit, a flip bucket or ski-jump type of dissipator are generally the most economical design for energy dissipation at high dams. Flip buckets may be located at the base of an overflow spillway, at the end of a chute or tunnel spillway or at mid- or bottom-outlets. Utilising high velocity approach flow, the action of the bucket flips spillway flows to downstream river channels and away from major structures. The dissipation of energy does not take place in the bucket itself (except at low flows) but in the air and in the river bed where severe erosion can be expected.

One characteristic of flip buckets is a high concentration of energy accompanied by very high flow velocity. It is common for flow velocity to reach 50 m/s and for the discharge per unit width to reach 200 m³/s/m, thus attaining an energy level of about 250 MW per metre of width.

In the case of tunnel spillways, the energy level can be even higher; at the Glen Canyon Project, for example, the energy was about 390 MW per metre of width. In comparison, the energy was only 38 MW per metre at Grand Coulee's roller bucket stilling basin.

4.2 Bucket Geometry and Flow Behaviour

Flip buckets have been designed in various shapes and forms. Some are cylindrical, some have lateral contractions or expansions, some use plane shapes,[13] and some, such as those at Fontana Dam[68,94] and at P. K. Le Roux Dam[5] have complex geometrics which almost defy description. However, all were designed with one common objective: to discharge the flow from the spillway into the river so as to achieve the greatest dispersion possible at all discharges. This approach minimises flow energy per unit area and reduces tendencies for eddy currents to develop which would erode channel banks. With very few exceptions, flip buckets are tailor made for a given project and the designs must be confirmed with the aid of hydraulic models.

The key parameters for the design of a cylindrical flip bucket are the approach-flow velocity and depth, the radius of the bucket and the lip angle. These parameters dictate the hydrodynamic forces acting on a bucket and the nappe trajectory. Balloffet[7] (Fig. 13) developed a theoretical equation for determining the maximum pressure head, h, in a two-dimensional circular bucket, assuming that the flow in the bucket is irrotational, as follows:

$$h = d + \frac{V_1^2}{2g}\left(1 - \frac{(R-d)^2}{R}\right) \qquad (3)$$

where d can be computed from

$$d = q/\sqrt{(2gH)} \qquad (4)$$

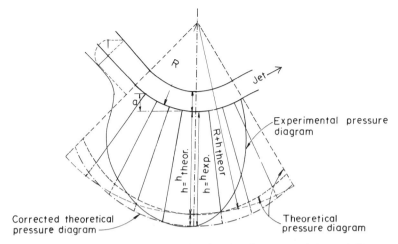

FIG. 13. Typical pressure distribution in a flip bucket (after ref. 7).

Here, q is the discharge per unit width, V_1 is the surface velocity in the bucket, R is the bucket radius and g is the gravitational acceleration. Equation (3) was compared with US Army Corps of Engineers' chute spillway model data of Pine Flat and Hartwell Dams and with USBR's tunnel spillway data for Flaming Gorge, Glen Canyon and Whiskeytown Dams. The results showed that the computed h values were only 2% and 4% lower than the experimental data. In applying eqn. (3) for a tunnel spillway, d and V_1 are taken as the water depth and the corresponding flow velocity at the entrance to the flip bucket. Figure 13 shows a typical pressure distribution. As shown, the pressure rise occurs at about two depths upstream from the point of tangency and the pressure reaches a maximum at or near the lowest point of the bucket. Balloffet also indicated that the lip angle does not affect the maximum pressure but the location of the maximum pressure tends to shift downstream as the lip angle increases.

Boundary-generated vorticity will also produce fluctuating pressures in the bucket. According to Kraichnan (see ref. 87), the rms of the pressure fluctuation, $\sqrt{(\overline{p'^2})}$, can be expressed by

$$\sqrt{(\overline{p'^2})} = \beta C_f \rho \frac{V_m^2}{2} \qquad (5)$$

where β is a coefficient varying from 3 to 5, C_f is the friction factor,

V_m is the average velocity and ρ is the water density. With $C_f = 0.013$, the rms of the fluctuating pressure is about 2·5 to 4% of the velocity head, $V_m^2/2g$. For a design with an average velocity of 50 m/s, the rms pressure is about 5 m of head.

The authors are unaware of any systematic tests which define the required bucket radius for proper projection of flow downstream. Rhone and Peterka[77] indicated that the radius should be at least four times the maximum depth of flow. A model test for the Kettle Project, Nelson River, Manitoba, Canada[101] revealed that when R/d was less than 3, the flow was not properly trained by the bucket and the distance at which the nappe impinged on to the river was actually closer to the bucket than that at lower discharge. The model test for the Guri Expansion Project[23] resulted in a flip bucket with $R/d = 3.33$. From this evidence, it seems clear that an R/d of 3 or greater should be maintained; the authors would recommend an R/d of not less than 4 to be conservative.

A bucket lip may be subjected to negative pressure and cavitation damage if the shape is improperly designed and if the lip is positioned below the tailwater. The damage at the Guri Stage I flip bucket is a case in point.[23] In this design, the lip was submerged. Field records revealed that cavitation eroded as much as 10 m from the tip of the lip of one of the spillways over a three-year period. A follow-up model test showed a negative pressure of about −7 psig at a point 13 cm upstream from the lip. To correct the problem, a small wedge 0·75 m long was added to the lip, as shown in Fig. 14, which maintained positive pressures in the bucket. The modification was satisfactory from a hydraulic viewpoint; structural difficulties are described by Chavarri.[23] A similar wedge was provided for the flip bucket lip at Itaipu.[91]

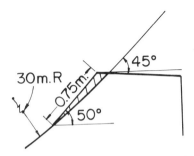

FIG. 14.   Modifications to the Guri flip bucket (after ref. 23).

Placing the lip above the tailwater is good design practice because it provides an opportunity for inspection of the bucket after each major flood and for repair, if necessary, without a major cofferdamming effort.

The bucket radius and the lip angle affect the sweep-out discharge, the discharge at which flip action takes place. Below this discharge a hydraulic jump occurs in the flip bucket and the lip functions as an overflow weir. Such a phenomenon is of considerable importance to the design of a flip bucket, especially for an ungated spillway, because frequent floods are usually less than the sweep-out discharge and can cause severe erosion at the foundation supporting the flip bucket. As the flood recedes, there exists a sweep-in discharge below which hydraulic jump reappears in the bucket. As may be expected, the sweep-out flow is higher than the sweep-in flow.

4.3 Dispersion Blocks

Dispersion blocks have been used frequently at the end of buckets to break up a solid nappe into jets. This increases air entrainment and the impact area in the river channel and thereby reduces downstream erosion. Among many of the examples are the dispersion blocks for the spillways of Oroville Dam in the USA, M'Jara Dam in Morocco[69] and Al-Ibtissam Dam in Algeria.[12] Large dispersion blocks were used at Ilha-Solteria in Brazil, at Alcantra in Spain,[103] and at Sobron, also in Spain; there was insufficient tailwater at Sobron for a hydraulic jump.[31] Dispersion blocks have also been used in the repair of Edgard de Souza Dam in Brazil[2] and in remedial measures at Langbjorn in Sweden.[25a] Ski-jump blocks with aeration have been used at several Swedish dams.[25a] Examples of dispersion blocks at bottom outlets include St. Croix in France[104] and P. K. Le Roux Dam in South Africa.[35]

For high-head dams, dispersion blocks will be subjected to very high velocity and cavitation potential. At Itaipu in Brazil,[91] dispersion blocks were considered and tested but were rejected because the risk of cavitation was judged to outweigh the benefits in reduction of downstream erosion.

4.4 Jet Trajectory

The trajectory of flow leaving a flip bucket depends primarily upon the lip angle, θ, and the exit velocity, V_0. Neglecting air resistance, the trajectory can be determined by the equations for the path of a projectile. The equation for the throw distance at the spillway lip elevation, L_0, is

$$L_0 = \frac{V_0^2}{g} \sin 2\theta \tag{6}$$

In normal practice, the angle θ ranges from 20 to 45°. The angle is selected for a desirable distance, L_0, and angle of entry into the stream. With a steep angle, the vertical velocity component at the point of entry will be large and the jet will cause deep-channel bottom erosion. As the angle becomes flatter, the horizontal velocity component will be higher and will increase drawdown and forward velocity. Excessive forward velocity tends to increase downstream bank erosion. In general, the selection of an appropriate lip angle should be investigated in a hydraulic model.

Equation (6) and model tests of jet trajectories do not show the effect of air resistance. Kawakami[39] presented results of some field investigations of jet trajectories for a ski-jump spillway and introduced a coefficient related to air resistance, k, for the following trajectory equations:

$$y = \frac{1}{gk^2} \ln (\cos \gamma + \tan \alpha \sin \gamma) \tag{7}$$

$$L_1 = \frac{1}{gk^2} \ln (1 + 2k\alpha V_0 \cos \theta) \tag{8}$$

where

$$\alpha = \tan^{-1} (kV_0 \sin \theta)$$

$$\gamma = \frac{\exp (gk^2 x) - 1}{kV_0 \cos \theta}$$

and x and y are Cartesian coordinates, V_0 is in m/s and θ is as defined on Fig. 15(A). L_1 is the throw distance which corresponds to L_0 in eqn. (6); Fig. 15(B) shows an empirical relationship between V_0 and k. The data were used to develop L_1/L_0 as a function of V_0 as shown in Fig. 15(C). From this result, it appears that the effect of air resistance is small whenever V_0 is less than about 20 m/s, but as the velocity increases to 40 m/s the throw distance could be reduced by as much as 30% from the theoretical value given by eqn. (6). Application of Fig. 15(C) to the Fontana Dam tunnel spillway data also yields reasonable agreement.

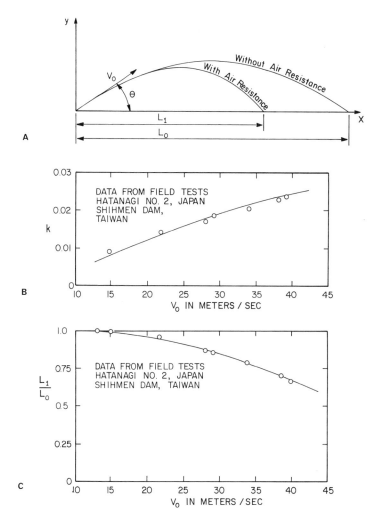

FIG. 15.   Jet trajectory with air resistance (after ref. 39).

Kawakami's results provide a basis for estimating effects of air resistance. In reality, factors such as the thickness and shape of the jet and the initial level of turbulence all play important roles in the manner in which the jet is broken into droplets by entrained air. Clearly, more field data are needed to delineate these effects.

4.5   Drawdown

The plunging of a jet at flat angles of entry into the downstream channel tends to create an ejector effect which depresses the water level upstream from the impingement area. The magnitude of this drawdown is an important design parameter since it may affect powerhouse operation. Rhone and Peterka[77] reported drawdown as much as 7·5 m in both Hungry Horse and Glen Canyon tunnel spillways at their respective design discharges and provide data for preliminary estimates of drawdown.

4.6   Erosion

The erosion characteristics downstream from flip buckets have been the subject of numerous studies, and a host of relationships have been proposed for estimating the maximum depth of scour produced by a plunging jet. The equations by Schoklitsch (see ref. 24), Veronese,[97] Damle,[26] Martins,[47,48] Wu,[107] Chee and Padiyar,[24] and Chee and Kung[25] are all of the general form

$$d_s = \frac{Cq^x H^y \alpha^w}{d^z} \qquad (9)$$

where d_s is the maximum scour depth measured from the water surface (m), q is the discharge per metre at the crest of a drop structure or at a flip bucket exit ($m^3/s/m$), H is the height of drop from the upstream to the downstream water surface (m), d is the particle size of the material (mm), and α is the angle (degrees) that the flip bucket makes with the horizontal.

The coefficient C and the exponents w, x, y and z, summarised in Table 2 show that the ultimate scour depth is primarily a function of

TABLE 2
SUMMARY OF EQUATIONS OF MAXIMUM EROSION DEPTH

Author	Ref.	C	x	y	z	w
Schoklitsch	(see 24)	4·71	0·57	0·2	0·32	0
Veronese	97	1·9	0·54	0·225	0	0
Damle	26	0·65	0·5	0·5	0	0
Martins	48	1·5	0·6	0·1	0	0
Wu	107	1·18	0·51	0·235	0	0
Chee & Kung	25	2·22	0·60	0·20	0·1	0·1
Chee & Padiyar	24	3·35	0·67	0·18	0·063	0

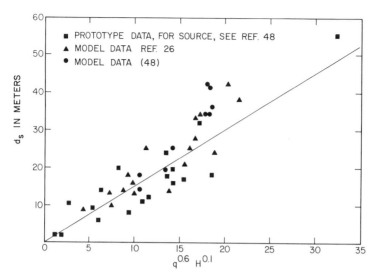

FIG. 16.   Scour depth from plunging jets (after ref. 43).

discharge, q. The head, H, plays only a secondary role and the particle size, d, and lip angle, α, are not particularly significant. Only Schoklitsch and Chee and Padiyar introduced d as a parameter and only Chee and Kung included α as a parameter. In Schoklitsch's equation, d is the d_{90} size, while in Chee and Padiyar's and Chee and Kung's expressions, d is the average particle size. The equations by Chee and Padiyar and Chee and Kung were derived purely from laboratory testing using sand or gravel. The others were obtained primarily from field data. Martins' relationship was based on 18 field observations, Damle's model data, as well as other model data available in the literature; Fig. 16 shows his data compilation and indicates the general scatter involved in scour data.

Taraimovich,[90] based on extensive field and laboratory data, proposed that the maximum erosion, t_{max}, measured below the original channel bottom can be determined by

$$t_{max} = 6h_{cr} \tan \alpha_1 \qquad (10)$$

where h_{cr} is the critical depth at spillway outlet and α_1 is the upstream angle of the scour hole as defined in Fig. 17. Taraimovich further suggested relationships for the mean angle of the jet plunging into the

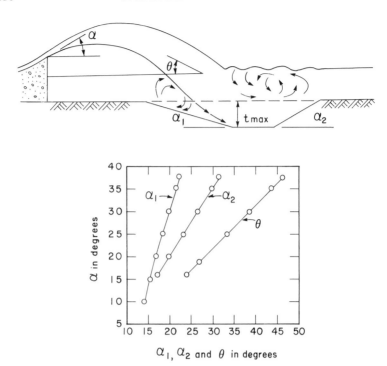

FIG. 17.   Scour hole relationships (after ref. 90).

pool, θ, and the downstream angle of the scour hole, α_2 and α_1, as a function of the angle that the lip of the flip bucket makes with the horizontal. From this plot it may be concluded that the scour hole geometry is not very sensitive to the angle of flip bucket, α. Furthermore, it can also be noted that θ is always larger than α, an expected effect of air resistance on the trajectory of plunging jets.

Chee and Padiyar and Chee and Kung also gave some relationships which provided an estimate of the scour hole dimensions in non-cohesive material; their results were in general agreement with those of Taraimovich as far as the slopes of the scour hole were concerned.

An extensive review of scour and erosion associated with energy dissipators is beyond the scope of this chapter. The references cited in Table 2 provide an overview of this complex subject. The use of relationships such as those in Table 2 should be restricted to the range of q and H used in developing the equations. For preliminary design, Martins' expression probably provides a reasonable estimate of the ultimate depth of scour. In the final analysis, a model study will be required as discussed in Section 9.

5 PLUNGE POOLS AT OVERFLOW STRUCTURES

Overflow spillways at arch dams may result in free-fall nappes, or in the case of gated outlets and orifices, in plunging jets. Typical examples of energy dissipators for arch dam spillways include: (1) impact on a slab or apron with a cushioning pool formed either by a secondary weir close to the dam, e.g. Vouglans[106] and Morrow Point[36] or by sufficient tailwater, e.g. P. K. Le Roux Dam;[5] (2) formation of a scour hole with sufficient tailwater provided by a weir located well downstream from the dam, e.g. Muhdiq;[106] and (3) formation of a scour hole in the natural channel, e.g. Kariba.[76]

For basins with aprons, the determination of the pool depth and dimensions and the forces acting on the apron are the principal factors in the hydraulics of the design. The hydrodynamics of a freely falling jet or nappe plunging into a pool are somewhat similar to those of an unconfined submerged jet, as summarised by Hartung and Hausler.[32] The depths of plunge pools on slabs or aprons are usually small in comparison with the depths necessary for any appreciable diffusion of the jet to occur. The centreline velocity of an axisymmetric jet does not even begin to decrease until the jet has penetrated at least 5 to 6 jet diameters, D, below the pool surface. Consequently, the mean and fluctuating pressures, in metres of water, on the slab can be an appreciable percentage of the distance from headwater to tailwater. Studies for Morrow Point Dam[41] showed maximum pressure heads of about one-third the height of fall (110 m) under a pool with a depth about one-fifth the height of fall. Even at heads of the order of 50 m the forces are impressive. At Granget Dam, for example, with $q = 40$ m^3/s/m, blocks of concrete and debris weighing more than 10 tons were moved out of the basin. A discussion of the damage sustained and repairs required are presented in ref. 105.

For basins without aprons, the determination of the scour and extent of the scour hole is the principal concern. Axisymmetric jets possess sufficient energy for erosion after penetrating about $20D$ into a pool. Since the velocity in two-dimensional jets such as a nappe decays more slowly than that in axisymmetric jets, erosion can occur at even greater depths up to $40B$, where B is the thickness of the nappe at the entry into the pool. An analysis of scour depth using observations on free-falling jets in a pool was presented by Hartung and Hausler.[32] The scour hole at Kariba was used as a case history; it is certainly an excellent example of the erosion potential from plunging jets. As shown on Fig. 18, the depth of scour is now more than 75 m, almost two-thirds the height of the dam; it has not yet reached equilibrium.

One of the more recent innovations in the design of energy dissipators for overflow spillways is the use of aerated nappe dispersers. Dispersers aerate and spread the jet so that forces on the basin slab or the depth of erosion are considerably reduced. Although this principle was developed in 1939 by Roberts, the feasibility of such devices for large-scale applications[5,105] was only recently demonstrated in the construction of Hendrik Verwoerd and P. K. Le Roux Dams. The central overflow spillway of the P. K. Le Roux Dam ($q = 76 \text{ m}^3/\text{s/m}$) is equipped with nappe splitters and a sill as illustrated in Fig. 19. The swirling motion imparted by the splitters causes wide dispersal of the nappe as it leaves the platform located below the splitters. Since the overflow heads employed at P. K. Le Roux (about 10 m) are higher than those used by Roberts, vents were provided to ensure the aeration which is essential to the proper operation of the splitters. A comparison of erosion in a model study using an erodable bed showed

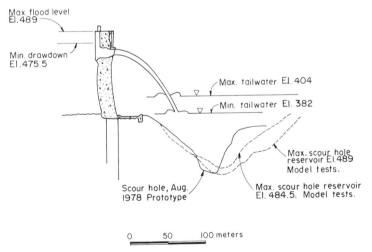

FIG. 18.   Scour hole at Kariba (after ref. 76).

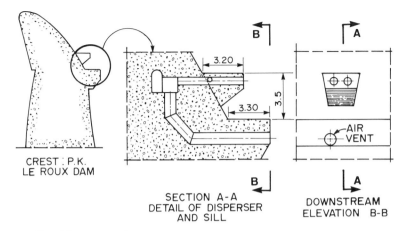

CREST : P.K.
LE ROUX DAM

SECTION A-A
DETAIL OF DISPERSER
AND SILL

DOWNSTREAM
ELEVATION B-B

FIG. 19.   Nappe dispersers for P. K. Le Roux Dam (after ref. 105).

that the depth of erosion without the splitters was almost twice as great as the depth with the splitters and that the bottom of the scour hole was much closer to the dam.

The decrease in scour with aeration was also observed by Johnson[37] who conducted a laboratory investigation of the effect of entrained air on the scouring capability of water jets. He concluded that an aerated water jet was much more rapidly diffused than a non-aerated jet after it entered the pool. The depth of tailwater required for no scouring with an aerated jet was approximately half the tailwater depth required for a non-aerated flow with the same discharge. Novak and Čábelka[63] also discuss the effect of entrained air on energy dissipation. There is a need for a systematic study of the mean and fluctuating pressures on slabs under plunging jets as a function of pool depth and quantity of entrained air to help quantify these effects for design.

Pre-excavated plunge pools have also been used to provide a deeper initial pool and to get the erosion started in the right direction, such as at Crystal Dam[82] and Manicouagan 3.[14] The underlying geology sometimes causes directions other than those intended. At Tarbela, for example, an igneous intrusion which was more erosion resistant than the surrounding rock completely changed the development of the service spillway's pool;[46] extensive rehabilitative work was required.

6 CAVITATION AND AERATION

6.1 Cavitation in Energy Dissipators

A review of past and recent experience with cavitation and energy dissipators shows that many of the problems of the past are still present. The most persistent problems with cavitation in dissipators are caused generally by offsets or changes in alignment that result from construction activities. Transitions from tunnel or sluice liners such as at Dworshak and Libby Dams,[74] and Tarbela's stilling basin 4,[45] irregularities in floors caused by misaligned forms and offsets at construction joints are typical examples of continuing problems.

Cavitation on chute blocks and baffle blocks[21] is expected in high velocity flow, and as a general rule these appurtenances should be avoided in dissipators at high dams. Cavitation can also occur with submerged flip buckets, as demonstrated by the recent experience at Guri.[23]

Estimates of the surface tolerances necessary to prevent cavitation have been presented by Ball[6] and Wang and Chou.[100] Results for several types of offsets are shown in Figs. 4, 5, 6, 7 and 8 of Chapter 4. With velocities greater than 35 m/s, the construction tolerances required become extremely difficult to maintain. The results of Ball *et al.* have been obtained for incipient cavitation conditions. Incipient cavitation refers to the onset of cavitation as detected by a hydrophone or other sensor. Cavitation more severe than just an incipient condition is required for excessive damage to occur. Unfortunately, there is no information available on the critical cavitation indices for which damage occurs for offsets of practical importance in the design of energy dissipators. The use of Ball's or Wang and Chou's criteria does ensure that cavitation will not occur. Since the region between incipient cavitation and critical cavitation is unknown (it is also probably rather limited), the authors do not recommend encroachment on these criteria until further studies have been made.

6.2 Pressure Fluctuations and Cavitation

Cavitation is a phenomenon that does not scale according to the Froude law; effects of cavitation on the flow cannot be investigated in models commonly employed to study energy dissipators because the vapour pressure is the same in both the model and the prototype. One consequence of this lack of similitude is that the absence of cavitation in the model does not ensure the absence of cavitation in the prototype. Even the determination that there are positive mean pressures in the model does not ensure that there will be no cavitation in the prototype. Fluctuating pressures in energy dissipators can be very large, especially where flows around chute blocks, baffle blocks and sills are concerned, and instantaneous pressures can easily drop below vapour pressure, resulting in cavitation conditions.

Models can, however, be used to investigate whether or not cavitation will occur. The fluctuating pressures can be measured, analysed and scaled to prototype conditions to ascertain whether vapour pressure and cavitation can occur. If they do not, then there will be no cavitation in the prototype structure. There are few general data available for estimating the onset of cavitation produced by turbulence in energy dissipators. Some approaches to the problem are presented by Narayanan[61] and Lopardo.[44] For specific basins, appropriate measurement of pressure fluctuations will have to be made during the model studies.

6.3   Use of Aeration to Control Cavitation

The use of aeration to control cavitation is not a new idea, but with today's high velocity flows, aeration is used increasingly in high-head structures. The basic principle, as outlined in detail in Chapter 4, is to cushion the cavitation with an admission of air in cavitation-prone areas, usually through slots or offsets in the flow that are constructed in the walls or floor of the basin (Fig. 9, Chapter 4). Noteworthy applications of this technique are the repair of Basin 3 at Tarbela as described by Lowe,[46] and in the design of the outlet works at Nurek.[70]

At first, aeration was viewed as a panacea for cavitation problems in high-velocity flow. In retrospect, construction of aeration facilities is not without cost; cavitation effects can also be minimised by careful design and control of tolerances and material during construction, as demonstrated by past experience. In general, where maintenance of tolerances and control of materials is suspect, the use of aeration would appear prudent. The duration of high-velocity flows is another factor—some damage may be acceptable for infrequent use, such as extreme flood events, but certainly not in cases with annual long duration flows. References useful in the design of aeration slots are presented in Chapter 4.

Aeration of dispersion blocks is a separate question. Here the objective is to aerate the jet to promote dispersion in the atmosphere (Fig. 19), and reduce loading or scour in the plunge pool or basin and often at the same time to reduce potential for cavitation. Injecting this air in regions of high velocity accomplishes both of these objectives.

6.4 Cavitation-Resistant Materials

Steel lining is an expensive but effective method to resist cavitation. Steel liners have been used successfully at sluice outlets and in energy dissipators for valves such as those illustrated in Fig. 20, for example.

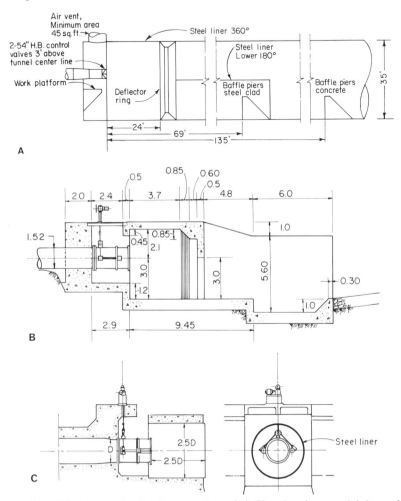

FIG. 20.   Dissipators for fixed cone valves. (A) Chamber in tunnel (after ref. 98); (B) single chamber dissipator; (C) hood for fixed-cone valve.

Armouring of chute blocks and baffle piers is generally not very successful. The fluctuating pressures are quite large and vibration of the plates, or failure of the fasteners, usually results in short-lived protection, especially at high-head structures.

The more recent innovations in concrete technology for resisting cavitation include the development of epoxy mortars and concrete, steel fibre reinforced concrete, polymerised concrete and polymerised steel fibre reinforced concrete. Tests of various specimens at the Corps of Engineers Detroit Dam facility as described by Lowe *et al.*[46] showed that steel fibre reinforced concrete and polymerised concrete took three times as long to reach 75 mm erosion depth as conventional concrete. The polymerised steel fibre reinforced concrete was most erosion resistant; the depth of erosion reached 25 mm after 10 h and remained constant for the remainder of the 200-h test.

Repairs using epoxy mortar and epoxy concrete at Dworshak Dam[74] and Tarbela[46] have not been very satisfactory. Failure of patches with epoxy mortar was attributed to an order of magnitude higher coefficient of thermal expansion of the epoxy mortar in comparison with conventional concrete. Repairs with fibrous concrete at Dworshak Dam seem to be holding up well. At Tarbela, future repairs will probably be made with fibrous concrete. An overlay of steel fibre reinforced concrete was used in the repair of basin 3 at Tarbela; two of the overlay slabs were constructed of conventional concrete so that a comparison of the behaviour of the two types of concrete could be made in the future.

7 HIGH PRESSURE OUTLETS

7.1 Hollow Jet Basins

Valves for control of flow at low-level outlets include fixed-cone dispersion valves, hollow jet valves and high pressure slide gates. Hollow jet valves may discharge above tailwater into the river where the rock is good. The USBR has developed a standard stilling basin for hollow jet valves.[68] Prototype experience with this dissipator has been mixed. At Navajo Dam, for example, debris was swept back into the basin resulting in extensive damage due to abrasion.[3] Modifications included cladding of the sloping chute, removal of the converging wedges and construction of a slab and a rock trap at the downstream end of the basin. At Trinity Dam, damage consisted of severe abrasion of the floor and sidewalls; the centre dividing wall failed along a construction joint. Laboratory tests showed fluctuating pressures considerably greater than assumed in the design. Riprap downstream from this structure was grouted, and the centre wall was reinforced and repaired. The basin at Yellowtail was constructed with a cover slab 1 m thick extending the full length of the basin. The divider wall was instrumented; the maximum differential fluctuation was about 7 m of water and no damage has occurred in the operation of the basin. Use of the basin at heads higher than those presently in successful operation will require a model study to evaluate the dynamic forces on the walls, the necessity for cladding the sloping chute and the potential for material to be swept back into the basin. Waves downstream from the structure may also present potential channel erosion problems in some cases.

7.2 Dissipators for Fixed-Cone Valves

The fixed-cone dispersion valve (sometimes referred to as the Howell–Bunger valve) was designed for free discharge above tailwater as a lighter, less expensive alternative to the hollow jet valve.

High-head dissipators for this valve include those developed for Oroville[98] and Portage Mountain[96] (Fig. 20(A)). For heads of about 100 m a multiple chambered dissipator has been developed that reduces wave action at the outlet to about 10 cm; at heads of 30 m or less, a single-chambered dissipator has been used (Fig. 20(B)). Hoods, as illustrated in Fig. 20(C) have also been used to form a hollow jet discharge to reduce spray at heads up to 150 m. Other dissipators include those developed for Fontana,[94] the outlet at Ramganda[30] and New Melones.[50]

The use of submerged fixed-cone valves for energy dissipation is not good design practice. Since the valve was designed for free discharge, its light-weight construction was never intended to resist the dynamic loading caused by the jet entrainment and cavitation under submerged operation. The authors are not aware of any installations of submerged fixed-cone valves with successful, extensive, long term operating experience throughout the entire range of flow for which the facility was designed. In cases where unacceptable vibration has occurred, provision of air vents has been used with mixed success to reduce the back flow around the valve in an attempt to provide a protective cushion of air in which the valve operates.

A typical example of problems with a submerged valve was described by Broehl and Fisch.[17] In this case, modifications to a valve used as a turbine pressure relief valve included doubling the thickness of the vanes and redesigning the submerged chamber. The changes were not completely successful because the valve still vibrated excessively; it has never operated satisfactorily when fully open and is seldom used.

In addition, fixed-cone valves are also sensitive to approach flow conditions. Highly turbulent flow, or skewed velocity distributions such as caused by the proximity of bends, Y-branches or tees, can result in unequal loading and subsequent failure of the vanes.[53] A recent design change in the vane configuration was tested extensively by the Corps of Engineers,[49] and used in the valves supplied for New Melones Dam. Although the design change increased the discharge coefficient in comparison with a conventional design, a shift in hydraulic control from the valve sleeve to the valve body limits the maximum opening to about 80%; since a conventional valve opens to about 84%, the new design has a slightly lower maximum capacity than a conventional valve of the same size.

7.3 Sudden Expansion Dissipators

Chamber dissipators with internal baffling have also been described by Widmann[102] for use with slide-gate outlets. This type of dissipator is suited to heads of about 120 m and discharges up to about 100 m³/s. Extrapolation to higher heads would require extensive model studies.

For irrigation outlets and fish releases under high heads where relatively small releases (5–10 m³/s) are required, vertical stilling wells using a standard sleeve valve as described by Burgi[20] or a multiport sleeve valve as described by Watson[99a] and Burgi[20a] provide a compact means of dissipating energy.

Sudden expansion energy dissipators are an innovation that has appeared in the last 15 years. These dissipators use the principle of energy loss at a sudden enlargement for dissipation. Cavitation occurs well away from the boundaries and thus does not result in damage to the structure. The most noteworthy example is that at Mica Dam.[52,80] which dissipates about 135 m of head at a discharge of 850 m³/s. The same principle was also used in the outlet works at New Don Pedro Dam (Fig. 21). The three expansion chambers were designed to pass about 200 m³/s and dissipate about 45 m of head. The remainder of the 170 m gross head is dissipated in pipe resistance and the 9·14-m diameter tunnel downstream from the gates.

F. A. LOCHER AND S. T. HSU

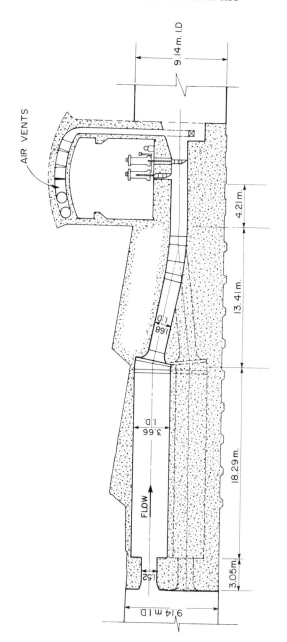

FIG. 21. Sudden expansion dissipator, New Don Pedro Dam.

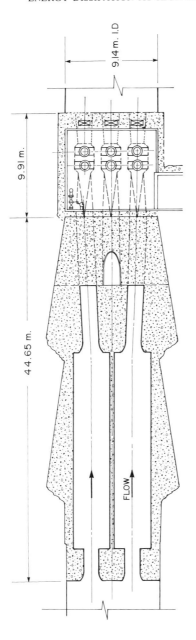

PLAN - SECTION

Fig. 21—contd.

8 ENVIRONMENTAL FACTORS AND DISSIPATOR DESIGN

The effects of dams and reservoirs on the environment have been the subject of many papers and symposia. Here, we shall consider only the effects that may have a direct bearing on the design of energy dissipators.

One of the principal effects of how the energy is dissipated is the problem of nitrogen supersaturation in the water and the subsequent effects on fish life. Nitrogen supersaturation occurs when aerated flows plunge or are diffused deeply in pools or stilling basins. Fish are killed when the dissolved gas comes out of solution in their circulatory system or tissues—in essence, the 'bends' as experienced by human divers. This potential problem received a great deal of attention in the Pacific Northwest of the United States where the salmon fishery is an important factor in the local economy.

In the Columbia Basin, studies have shown that passage of juvenile fish through turbines and predation are much more important factors in fish mortality than effects of nitrogen supersaturation, because the regulation of the Columbia River has significantly reduced the quantity flowing over spillways in the system. For other areas, such as Alaska, the problem may still exist, and mitigation of the potential impact will have to be considered in design. One solution is to prevent aerated flows from plunging deeply into the stilling basin by using deflector blocks. The flow deflectors are designed to be effective at normal flows and to deflect the spillway flow along the surface of the receiving pool. Under flood flows, the blocks are ineffective in deflecting the flow and may be damaged or sacrificed. Deflector blocks have been installed at Lower Granite Dam. Results of studies by the US Army Corps of Engineers show some promising mitigation of effects of nitrogen supersaturation.[84]

Another solution is to prevent aeration in the first place. In cases where the fish are by-passed by other means, or only the downstream water quality is of concern, a high-capacity outlet using sudden expansion energy dissipators with submerged outlets will prevent supersaturation and should result in water quality equal to that passing through the turbines.

Spray from flip bucket flows can cause saturation of surrounding slopes and result in landslides that block access roads or cause excessive turbidity in the flows downstream from the dam. Erosion from plunging jets, flip buckets, or other outlets may result in unacceptable water quality downstream from the structure. In environmentally sensitive areas such considerations may govern the choice of dissipator. In general, environmental factors that influence the design of energy dissipators are best incorporated in the conceptual layout of the project. Sound engineering judgement, experience, and a sensitivity to the environmental politics of the site are prerequisites for a successful design in this era. A very large measure of patience is also helpful.

9 MODEL STUDIES

The process of dissipating large amounts of energy in flows from spillways is an extremely complex flow phenomenon involving a three-dimensional, turbulent, two-phase flow that depends on the topographic and geologic conditions at the site. A reduced-scale model is usually used to study a proposed design and to aid in developing a final design. Often, the model is also used to develop guidelines for spillway operation. For example, extensive studies may be required to establish the operating sequence for a gated spillway with hydraulic jump or roller bucket basin at other than design flow conditions. When only some of the gates are in operation, flow conditions in the basin can result in eddies which transport material from downstream areas back into the basin; a ball-milling action can then result in damage to the floor, bucket or baffle blocks.

The basic requirement of a model is to reproduce, as accurately as possible, the flow dynamics of the prototype. The general modelling procedures for an energy dissipator are well established, as described by Novak and Čábelka.[63] Normally, geometric similarity is preserved and the discharge and dynamic relationships are scaled on the basis of the Froude law. In this section, a brief discussion of scale effects, erosion testing and use of the computer for data acquisition and analysis will be presented.

A 'scale effect' is a term that is applied to an observed discrepancy between the hydrodynamic behaviour in a model and the prototype caused by the fact that not all of the forces in the prototype can be properly modelled in a reduced scale model. Scale effects, however small they may be, always exist unless a 1 : 1 scale model is used. The first step towards minimising scale effects is to properly select a model scale and a model material. For modelling of a spillway dissipator, normally a scale ratio in the range of 1 : 25 to 1 : 100 is used with 1 : 50

to 1:75 being the most common choice. A minimum water depth about 5 cm should be maintained so that the flow remains turbulent and surface tension effects are small. This will reduce scale effects of the Reynolds number and Weber number. Other constraints include laboratory flow capacity and space, instrumentation, etc.

Perhaps the most significant scale effect in the modelling of a dissipator is the phenomenon created by entrained air which occurs in flip bucket nappes, in hydraulic jump basins and in plunge pools. Scale effects also occur when air is introduced to mitigate cavitation or to aerate plunging jets in an attempt to minimise erosion in a plunge pool or for reducing dynamic forces acting on the apron of such a pool. In this type of modelling, scale effects stem from the fact that the jet in a model does not entrain air as readily as in the prototype and that air bubbles tend to be the same size regardless of the scale differences. Therefore, one finds proportionally that a model dissipator tends to have a smaller air volume but larger bubble sizes than the prototype bubbles. Based on Kawakami's data on effect of air resistance on flip bucket jet trajectories[39] and on Johnson's results[37] on effects of air entrainment on scour, it seems reasonable to conclude that a reduced-scale model will produce a relatively longer jet throw distance, deeper erosion, higher apron impact pressures and less bulking. Clearly, scale effects vary with the flow phenomena under investigation and should be assessed on an individual basis. One method which has been used to evaluate scale effects is to compare models of at least two different scales. This procedure permits extrapolation of model results with a higher level of confidence. Some recent work indicates that a scale ratio of 1:15 is sufficient for modelling air slots (see Chapter 4).

Determination of scour in plunge pools or in areas downstream from hydraulic jump basins requires knowledge of and proper simulation of soil and rock characteristics such as soil cohesiveness and boulder size, rock joint patterns, and the degree of weathering and crushing strength. The acceptability of any design requires a qualitative evaluation of a combination of hydraulic, geologic and soil parameters that often requires expert opinion from all three areas.

The selection of material to simulate a prototype erosion condition is certainly more of an art than a science. Sand or crushed stones are used typically because of their availability. However, these materials have a low angle of repose and do not simulate vertical banks which occur in natural soil and especially in rock. The failure to properly represent flow boundaries will lead to erroneous erosion patterns and scour depths. In an attempt to simulate such erosion conditions, special materials such as lean sand–cement mixtures, mixtures of bentonite or other clay–sand mixtures are used. The selection of material and mix is an art that depends upon individual experience and preference. The limitations of the material used in the model and the knowledge of the geology of the site precludes an exact modelling of prototype conditions. Results of these studies are qualitative and depend a great deal on the skill and experience of those performing the model study.

The study of the effects of turbulence and fluctuating forces in hydraulic structures has been facilitated by significant advances in electronic instrumentation and the use of on-line, real-time analysis with digital computers. As the cost of microprocessors continues to decrease, the use of sophisticated techniques for control and analysis in laboratory research increases. It does not necessarily follow that our understanding of the phenomena increases in proportion to the power of the instrumentation that is employed, particularly in view of the difficulties involved in ensuring that high quality data emerge from the myriad of 'black boxes' that surround many of today's researchers.

Nevertheless, the variety of electronic instrumentation available is certainly impressive. Sensors such as strain gauges, load cells and pressure transducers can be interfaced with microcomputers which can be programmed to sample multiple channels of data at specified rates and store the information on disks. The data can then be retrieved for processing. Alternatively, the analogue data can be recorded on magnetic tape either in the field or laboratory, and played back later for digitising and analysis. Special-purpose equipment for spectral analysis, correlation and other signal conditioning is also available.

The most versatile piece of equipment is, however, the programmable digital computer, with analogue to digital and digital to analogue capabilities. Using appropriate software, the computer can perform any of the functions available with the special-purpose equipment. In addition it can be used for controlling or setting experimental conditions. An exceptional range of analyses can be performed on the characteristics of fluctuating forces, pressures and velocities.

The capability of obtaining a much more detailed picture of the hydrodynamic loading acting on structures will undoubtedly be one of the most significant developments in improving the design of energy dissipators in the future.

REFERENCES

1. AKBARI, M. E., MITTAL, M. K. and PANDE, P. K. Pressure fluctuations on the floor of free and forced hydraulic jumps, *Proc. Int. Conf. on Hydraulic Modelling of Civil Engineering Structures*, BHRA, Coventry, 22–29 September, 1982, paper C1, 87–96.

2. ANASTASI, G., BISAZ, E., GERODETTI, M., SCHAAD, F. and SOUBRIER, G. Essais sur modele hydraulique et etudes d'evacuateurs par rapport aux conditions de restitution, 13*th* ICOLD, New Delhi, 1979, Q50, R32, pp. 515–58.

3. ARTHUR, H. G. and JABARA, M. A. Problems involved in operation and maintenance of spillways and outlets at Bureau of Reclamation dams, 9*th* ICOLD, Istanbul, 1967, Q33, R5, pp. 73–93.

4. AUBIN, L., LEFEBVRE, D., MCNEIL, N. and STOIAN, A. Les evacuateurs de crue des amenagements hydroelectriques LG2 et LG1 du complex La Grande, 13*th* ICOLD, New Delhi, 1979, pp. 121–42.

5. BACK, P. A. A., FREY, J. P. and JOHNSON, G. P. K. Le Roux Dam: spillway design and energy dissipation, 11*th* ICOLD, Madrid, 1973, Q41, R76, pp. 1439–68.

6. BALL, J. W. Cavitation from surface irregularities in high velocity flow, *J. Hyd. Div. ASCE*, **102** (HY9) (Sept., 1976), 1283–97.

7. BALLOFFET, A. Pressures on spillway flip buckets, *J. Hyd. Div. ASCE*, **87** (HY5) (Sept., 1961), 87–98.

8. BASCO, D. R. *Trends in baffled hydraulic jump stilling basin designs of the Corps of Engineers since 1947*, Misc. Paper H-69-1, US Army Engineers Waterways Experiment Station, Vicksburg, January, 1969.

9. BASCO, D. R. *An experimental study of drag forces and other performance criteria of baffle blocks in hydraulic jumps*, Paper No. H-70-4, US Army Engineers Waterways Experiment Station, Vicksburg, May 1970.

10. BASCO, D. R. and ADAMS, J. R. Drag forces on baffle blocks in hydraulic jump, *J. Hyd. Div. ASCE*, **97** (HY12), Proc. Paper 8599 (December 1971), 2023–35.

11. BASCO, D. R. Optimized geometry for baffle blocks in hydraulic jumps, 14*th Int. Congress, IAHR*, Paris, 1971, Vol. 2, Paper B-18, 141–8.

12. BELBACHIR, K. and LAFITTE, R. Evacuateur de crue du barrage Al-Ibtissam, 13*th* ICOLD, New Delhi, 1979, Q50, R54, 911–57.

13. BILLORE, J., JAOUI, A., KOLKMAN, P. A., RADU, M. and deVRIES, A. H. Recherches hydrauliques pour la derivation provisoire, les deversoirs en puits et la vindange de fond du barrage de M'Dez au Maroc, 13*th* ICOLD, New Delhi, 1979, Q50, R62, 1085–1106.

14. BOUCHER, R. Dissipation d'energie par nappe plongeante pour le deversoir de l'amenagement hydro-electrique Manicouagan 3, 11*th* ICOLD, Madrid, 1973, Q41, R51, 915–33.

15. BOWERS, C. E. and TSAI, F. Y. Fluctuating pressures in spillway stilling basins, *J. Hyd. Div. ASCE*, **95** (HY6), Proc. Paper 6915 (November 1969), 2071–9.

16. BRIBIESCA, J. L. and VISCAINO, A. C. Turbulence effects on the lining of

stilling basins, 11*th ICOLD*, Madrid, 1973, Q41, R83, 1575–92.

17. BROEHL, D. J. and FISCH, J. Solution of vibration problems experienced with Howell-Bunger valves at Round Butte Dam, 9*th ICOLD*, Istanbul, 1967, Q33, R20, 333–46.

18. BROWN, F. R. Cavitation in hydraulic structures: problems created by cavitation phenomena, *J. Hyd. Div. ASCE*, **89** (HY1) (January 1963), Proc. Paper 3343, 99–112.

19. BUDWEG, F. M. G. Safety improvements taught by dam incidents and accidents in Brazil, 14*th ICOLD*, Rio de Janeiro, 1982, Q52, R73, 1245–62.

20. BURGI, P. H. Hydraulic design of vertical stilling wells, *J. Hyd. Div. ASCE*, **101** (HY7) (July 1975), 801–16.

20a. BURGI, P. H., GREEN, E. O. and THIBAULT, R. E. Multiport sleeve valve development and application, *J. Hyd. Div. ASCE*, **107** (HY1) (January 1981), 95–111.

21. ANON. Cavitation in hydraulic structures—A symposium, *Transactions ASCE*, **112** (1947), 2–124.

22. CENTER, G. W. and RHONE, T. J. Emergency redesign of Silver Jack Spillway, *J. Power Division ASCE*, **99** (PO2), Proc. Paper 10151 (November 1973), 265–79.

23. CHAVARRI, G., LOUIE, D. S., CASTILLEJO, N. and COLEMAN, H. W. Spillway and tailrace design for raising of Guri Dam using a large scale hydraulic model, 13*th ICOLD*, New Delhi, 1979, Q50, R12, 199–213.

24. CHEE, S. P. and PADIYAR, P. V. Erosion at the base of flip buckets, *Eng. J., Eng. Inst. Canada* (November 1969), 22–4.

25. CHEE, S. P. and KUNG, T. Stable profiles of plunge basins, *Water Resources Bull., J. Am. Water Resources Ass.*, **7**(2) (April 1971), 303–8.

25a. CORLIN, B. and LARSEN, P. Experience from some overflow and side spillways, 13*th ICOLD*, New Delhi, 1979, Q50, R37, 627–47.

26. DAMLE, P. M., VENKATRAMAN, C. P. and DESAI, S. C. Evaluation of scour below ski-jump buckets of spillways. Chapter in: *Model and Prototype Conformity*, Vol. 1, Central Water and Power Research Station, Poona, 1966, 154–63.

27. ESSERY, I. T. S. and HORNER, M. W. *The hydraulic design of stepped spillways*, Report No. 33 Construction Industry Research and Information Association (CIRIA), London, June 1971.

28. FRANKOVIC, B. Design criteria, operating rules, and monitoring the Drava River barrages, 14*th ICOLD*, Rio de Janeiro, 1982, Q52, R58, 985–91.

29. GOMASTA, S. K., MITTAL, M. K. and PANDE, P. K. Hydrodynamic forces on baffle blocks in hydraulic jump, *Proc. 17th Int. Congress, IAHR*, Baden-Baden, 1977, Vol. 4, Paper C-56, 453–59.

30. GOYAL, K. C., MAHESHWARI, K. M., JOSHI, V. K. and BHATIA, D. L. River closure flow and energy control at Ramganda Dam, 11*th ICOLD*, Madrid, 1973, Q41, R61, 1115–39.

31. GUINEA, P. M., LUCAS, P. and ASPURU, J. J. Selection of spillways and energy dissipators, 11*th ICOLD*, Madrid, 1973, Q41, R66, 1233–54.

32. HARTUNG, F. and HAUSLER, E. Scours, stilling basins and downstream

protection under free overfall jets at dams, 11th *ICOLD*, Madrid, 1973, Q41, R3, 39–56.

33. HERBRAND, K. and KNAUSS, J. Computation and design of stilling basins with abruptly or gradually enlarged boundaries, 11th *ICOLD*, Madrid, 1973, Q41, R4, 57–79.

34. HERBRAND, K. and SCHEUERLEIN, H. Examples of model tests dealing with special problems and design criteria at large capacity spillways, 13th *ICOLD*, New Delhi, 1979, 161–76.

35. HOLLINGWORTH, B. E. and ROBERTS, C. P. R. Model tests on a high head bottom outlet gate for vibrations and cavitation, 13th *ICOLD*, New Delhi, 1979, Q50, R4, 45–63.

36. JABARA, M. A. and LEGAS, J. Selection of spillways, plunge pools and stilling basins for earth and concrete dams, 11th *ICOLD*, Madrid, 1973, Q41, R17, 269–87.

37. JOHNSON, G. The effect of entrained air on the scouring capacity of water jets, 12th *Int. Congress, IAHR*, Fort Collins, 1967, Vol. 3, Paper C26, 218–26.

38. KARKI, K. S. Supercritical flow over sills, *J. Hyd. Div. ASCE*, **102** (HY10), Proc. Paper 12480 (October 1976), 1449–59.

39. KAWAKAMI, K. A study on the computation of horizontal distance of jet issued from a ski-jump spillway, *Trans. JSCE*, **5** (1973).

40. KHADER, M. H. A. and ELANGO, K. Turbulent pressure field beneath a hydraulic jump, *J. Hyd. Res. IAHR*, **12**(4) (1974), 469–89.

41. KING, D. L. *Hydraulic Model Studies for Morrow Point Dam*, Monograph No. 37, USBR Eng., 1967.

42. LOCHER, F. A. *Some characteristics of pressure fluctuations on low-ogee crest spillways relevant to flow-induced structural vibrations*, US Army Engineers Waterways Experiment Station, Vicksburg, Contract Report No. H-71-1, February 1971.

43. LOPARDO, R. A., ORELLANO, J. A. and VERNET, G. F. Baffle piers subjected to flow-induced vibration, *Proc. 17th Intl. Congress IAHR*, Baden-Baden, 1977, Vol. 4, Paper C55, 445–52.

44. LOPARDO, R. A., DEL LIO, J. C. and VERNET, G. F. Physical modelling of cavitation tendency for macro turbulence of hydraulic jump, *Proc. Int. Conf. on Hydraulic Engineering Structures*, BHRA, Coventry, 22–29 September, 1982, paper C1, 109–21.

45. LOWE, J., BANGASH, H. D. and CHAO, P. C. Some experiences with high velocity flow at Tarbela Dam project, 13th *Int. Cong. Large Dams*, New Delhi, 1979, Q50, R13, 215–47.

46. LOWE, J., CHAO, P. C. and LUECKER, A. R. Tarbela service spillway plunge pool development, *Water Power and Dam Construction* (Nov. 1979), 85–90.

47. MARTINS, R. B. Contribution to the knowledge on the scour action of jets on rocky river beds, 11th *ICOLD*, Madrid, 1973, Q41, R44, 799–814.

48. MARTINS, R. B. Scouring of rocky river beds by free-jet spillways, *Water Power and Dam Construction* (April 1975), 152–3.

49. MAYNORD, S. T. and GRACE, J. L. *Fixed cone valves, New Melones Dam*,

California, US Army Engineers Waterways Experiment Station Tech. Report, HL-81-4, April 1981.

50. MAYNORD, S. T. *Flood control and irrigation outlet works and tailrace channel for New Melones Dam, Stanislaus River, California*, US Army Engineers Waterways Experiment Station, Vicksburg, Technical Report No. HL-81-6, September 1981.

51. McCORQUODALE, J. A. and GIRATALLA, M. K. Supercritical flow over sills, *J. Hyd. Div. ASCE*, **98** (HY4), Proc. Paper 8846 (April 1972), 667–79.

52. MEIDAL, P. and WEBSTER, J. L. Discharge facilities for Mica Dam, 11*th ICOLD*, Madrid, 1973, Q41, R50, 893-914.

53. MERCER, A. G. Vane failures of hollow cone valves, *IAHR Symposium, Section for Hydraulic Machinery, Equipment and Cavitation*, Paper G4, Stockholm, 1970.

54. MERMEL, T. W. Major dams of the world, *Water Power and Dam Construction* (May 1982), 93–103.

55. MINAMI, I. and AKI, S. A consideration on the supervision of a concrete arch dam in the flood time, 10*th ICOLD*, Montreal, 1970, Q38, R8, 113–140.

56. MOUELHI, M., MARINIER, G., MORUEZ, J. P. and ALAM, S. Evacuateur de crue du barrage de Sidi Saad, 13*th ICOLD*, New Delhi, 1979, Q50, R5, 65–84.

57. NARASIMHAN, S. and BHARGAVA, V. P. Pressure fluctuations in submerged jump, *J. Hyd. Div. ASCE*, **102** (HY3), Proc. Paper 12004 (March 1976), 339–50.

58. NARAYANAN, R. and SCHIZAS, L. S. Force fluctuations on sill of hydraulic jump, *J. Hyd. Div. ASCE*, **106** (HY4), Proc. Paper 15368 (April 1980), 589–99.

59. NARAYANAN, R. and SCHIZAS, L. S. Force on sill of forced jump, *J. Hyd. Div. ASCE*, **106** (HY7), Proc. Paper 15552 (July 1980), 1159–72.

60. NARAYANAN, R. Pressure fluctuations beneath submerged jump, *J. Hyd. Div. ASCE*, **104** (HY9), Proc. Paper 14039 (September 1978), 1331–42.

61. NARAYANAN, R. Cavitation induced by turbulence in stilling basin, *J. Hyd. Div. ASCE*, **106** (HY4) (April 1980), 616–19. See also discussion by Blazejewski, ibid (February 1981), 244–5.

62. NOURESCU, N., CONSTANTINESCU, C. and RADU, M. Evacuation des debits maximum et dissipation de l'energie dans des barrages en Roumanie, 11*th ICOLD*, Madrid, 1973, Q41, R29, 527–37.

63. NOVAK P. and ČÁBELKA, J. Chapter 7, Models of weirs, dams and hydroelectric power stations, in: *Models in Hydraulic Engineering*, Pitman Publishing Co., 1981.

64. OHASHI, K., SAKABE, I. and AKI, S. Design of combined hydraulic jump and ski-jump energy dissipator of flood spillway, 11*th ICOLD*, Madrid, 1973, Q41, R19, 311–33.

65. OSWALT, N. R., PICKERING, G. A. and HART, E. D. Problems and solutions associated with spillways and outlet works, 13*th Int. Cong. on Large Dams*, New Delhi, 1979, Q50, R15, 273–91.

66. PALTA, B. R. and AGGARWALA, S. K. Operation and maintenance of Bhakra Dam spillway, 9th ICOLD, Istanbul, 1967, Q33, R43, 745–56.
67. PENNINO, B. J. and LARSEN, J. *Measurement of flow-induced forces on floor blocks, Pit 6 Dam model study*, Alden Research Laboratories Report No. 109-77/M303CF, Worcester Polytechnic Institute, July 1977.
68. PETERKA, A. J. *Hydraulic Design of Stilling Basins and Energy Dissipators*, Engineering Monograph No. 25, USBR, July 1963.
69. QUINTELA, A. C., MOHAMED, J., MAGALHAES, A. P., de ALMEIDA, A. B. and de COSTA, J. V. L'evacuateur de crue et les vindanges de fond du barrage de M'Jara, 13th ICOLD, New Delhi, 1979, Q50, R40, 691–711.
70. QUINTELA, A. C. Flow aeration to prevent cavitation erosion, *Water Power and Dam Construction* (January 1980), 17–22.
71. RANGA-RAJU, K. G., KITAAL, M. K. and VERMA, M. S. Analysis of flow over baffle blocks and end sills, *J. Hyd. Res.*, IAHR, **18**(3) (1980), 227–41.
72. RAJARATNAM, N. Hydraulic jumps. In: *Advances in Hydroscience*, Vol. 4, V. T. Chow, Ed., Academic Press, New York, 1967, 198–280.
73. RAMOS, C. M. Statistical characteristics of the pressure field of crossed flows in energy dissipation structures, 13th ICOLD, New Delhi, 1979, Q50, R24, 402–16.
74. REGAN, R. P., MUNCH, A. V. and SCHRADER, E. K. Cavitation and erosion damage of sluices and stilling basins at two high-head dams, 13th ICOLD, New Delhi, 1979, Q50, R11, 177–98.
75. RESCH, F. J., LEUTHEUSSER, H. J. and COANTIC, M. Study of the kinematic and dynamic structure of the hydraulic jump, *J. IAHR*, **14**(4) (1976) 293–319.
76. RHODESIAN COMMITTEE ON LARGE DAMS, General Report, 13th ICOLD, New Delhi, 1979, G.P.-R.S. 3, Vol. 4, 303–22.
77. RHONE, T. J. and PETERKA, A. J. Improved tunnel spillway flip buckets, *Transactions ASCE*, **126**, Part 1 (1961), 1270–91.
78. ROUSE, H., SIAO, T. T. and NAGARATNAM, S. Turbulence characteristics of the hydraulic jump, *Transactions ASCE*, **124** (1959), 926–50.
79. RUDAVSKY, A. B. Selection of spillways and energy dissipators in preliminary planning of dam developments, 12th ICOLD, Mexico City, 1976, Q46, R9, 153–80.
80. RUSSELL, S. O. and BALL, J. W. Sudden-enlargement energy dissipator for Mica Dam, *J. Hyd. Div. ASCE*, **93** (HY4), Proc. Paper 5337 (July 1967), 41–56.
81. SANCHEZ BRIBIESCA, J. L. and FUENTES MARILES, O. A. Experimental analysis of macroturbulence effects on the lining of stilling basins, 13th *Int. Congress on Large Dams*, New Delhi, 1979, Q50, R6, 85–103.
82. SCHERICH, E. T., ROSSILLON, E. C., LEGAS, J. and RHONE, T. J. Contemporary design of major spillways and energy dissipators, 13th ICOLD, New Delhi, 1979, Q50, R36, 605–25.
83. SCHIEBE, F. R. and BOWERS, C. E. Boundary pressure fluctuations due to macro-turbulence in hydraulic jump, *Proc. Symposium on Turbulence in Liquids*, University of Missouri, Rolla, 1971, 134–9.
84. SMITH, H. A. A detrimental effect of dams on environment: nitrogen supersaturation?, 11th ICOLD, Madrid, 1973, Q40, R17, 237–53.

85. SPOLJARIC, C., MAKSIMOVIC, C. and HAJDIN, G. Unsteady dynamic force due to pressure fluctuations on the bottom of an energy dissipator, *Proc. Int. Conf. on Hydraulic Modelling of Civil Engineering Structures*, BHRA, Coventry, 22–24 September, 1982, paper C2, 97–107.
86. STRASSBURGER, A. G. Spillway energy dissipator problems, 11*th ICOLD*. Madrid, 1973, Q41, R16, 249–68.
87. STUTZ, R. O., GIEZENDANNER, W. and RUEFENACHT, H. P. The ski-jump spillway of the Karakaya hydroelectric seheme, 13*th ICOLD*, New Delhi, 1979, Q50, R33, 559–76.
88. SURYAVANSHI, B. D., VAIDYA, M. P. and CHOUDHURY, B. Use of chute blocks in stilling basin—An assessment, 11*th ICOLD*, Madrid, 1973, Q41, R56, 1011–36.
89. SUZUKI, Y., SAKURAI, A. and KAKUMOTO, N. A design of a chute spillway jointly serving as the roof slab of a hydropower station and its review on the vibration during flood, 11*th ICOLD*, Madrid, 1973, Q41, R21, 365–90.
90. TARAIMOVICH, I. I. Deformations of channels below high-head spillways on rock foundations, *Hydrotechnical Construction* No. 9 (September 1978), 38–42. (Translated from *Gidrotekhnicheskoe Stroitel'stvo*.)
91. TARRICONE, N. L., NEIDERT, S., BEJARANO, C. and FONSECA, C. L. Hydraulic model studies for Itaipu spillway, 13*th ICOLD*, New Delhi, 1979, Q50, R43, 749–66.
92. THOMAS, H. Cavitation on baffle pier below dams, *Proc. Second Hydraulics Conference*, State University of Iowa, Iowa City, June 1942.
93. TORRES, W. J. On the design of forced spatial hydraulic jump energy dissipators, *Proc. 18th Int. Congress IAHR*, Cagliari, Italy, Sept. 1979, Vol. 4, paper C.A.7, 55–62.
94. TVA, *Fontana Project Hydraulic Model Studies*, Technical Monograph No. 68, Tennessee Valley Authority, Knoxville, 1953.
95. TYAGI, D., PANDE, P. K. and MITTAL, M. K. Drag on baffle walls in hydraulic jump, *J. Hyd. Div. ASCE*, **104** (HY4), Proc. Paper 13677 (April 1978), 515–25.
95a. US Army Corps of Engineers *Hydraulic Design of Spillways*, EM 1110-2-1603, March 1965.
96. US Bureau of Reclamation *Hydraulic model studies of Portage Mountain development low-level outlet works, British Columbia, Canada*, Hydraulics Branch Report No. Hyd-562, June 1966.
97. US Bureau of Reclamation *Design of Small Dams*, 1974, 410.
98. US Bureau of Reclamation *Hydraulic model studies of the river outlet works of Oroville Dam—California*, Hydraulics Branch Report No. Hyd-508, October 1963.
99. VASILIEV, O. F. and BUKREYEV, V. I. Statistical characteristics of pressure fluctuations in the region of hydraulic jump, *Proc. 12th Congress, IAHR*, Fort Collins, Colorado, 1967, Vol-2, Paper B1, 1–8.
99a. WATSON, W. W. Evolution of multijet sleeve valve, *J. Hyd. Div. ASCE*, **103** (HY6) (June 1977), 617–31.
100. WANG, X. R. and CHOU, L. T. The method of calculation of controlling (or treatment) criteria for the spillway surface irregularities, 13*th ICOLD*, New Delhi, 1979, Q50, R56, 977–1003.

101. Western Canada Hydraulic Laboratories Ltd *Manitoba Hydro Nelson River Development Kettle Project Final Report: Hydraulic Model Studies of Overflow Spillway*, Port Coquitlam, Jan. 1969.

102. WIDMANN, R. Bottom outlets with stilling caverns at high dams, 11*th ICOLD*, Madrid, 1973, Q41, R40, 719–26.

103. WORKING GROUP, FRENCH COMMITTEE ON LARGE DAMS Les ouvrages d'evacuation definitifs des barrages, 11*th ICOLD*, Madrid, 1973, Q41, R35, 645–70.

104. WORKING GROUP, FRENCH COMMITTEE ON LARGE DAMS Les evacuateurs de crue du barrage de Villerest, 13*th ICOLD*, New Delhi, 1979, Q50, R35, 591–604.

105. WORKING GROUP, FRENCH COMMITTEE ON LARGE DAMS Quelques problemes particuliers posés par les deversoirs a grande capacité: tapis de protection, dissipation d'energie par deflecteurs et aeration et cavitation produite par les ecoulements a grande vitesse, 13*th ICOLD*, New Delhi, 1979, Q50, R38, 649–73.

106. WORKING GROUP, FRENCH COMMITTEE ON LARGE DAMS Ouvrages d'evacuation de grande capacite, 13*th ICOLD*, New Delhi, 1979, Q50, R61, 1063–83.

107. WU, C. M. Scour at downstream end of dams in Taiwan, *IAHR Int. Symposium on River Mechanics*, January 1973, Bangkok, Paper A-13, 137–42.

108. DOMANSKY, L. K., FERINGER, B. P., GOUN'KO, F., ROUBINSTEIN, G. L. and SOLOVIEVA, A. G. Evacuation de l'eau et la glace en periodes de construction et d'exploitation des grands barrages sur les grands fleuves de Siberie, 11*th ICOLD*, Madrid, 1973, Q41, R39, 703–17.

INDEX

Added damping, 4, 21–4, 63
Added mass, 4, 9, 11–20, 35, 43, 61–3, 69
  computation methods, 16–17
  computation results, 17–20
Added negative damping, 63
Added rigidity, 4, 20–1, 63
Aerated flow, 116–19
  calculation of, 122
  non-uniform, 119–23
  open channels, in 116–23
Aeration, 113–58
  cavitation control, 221
  decrease in scour with, 219
  dispersion blocks, of, 221
  hydraulic structure elements, of, 140–5
  outlet from turbine draft tubes, at, 154
  sluice gates or tainter gates, 141
Aeration facilities, 175
Aeration flow, transition phenomena, 123–39
Aeration mechanism, 119
Aeration ramps, 167
Aeration ratio, 117, 119
Aeration zone length, 146
Air
  conduit systems, 180
  cushion, 97, 99, 137
  entrainment, 155, 174, 175, 177–8, 180
    causes of, 113–15
    hydraulic jump in closed conduit, 135

Air—*contd.*
  vents, 140–5
Air–water discharge, 128
  ratio, 115, 124, 125, 139, 144, 149
Air–water mixtures, 115, 130
Al-Ibtissam, 207
Amplification function, 6
Anderson Ranch, 206

Baffle blocks, 199–204
Bath-tub plug, 64, 65
Bending vibration, 14
Body-controlled excitation, 1
Boundary-layer theory, 171
Boussinesque coefficient, 123
Bratsk Dam, 167, 174
Bridge decks, 26
Butterfly valve, 47

Cascade weir, 151
Castro Dam, 189
Cavitation, 101–7, 162, 167
  determining factors, 103
  developed, 102
  energy dissipators, in, 220
  gate slots, due to, 104
  incipient, 102, 103
  remedies for, 105–7
  wall roughness, due to, 104
  wall surface irregularities, due to, 105
Cavitation control, 170–6, 221
Cavitation damage, 105, 166, 167, 169, 174, 175, 180